Richard J Kulda
Oct 1952

Catholicism and American Freedom

Catholicism and American Freedom

By JAMES M. O'NEILL

Chairman, Department of Speech, Brooklyn College
Author of *Religion and Education Under The Constitution*

The first law of history is not to dare to utter falsehood; the second, not to fear to speak the truth.

—POPE LEO XIII

On opening the Vatican Archives to the scholars of the world, August 18, 1883.

HARPER & BROTHERS · NEW YORK

CATHOLICISM AND AMERICAN FREEDOM

D-B

Library of Congress catalog card number 51-11945

To Edith

CONTENTS

Preface ix

I. THE HISTORICAL RECORD

1. American Beginnings 3
2. The Framing of the Constitution 17
3. Catholic Support of American Freedom 29

II. CATHOLIC BELIEF AND PRACTICE

4. The Separation of Church and State 41
5. Democracy 59
6. Religious Freedom 74
7. Catholic Education 93
8. Catholic "Censorship" 115
9. Catholics and Social Policies 129
10. Catholics and "Medicine" 148
11. Papal Infallibility 159

III. BLANSHARD'S ATTACK ON AMERICAN CATHOLICS

12. The Blanshard Documentation 181
13. Blanshard on the Knights of Columbus Advertisements 200
14. Blanshard's "Catholic Plan for America" 214
15. Opinions of Blanshard's Book 224
16. Blanshard's Attack on Religion 246
17. The Blanshard Plan for America 259

Appendix 269

Bibliography 273

Index 283

PREFACE

This book is written in defense of American Catholics. It is offered in answer to current attacks on American Catholics as enemies of American freedom. Obviously Catholics and Catholicism (or Protestants and Protestantism) or almost any other religious group, may, under the right conditions, be the subject of controversy with complete propriety on the part of all concerned. But in order to meet ordinary standards of ethical and competent discussion, it must be fair, informed, and accurate. This volume, I believe, will meet such standards.

Mr. Paul Blanshard's recent book, *American Freedom and Catholic Power,* is the most elaborate current attack. The uncritical praise and consequent wide acceptance of Mr. Blanshard's misrepresentations make imperative a somewhat detailed answer. If not so answered, that book can do incalculable harm. The answer here presented is of course not an official answer of the Catholic Church. It is my answer. I was not asked or commissioned to undertake this task by anyone representing the Catholic Church or any Catholic agency, organization, or institution. So far as I can recall, no one (except my wife) knew of this project until after the contract had been signed with the publishers. Cordial and helpful advice and information have come from many—priests and laymen. But I alone decided what use to make of such help.

I write as a layman—as one who is neither a philosopher nor a theologian. For over forty years I have been professionally a student and teacher of rhetoric, particularly of argumentation and debate. When Mr. Blanshard's original articles were announced by *The Nation,* I subscribed to that journal. At first the articles were interesting. However, I soon became so bored by the bad argument that I never finished the reading.

The Blanshard articles had most of the worst faults of argument known to the students of rhetoric from Aristotle down to the latest high school text. Particularly evident were the inaccurate use of words, unsupported assertions, inaccurate interpretations, the apparent absence of information, the offering of inept remarks of individual Catholics as *official Catholic doctrine,* and the repetition of charges that have been answered again and again.

When Mr. Blanshard's book appeared, and was praised as sound, unbiased, carefully documented, and scholarly by men who had reputations for responsible scholarship, my interest revived. I bought the book and studied it with care. All the faults mentioned above are in the book in profusion. On reading Mr. Blanshard's volume, the temptation to write an answering argument was so great that I at once began work on this book.

Mr. Blanshard's basic thesis is that the Catholic Church is an enemy of American freedom. He tries to persuade his readers of the soundness of this thesis by his treatment of many aspects of alleged Catholic belief and practice.

My position is that Mr. Blanshard's basic thesis is false, and that the discussion of the belief and practice of American Catholics which he presents in support of his thesis is so biased and inaccurate as to be substantially worthless. Anyone, of any religion or of none, with some knowledge of the Church's doctrines, and of the history and practices of American Catholics, should have known that the book's central thesis is false; and anyone with elementary knowledge of the principles of argument and proof should have known that Mr. Blanshard does not prove his case.

My purpose is not to convert my readers to Catholicism. The objective here is not that everyone should believe in the Catholic Church, but that no one should believe in Mr. Blanshard. In so far as I can accomplish this objective, I believe that I will be helping Americans to find it easier to live in harmony and *in freedom* without the dividing and corroding influence of untruth, ignorance, suspicion, and hatred. Further, I am trying to answer *only a part* of Mr. Blanshard's attack. No one book could answer all of his false accusations, misinterpretations, and insinuations.

If the Blanshard book is so bad, a reader may well ask, why take it so seriously? The answer is, because it has been *praised and promoted* by men who, on account of the positions they occupy and the ideals they advocate, should have been expected to expose its antireligious, anti-Catholic bias, its basic freedom-smothering philosophy of the omnipotent state, and its erroneous scholarship. The betrayal of American scholarship by the encomiums heaped on Mr. Blanshard's book has done more to produce what has been called the "tension" between Catholic and non-Catholic Americans than all of Mr. Blanshard's inaccuracies and insults put together.

Perhaps some knowledge of Mr. Blanshard's education and career would assist those who may be interested in estimating the extent of his lapses in attitude and workmanship. He is no uncouth "kleagle" hiding in a bed sheet who would almost certainly be ignored by cultivated Americans. Mr. Blanshard's record doubtless made it easier for a number of cultivated Americans to praise his volume (with or without reading it) as possessing the exact virtues the absence of which constitutes the book's outstanding vices. He is a thoroughly literate man, a Congregational minister, a lawyer, and a professional writer, former associate editor of *The Nation,* and the author of a number of books. He is a graduate of the University of Michigan, a member of Phi Beta Kappa, and has done postgraduate work at Harvard, Union Theological Seminary, and Columbia University. He has also held important public positions, particularly that of commissioner of accounts in Mayor LaGuardia's administration in New York City.

It will be appropriate, since I give something of Mr. Blanshard's background and experience, to give a brief outline of my own. I have been a practicing Catholic all my life. I have lived for considerable periods of time in eleven different states from Maine to California, both included. Throughout these periods I have been interested in Catholic affairs, a reader of Catholic periodicals, and a listener to Catholic sermons. While I have never been either a student or a teacher in a Catholic educational institution of any kind, all my six children attended at one time or another both Catholic parochial schools and public schools. I have been a teacher for forty-five years (thirty-nine in public education) in eight different states. I have taught in every grade and level of public education from first grade in a country district school to university seminars open only to graduate students.

My belief in American freedom and civil liberties is *in toto* doubtless the result of my total training and experience. However, my particular interest in recent years in the Constitution and the Bill of Rights is a direct outgrowth of my experience as a member of the Committee on Academic Freedom of the American Civil Liberties Union for twelve years, during the last four of which I was its Chairman.

The manuscript of this book was completed and in the publisher's hands before Mr. Blanshard's second book appeared. However, in order to keep this volume down to the agreed price, I took the manuscript back and cut out 130 pages. Before this task was completed, Mr. Blanshard's second book was published. I discussed with Harpers' editors the possibility of adding a section on that book, but it was finally decided to print only my review of *Communism, Democracy, and Catholic Power,* which I wrote for the New York Herald Tribune *Book Review,* June 10, 1951. This review will be found in the Appendix.

My thanks are particularly due to President Harry D. Gideonse, of Brooklyn College, and to Deans William R. Gaede and Thomas E. Coulton for making most helpful arrangements to allow me uninterrupted periods for work on this volume, especially library work in New York and Washington; to Professors Humphrey Bousfield, Librarian of Brooklyn College, Eugene P. Willging, Librarian of Catholic University of America, and Phillips Temple, Librarian of Georgetown University; to Mr. Edward J. Heffron, formerly Director of Public Relations of the National Conference of Christians and Jews; to the Reverend Robert E. Southard, of St. Louis University, the Very Rev. Msgr. Thomas J. McCarthy, and the Reverend W. E. McManus of the National Catholic Welfare Conference.

To all of these, and to the many writers to whom I refer or from whom I quote, my best thanks. To my wife, Edith Winslow O'Neill, I am indebted for many illuminating suggestions in regard to the use of language, and for the assistance of her keen understanding and appreciation of Catholic doctrine.

J. M. O'NEILL

Lakeville, Connecticut
February, 1952

I

The Historical Record

1

AMERICAN BEGINNINGS

THE beginnings of Catholicism in America are coincident with the American beginnings of Christianity and education. This is true not only as it applies to the Western Hemisphere or to North America; it is true of the area known today as the continental United States.

Whether one wishes to credit the discovery of America to Columbus or to the Norsemen (or possibly to legendary Irishmen), it must be credited to Catholic discoverers.

In the ninth century A.D. Scandinavians from Norway occupied Iceland, driving out the Christian Irish colonists who had been living there in isolation for almost two centuries. These Celtic wanderers were bold and skilful navigators in their skin-covered boats, and the sea-voyage from Iceland to Greenland, or from Greenland to the Labrador, is much shorter than that from Ireland to Iceland. Hence, it is possible that Irish from Iceland were the first Europeans to reach the American continent. If so, they were absorbed or exterminated by the Indians, leaving no trace that has been uncovered. However that may be, it is a matter of historic record that in the late tenth century a tough Norseman from Iceland named Eric the Red discovered Greenland, and founded on the west coast a colony named Brattahild that flourished for several centuries by raising cattle and exporting walrus ivory and white falcons to Norway. In the year A.D. 1000, Eric's son Leif the Lucky, returning to Greenland from a visit to Norway, was driven out of his course, reached a coast where wild grapes grew, and finally made Brattahild, rather the worse for wear.

A few years later another Icelander named Thorfinn Karlsefni, with a group of Eric the Red's kindred and neighbors, explored the coast of this "Wineland the Good," and attempted to found a colony. They spent two winters in an estuary of the North American coast, but the natives, whom they called Skrellings, proved so hostile that the Norsemen gave up and returned to Greenland. Their adventures were related in two sagas which were first written down in the fourteenth century, and which make a most entertaining story.[1]

On October 9, 1949, a bronze statue of Leif Ericson was unveiled on the grounds of the State Capitol at St. Paul, Minnesota. There were present Governor Youngdahl of Minnesota, Ambassador Morgenstierne of Norway, Vice-Consul Valdimar Bjornson for Iceland, Colonel Bernt Balchen, and many other notable personages. I quote from Mr. Bjornson's address on that occasion as reported in an article[2] about Scandinavian-Catholic-American relations many centuries ago.

Leif Ericson had two priests with him, intending to Christianize his pagan father, Eric the Red, and the rest of his family, then in Greenland, when he stumbled upon the North American mainland. . . . Let us never forget that in the period of which we're speaking now, more than nine hundred years ago, when we say Christian we might equally well say Catholic. For Christianity had no exponent in the world then other than the Catholic Church. Students at St. Olaf College, or people interested in that institution, ought to be particularly aware of the fact—for that Lutheran institution is named for a Catholic saint. . . .

The Icelandic sagas contain the detailed record. They are the best sources as to the Viking voyages of discovery.

But for the purposes of this discussion I would rather use other sources than the sagas—corroborative sources that show the record they preserve is more than a succession of boastful claims about long-departed ancestors. The best such evidence as to both the discovery of America and the early attempt at colonization is to be found in Catholic sources . . . the Catholic Encyclopedia. Take a look at it sometime, whether you happen to be Catholic or Protestant, and in doing so look on page 415 of the first volume. The heading is: "America—Pre-Columbian Discovery of." And then follows, over seven pages of its finely printed text, one of the best and most authoritative brief treatments of Leif Ericson's discovery of America that have been printed in the English language.

---

[1] Morison, Samuel Eliot, and Commager, Henry Steele, *The Growth of the American Republic* (New York: Oxford University Press, 1950), pp. 9–10.

[2] Harrigan, Edward A., "A Catholic Looks at Lutherans." Reprinted from *America,* Dec. 3, 1949, in *St. Ansgar's Bulletin* (New York, 40 West 13th St., June, 1950), pp. 1–3.

Mr. Bjornson then quoted excerpts:

> Of all the alleged discoveries of America before the time of Columbus, only the bold voyages of exploration of the fearless Vikings to Greenland and the American mainland can be considered historically certain. Although there is an inherent probability for the fact of other pre-Columbian discoveries of America, all accounts of such discoveries (Phoenician, Irish, Welsh, and Chinese) rest on testimony too vague or too unreliable to justify a serious defense of them. . . .

A further indication of the early westward reach of the Catholic Church is the fact that "in 1112 the See of Gardar [in Greenland] was erected by Pope Paschal II and Eric was appointed the first bishop." [3]

In addition to the Norse explorations mentioned above, and the voyages and discoveries of Columbus, it is interesting to remember that the first English explorers to touch the mainland of North America were also Catholics. In 1497 Cabot led a company of English-speaking Catholics to the northern shores of North America. Before 1502 a priest "crossed the Atlantic to administer the rites of religion, offer the holy sacrifice, and announce the gospel in our tongue." [4]

The Spanish Catholics first touched the southern shores of the present United States. Says Shea: "On Easter Sunday, called in Spanish *Pascua Florida* Juan Ponce de León sighted the Southern coast of North America. He landed on April 2, 1513, and named the land 'Florida.' " [5] To the Spanish Catholics must also go the distinction of establishing the first schools of any kind on land that was to become a part of the United States of America. They were inevitably, under the conditions of their founding, Catholic religious schools. These schools were for both Indians and whites—an ancient precedent in the "deep South" for racial equality and nonsegregation in education. These earliest attempts at formal education, however, did not start an unbroken story of educational history.

---

[3] Shea, John Gilmary, *The Catholic Church in Colonial Days* (New York: John G. Shea, 1896), Vol. I, p. 11.

[4] *Ibid.*, p. 12, referring to Harrisse's *Jean et Sebastian Cabot* (Paris, 1882), p. 270.

[5] *Ibid.*, p. 101.

The educational work of the Franciscans began on a systematic foundation in 1594, when twelve friars arrived from Spain to aid four already present. Missions were established in many places. By 1634 there were 35 friars with 44 missions and 30,000 converts. Twelve years later the missionaries had increased to fifty. The work of conversion and civilization was pushed on. Even the establishment of a classical school was effected as early as 1606 in St. Augustine.

The work in Florida was not, however, to be of permanent duration. The Apalachees revolted against Spanish rule in 1703. The missions present only a history of stagnation or decay from the middle of the seventeenth century. In 1736 Bishop Tejada reopened the classical school in St. Augustine but it did not last long. In 1740 Governor Oglethorpe, of Georgia, led an expedition against Florida and a long war followed. The Franciscans once again in 1785 reopened a school in St. Augustine, but when Florida was annexed by the United States (1817) there was little left of the Catholic colony. Thus a period of approximately two centuries was characterized by barren results. It was the familiar story of a grand plan with but little accomplishment.[6]

The story of the first schools in New Mexico is much like that of the beginnings in Florida.

When Don Juan de Onate took possession of the New Mexico territory in 1598, he had in his company seven Franciscan friars. . . . Churches, convents, and schools were constructed. In a report to the king by Father Alonso de Benavides, an early historian of the Province, published in 1630, it is stated that several schools were in existence.[7]

The schools in both Florida and New Mexico antedated the first schools in the northern settlements.[8] These were the school of the Dutch Reformed Church, 1633, and the Boston Latin School, 1635. The latter is still in operation as a successful modern school after over three centuries of uninterrupted service.

After the English-speaking settlements and colonies were well established, the few Catholics in them were generally subjected to a great deal of both legislative and propagandistic hostility. The bitterness of generations of European persecution and savagery, indulged in by

[6] Burns, J. A., C.S.C., and Kohlbrenner, Bernard J., *A History of Catholic Education in the United States* (New York: Benziger Brothers, 1937), p. 24.

[7] *Ibid.*, p. 24.

[8] *Report of Bureau of Education* (Washington, 1903), Vol. I, p. 555. (Referred to by Burns and Kohlbrenner.)

both Catholics and Protestants, seems to have survived the ocean voyage to the new continent. Whether the honors were about even in the final score of the number of victims robbed, burned at the stake, hanged, tortured, and beheaded, or whether one side rather than the other was able to catch the larger number of victims, it would be difficult, distasteful, and irrelevant, to determine and report today. The horrors of the Spanish Inquisition, apparently well known and often mentioned in America, and the practice and teaching of Luther, Calvin and Knox, less often mentioned but also horrible,[9] do not come within the purview of this book. Neither American Catholics nor American Protestants have, so far as I know, sought to defend or justify the atrocities on either side.

Regardless of the irrelevance of the ancient conflicts of prejudice and persecution in Europe, it seems that the conditions under which the Catholics lived in America until long after the Revolutionary War are clearly relevant to the story of the relation of Catholics to American freedom. While religious freedom was well observed in Pennsylvania and Rhode Island, elsewhere, after the Catholics of Maryland became a helpless minority, the situation was one of almost universal discrimination against them.[10]

> In all the colonies, except Pennsylvania, the exercise of the Catholic religion was debarred or its public exercise restricted. In Rhode Island no restriction of law existed but no Catholics are known to have been there. In Pennsylvania alone did real and full religious liberty exist. Even here its members were civilly restricted by oaths required by the law of England from officials which Catholics could not take had any been chosen to office.[11]

---

[9] Anyone interested in a brief telling of this story, with ample references to historical documents, can find it in *The End of Religious Controversy* by the Rt. Rev. John Milner, D.D. (Baltimore: John Murphy and Co. (no date), pp. 305–316). This book was originally written in England in 1801–1802, in answer to a personal challenge to Dr. Milner, contained in a work called *Reflections on Popery* written by the Chancellor of the (Anglican) diocese of Winchester. It was later somewhat revised to answer also a publication called *The Protestant Catechism.* It was widely circulated and was hailed as an outstanding work in religious controversy in both England and America.

[10] Morison and Commager, *op. cit.*, p. 110.

[11] Griffin, Martin J., *Catholics and the American Revolution* (Ridley Park, the Author, 1907–1911), Vol. I, p. 3. See also Guilday, Peter, *The Life and Times of John Carroll* (New York: The Encyclopedia Press, 1922), Chap. V.

One or two examples must suffice to show what I mean by the persecution of Catholics in the colonies. The fact of such persecution hardly admits of controversy. Instances can be multiplied by reference to any reputable historian who deals with the social history of the colonial period.

In June of 1700 Massachusetts Bay provided by law that any Catholic priest, or missionary, who should be in the province after September 10, 1700, should be punished with "perpetual imprisonment"; if one so imprisoned should escape and be recaptured, "he shall be punished by death." [12]

Doubtless the most important events of the colonial period in relation to *Catholicism and American Freedom* occurred in the Catholic colony of Maryland.

Sir George Calvert, a prominent figure in the government of England in the reign of Queen Elizabeth and King James I, became a Catholic in 1624 at the age of forty-two. King James regranted him his lands in Ireland, relieved him of certain restrictions which generally applied to Catholics, and made him Baron of Baltimore in Ireland.[13]

Lord Baltimore's first venture in American colonization was in Newfoundland. A charter had been granted him in 1623 which made it possible for Catholics, as well as Protestants, to leave England without undue difficulties and which allowed them to hold land and have their own churches and priests in Newfoundland. When Baltimore first arrived in the new colony in 1627 he brought with him both

---

[12] *Acts and Resolves, Public and Private, of the Provisions of the Massachusetts Bay,* 21 Vols., Boston, 1869–1922, Vol. 1, pp. 423–424, Ch. 1, 1700 Laws. Quoted by Arthur J. Riley, *Catholicism in New England to 1788* (Washington: Catholic University Press, 1936), pp. 327–328.

This study of Catholicism in New England is a volume of nearly five hundred pages of detailed and organized information drawn from a great number of historical documents. The source of all material presented is cited in elaborate footnotes. This book is a dissertation submitted to the Faculty of the Graduate School of Arts and Sciences of the Catholic University of America in Partial Fulfillment of the Requirements for the Degree of Doctor of Philosophy by the Rev. Arthur J. Riley, Priest of the Archdiocese of Boston. This volume is a thoroughgoing treatment of Catholic activity and anti-Catholicism in the section and period covered.

[13] Shea, *op. cit.,* p. 30.

Protestants and Catholics including two Catholic priests; a chapel was built and Mass said regularly.

What was undoubtedly the first grant of religious freedom on this continent was Lord Baltimore's giving the Protestant colonists in Newfoundland a place of worship and a minister.

The Newfoundland colony was not a success, and Baltimore died before his charter for Maryland "passed the Great Seal of England." [14] His son, Cecil, the new Lord Baltimore, received the Maryland charter in 1632. He took a majority of Catholics, but some Protestants, to Maryland, leaving each group free to take their own clergymen. Priests accompanied the first settlers, but no Protestant minister came until some time later. The first Mass in Maryland was said on March 25, 1634. The Catholic Church was not "established" in Maryland. The priests were not supported by either Baltimore or the settlers, but took up lands and supported themselves like other settlers. The company of priests (Jesuits) grew and worked among the Indians as well as serving the Catholic settlers. When the Protestants built a chapel and secured a minister they were protected and interference with their religious freedom was punished.[15]

Leonard Calvert, brother of Lord Baltimore and governor of Maryland, died in June, 1647, and Lord Baltimore, the proprietor, appointed William Stone as governor. Under Stone the Maryland Assembly, at St. Mary's, in April, 1649, passed the famous *Act Concerning Religion.* The Assembly was constituted as follows:

Governor Stone	Catholic
The Council	2 Catholics
	2 Protestants
The Burgesses	6 Catholics
	3 Protestants
Total	9 Catholics
	5 Protestants

The *Act Concerning Religion* prescribed penalties for "calling an-

[14] *Ibid.,* p. 35.

[15] *Ibid.,* p. 49, relying on Scharf, *History of Maryland, Maryland Archives,* Boyman, *History of Maryland,* etc.

other by a sectarian name of reproach." While limited to Christians under conditions of time and place in which anything more inclusive would not have occurred to the lawmakers, this act was the first great piece of legislation providing for equality and freedom of religion in America. The heart of the act is as follows:

> And whereas the enforcing of conscience in matters of religion hath frequently fallen out to be of dangerous consequence in those commonwealths where it has been practiced, and for the more quiet and peaceable government of this province, and the better to preserve mutual love and unity amongst the inhabitants, no person or persons whatsoever within this province or the islands, ports, harbors, creeks, or havens thereunto belonging, professing to believe in Jesus Christ, shall from henceforth be any ways troubled or molested, or discountenanced for or in respect of his or her religion, nor in the free exercise thereof within this province or the islands thereunto belonging, nor any way compelled to the belief or exercise of any other religion, against his or her consent.[16]

King William made Maryland a royal province and sent out Sir Lionel Copley as governor in 1691. Copley assembled a legislature from which all Catholics were excluded, which immediately passed "An Act for the Service of Almighty God, and the Establishment of the Protestant religion, in this Province." Taxes were laid on all alike, Catholic and Puritan, and Friend, to build Anglican churches and support their ministers. But in 1702 the English acts of toleration were extended to Protestant dissenters in Maryland, leaving the Catholics only as the victims of intolerance in Maryland. The historian Professor William Warren Sweet, of the University of Chicago, makes this comment:

"This has been termed one of the sarcasms of history. Maryland, which had been founded for the sake of religious freedom by the toil and treasure of Roman Catholics, was now open to all who call themselves Christians save Roman Catholics." [17]

It is even greater irony that today after two and a half centuries of consistent support of religious equality and freedom (in spite of

---

[16] *Ibid.*, p. 70, relying on *Maryland Archives,* etc.

[17] *The Story of Religions in America,* 5th ed. (New York: Harper & Brothers, 1930), p. 64.

periods of discrimination against them) American Catholics are under bitter attack by mature, literate Americans as enemies of American freedom.

There were only a few Catholic priests in the country in colonial days and in the decade immediately following the Declaration; and these had no bishop or formal leader. However, on June 6, 1784, Pope Pius VI appointed Father John Carroll "Superior of the Mission in the thirteen United States of North America." In 1788 Father Carroll, joined by Father Robert Molyneaux and Father John Ashton, asked the Holy See "to erect a new episcopal see in these United States" and to allow the American priests to *elect* the first American bishop. This petition was approved in a letter from Cardinal Antonelli, dated in Rome, June 12, 1788. In conformity to this correspondence, an election was held at White Marsh, Maryland, at which twenty-six priests were present. Twenty-four votes were cast for John Carroll, only one besides his own was cast for another. The priests at White Marsh chose Baltimore as the first see in America. In November, 1789, Pope Pius VI erected the See of Baltimore, and named John Carroll as the first Catholic bishop of America.[18]

John Carroll played a large part in the diminishing of anti-Catholic prejudice in the decades of the Revolutionary War and the framing of the Constitution. His wide acquaintance with Europe, his many friends in France and England, and his close relationship to Daniel Carroll (his younger brother) and to his cousin Charles Carroll of Carrollton, combined with his own genuine patriotism, gave his leadership of the Catholic clergy of America an undoubted persuasiveness with non-Catholics of that time. Further his friendly relations with Benjamin Franklin and George Washington, and the example of their conduct toward him and other Catholics, must inevitably have been effective in softening the attitude of many who still misunderstood Catholicism and feared their Catholic fellow citizens.

In 1774 the English Parliament

---

[18] See Shea, J. G., *The History of the Catholic Church in the United States* (4 vols.), Vol. II, pp. 259, 326, 337.

. . . passed the last and most important act dealing with the West—the Quebec Act of 22 June 1774. This law, dictated by an enlightened liberalism rare in that or any other age, was intended to correct certain mistakes in the Proclamation of 1763, and to secure the loyalty of the French Canadians. To these it granted complete religious liberty and the restitution of their peculiar legal and political institutions.[19]

The Quebec Act produced a bitter storm among the Protestant colonists to the south and has been listed by some scholars as one of the major causes of the American Revolution.[20]

In February, 1776, the Continental Congress, in an attempt to bring Quebec in as a partner in the Continental Revolution, sent a commission to Canada to see what could be done. Franklin, its outstanding leader, and Samuel Chase represented Congress officially. Charles Carroll, who had been educated in France and spoke French fluently, was appointed as the third member. Then Congress passed a resolution asking the latter to persuade Father John Carroll to go with the commission to help persuade the French Catholics to join the Revolution. The commission failed to reverse the attitude of the Canadians, which had been strongly affected by the Quebec Act and the wave of intense anti-Catholicism that it had produced south of the Canadian border.[21] "In the protests against the Quebec Act of 1774 the colonists had abused the Catholic Church with a bigotry which the French Catholics could not forget when Congress urged them in 1775 to join the Revolution and make it continental." [22]

However, the friendship between Franklin and Carroll following their close association on that expedition had some interesting ex-

---

[19] Morison, Samuel Eliot, and Commager, Henry Steele, *The Growth of the American Republic* (New York: Oxford University Press, 1950), 4th ed., Vol. I, p. 145.

[20] See Van Tyne, Claude Halstead, "Influence of the Clergy and of Religious and Sectarian Forces on the American Revolution," in the *American Historical Review,* XIX, p. 44, and his *The Loyalists in the American Revolution* (New York: P. Smith, 1929), and also Peter Guilday, *op. cit.,* Chapts. VI and VII.

[21] See Maynard, Theodore, *The Story of American Catholicism* (New York: The Macmillan Co., 1948), Chap. 8, pp. 125 ff., and Guilday, *op. cit.,* Chapts. VI and VII.

[22] Van Doren, Carl, *Benjamin Franklin* (New York: Viking Press, 1938), p. 542.

pressions in later years. Throughout the expedition Franklin and John Carroll traveled together, as did Chase and Charles Carroll.

Franklin was seventy in 1776 and Carroll was thirty-nine. Concerning this association Van Doren quotes Franklin:

> "I find I grow daily more feeble, and I think I could hardly have got along so far but for Mr. Carroll's friendly assistance and tender care of me." (Eight years later the Papal Nuncio in Paris told Franklin that on his recommendation John Carroll would probably be made a bishop; and he became the first archbishop in America.) [23]

On June 9, 1784, Cardinal Antonelli in writing to Father Carroll to inform him that Pope Pius VI had appointed him "Superior of the Mission in the thirteen United States of North America," said: ". . . it is known that your appointment will please and gratify many members of that republic, and especially Mr. Franklin, the eminent individual who represents the same republic at the court of the Most Christian King . . ." On February 17, 1785, Father Carroll wrote to his friend Father Thorpe in Rome, thanking him for his "active and successful endeavours to render service to this country. I say successful, not because of your partiality, [which] as I presume, joined to that of my old and cheerful friend Dr. Franklin suggested me to the consideration of his Holiness; but because you have obtained some form of spiritual government to be adopted for us." [24]

Charles Carroll of Carrollton was a boyhood schoolmate of his cousin John, at the Jesuit school at Bohemia Manor in Maryland, and they both entered St. Omer's (in Belgium) in 1748. Charles remained at St. Omer's for seven years—until he was eighteen, when he left to study law in Paris and London. He returned to America in 1765 at the age of twenty-eight. From that time until the end of his long life in 1832, at the age of ninety-five, he was one of the leading citizens of the country. Charles Carroll was a strong force in helping to establish Catholic Americans as competent, faithful, and patriotic

---

[23] *Ibid.*, p. 547, referring to *The Writings of Benjamin Franklin,* Albert Henry Smythe, ed. (New York, 1905–1907), Vol. 10, p. 349.

[24] Guilday, *John Carroll,* pp. 203, 208.

citizens. He was the only Catholic signer of the Declaration of Independence. If it is interesting or important to consider proportions on the basis of religious affiliation, here as in the Constitutional Convention of 1787 (see pp. 17–18), the few Catholics in the country in having one signer were tremendously overrepresented. There was one Catholic signer to fifty-five non-Catholic signers. In the population of that time there was, at most, one Catholic to 133 non-Catholics.

Carroll's biographer, L. A. Leonard,[25] writes: "He was the richest man that signed the Declaration of Independence, the first man that signed, the only Roman Catholic that signed, and the last to die of those that signed it."

Carroll himself has left a statement of his objectives in signing the Declaration: political liberty, and religious equality and freedom. The fact that religious equality and freedom was in this statement limited to Christians should not be read as an indication of any personal narrowness or bigotry belonging particularly to Carroll as a man or as a Catholic. Even the idea of a government allowing equality before the law, and freedom of religious worship, opinion, and teaching, *to all denominations of Christians* was a relatively new and not yet widely accepted idea. Charles Carroll was pioneering in his thinking, as were the other Catholics of Maryland of that and earlier days. He wrote: [26]

> When I signed the Declaration of Independence, I had in view not only our independence of England, but the toleration of all sects professing the Christian religion and communicating to them all equal rights. Happily this wise and salutary measure has taken place for eradicating religious feuds and persecution, and become a useful lesson to all governments. Reflecting, as you must, on the disabilities, I may truly say on the proscription, of the Roman Catholics in Maryland, you will not be surprised that I had much at heart this grand design founded on mutual charity, the basis of our holy religion.

The reciprocal relations of admiration and respect between George

---

[25] Leonard, Lewis A., *A Life of Charles Carroll of Carrollton* (New York: Moffat, Yard and Co., 1918). Quoted by Theodore Maynard, *The Story of American Catholicism* (New York: The Macmillan Co., 1948), p. 128.

[26] Quoted from Shea, *History of the Catholic Church in the United States,* Vol. III, p. 421.

Washington and the American Catholics of the time bore excellent fruit in reassuring the Catholics after the Revolution that they were to be more fully accepted as full-fledged and loyal citizens, and in reassuring the non-Catholics that the Catholics deserved this status. One or two instances must suffice as indications of such relations.

As a part of the widespread anti-Catholic demonstrations in a number of the colonies, a custom had developed of celebrating what had started as "Guy Fawkes Day" as "Pope Day," in which, with appropriate ceremonies, the Pope would be burned in effigy. Washington learned that this custom was to be observed in the army and promptly issued an order forbidding it, "expressing his surprise that there should be officers and soldiers in this army so void of common sense as not to see the impropriety of such a step." Washington characterized the custom as "insulting" and "so monstrous as not to be suffered or excused." [27]

Following Washington's inauguration as the first President of the United States, a group of eminent Catholics under the leadership of Bishop Carroll, in December, 1789, sent the following letter [28] to the new President. After congratulation, the letter was as follows:

> It is your peculiar talent, in war and in peace, to afford security to those who commit their protection into your hands. In war you shield them from the ravages of armed hostility; in peace, you establish public tranquility, by the justice and moderation, not less than by the vigour, of your government. By example, as well as by vigilance, you extend the influence of laws on the manners of our fellow-citizens. You encourage respect for religion; and inculcate, by words and actions, that principle, on which the welfare of nations so much depends, that a superintending providence governs the events of the works, and watches over the conduct of men. Your exalted maxims, and unwearied attention to the moral and physical improvement of our country, have produced already the happiest effects. Under your administration, America is animated with zeal for the attainment and encouragement of useful literature. She improves her agriculture; extends her commerce; and acquires with foreign nations a dignity unknown to her before. From these events, in which none can feel a warmer interest than ourselves, we derive additional pleasure, by recollecting that you, Sir, have been

---

27 Shea, *op. cit.*, Vol. II, p. 147.

28 Guilday, *The Life and Times of John Carroll*, pp. 365–366.

the principal instrument to effect so rapid a change in our political situation. This prospect of national prosperity is peculiarly pleasing to us, on another account; because, whilst our country preserves her freedom and independence, we shall have a well founded title to claim from her justice, the equal rights of citizenship, as the price of our blood spilt under your eyes, and of our common exertions for her defence, under your auspicious conduct—rights rendered more dear to us by the remembrance of former hardships. When we pray for the preservation of them, where they have been granted—and expect the full extension of them from the justice of those States, which still restrict them: when we solicit the protection of Heaven over our common country, we neither omit, nor can omit recommending your preservation to the singular care of Divine Providence; because we conceive that no human means are so available to promote the welfare of the United States, as the prolongation of your health and life, in which are included the energy of your example, the wisdom of your counsels, and the persuasive eloquence of your virtues.

Washington replied on March 12, 1790, in part as follows: [29]

America, under the smiles of Divine Providence—the protection of a good Government—and the cultivation of Manners, Morals, and Piety—cannot fail of attaining, an uncommon degree of Eminence, in Literature, Commerce, Agriculture, Improvements at home, and Respectability abroad.

As Mankind becomes more liberal, they will be more apt to allow, that all those who conduct themselves worthy members of the Community, are equally entitled to the protection of Civil Government. I hope ever to see America among the foremost Nations in examples of Justice and Liberality. And I presume that your fellow-citizens will not forget the patriotic part, which you took in the accomplishment of their Revolution, and the establishment of their Government—or the important assistance, which they received from a Nation, in which the Roman Catholic Faith is professed.

I thank you, Gentlemen, for your kind concern for me. While my Life and Health shall continue, in whatever situation I may be, it shall be my constant endeavor to justify the favourable sentiments which you are pleased to express of my conduct. And may the Members of your Society in America, animated alone by the pure spirit of Christianity, and still conducting themselves, as the faithful subjects of our free Government, enjoy every temporal, and spiritual felicity.

---

[29] Guilday, *op. cit.,* p. 366.

2

THE FRAMING OF THE CONSTITUTION

CATHOLICS participated in the Constitutional Convention that drew up the original Constitution in Philadelphia in 1787. Two of the thirty-nine signers of the Constitution were Catholic citizens of considerable distinction and influence in their communities. In the nature of things, they had to be rather outstanding because they represented overwhelmingly Protestant states. These two were Daniel Carroll, of Maryland, and Thomas Fitzsimmons, of Pennsylvania. Charles Carroll, of Carrollton, a signer of the Declaration of Independence, was originally chosen to represent Maryland, but declined the appointment, because as a member of the state legislature of Maryland he felt that he ought to stay at home in order to attend to the business of the legislature, particularly to work against a threatened issue of paper money by the state.[1]

While it is of no great significance, perhaps it is interesting to note that, while there were only two Catholic signers of the Constitution and thirty-seven non-Catholic signers, this made Catholic representation in writing the Constitution about seven times as large in proportion to the Catholic population as was the non-Catholic representation in proportion to the non-Catholic population. The various estimates of the Catholic population of the United States in 1787 run from twenty-four to thirty thousand. The total population of the United States in 1787 is generally estimated to have been about four million.

[1] Farrand, Max, *The Framing of the Constitution* (New Haven: Yale University Press, 1913), p. 35.

To keep the proportions even, there should have been about 264 non-Catholic signers of the Constitution to balance the two Catholic signers. The two Catholic delegates to the Convention both signed the Constitution, and thirty-seven of the forty non-Catholic delegates present at the time of the signing. Gerry (Massachusetts), Mason and Randolph (Virginia), refused to sign:

> An overwhelming majority of the delegates present in mid-September approved of the final draft. Although a few extreme states' rights men who disapproved of the Convention's work, among them Luther Martin, Lansing, and Yates, had left in disgust well before the day of adjournment, both the nationalists and the moderate champions of states' rights signed the document. To lend an appearance of harmony Franklin suggested that the Convention submit its work to the nation over the formula: "Done in Convention by the Unanimous Consent of the states present," and this somewhat disingenuous proposal was adopted. Only three of the delegates then present refused to sign: Randolph, in the belief that the Constitution would fail of adoption and in the wish to be free to support a second convention; George Mason, in the conviction that the Constitution was too aristocratic; Elbridge Gerry, on the grounds that the new government would have too much irresponsible authority. On September 17, 1787, the remaining thirty-nine members affixed their signatures to the document.[2]

I have been able to find no evidence that the Constitution signed by Carroll and Fitzsimmons was not wholly acceptable to them, and in fact that they were not enthusiastic about it. They were apparently at least as enthusiastic about it as the general run of the other delegates. I have found no instance in which either of them argued against measures which were adopted or argued for measures which were disapproved. What evidence is available seems to indicate clearly that the Catholics of America at that time looked upon the Constitution as a distinct step forward in the promotion of freedom, democracy, and at least a beginning of the removal of what Jefferson called the "civil incapacitations" to which they had been so largely subjected in the colonies.

The prohibition of a religious test for any office or public trust un-

---

[2] Kelly, Alfred H., and Harbison, Winfred A., *The American Constitution* (New York: W. W. Norton & Co., 1948), p. 147.

der the United States government was clearly a matter of great satisfaction to the Catholics of the country, since they were obviously the chief potential beneficiaries of such a policy. As such the inclusion of this item in Article VI is impressive evidence that the old rancors had been considerably dissipated by the events from 1776 to 1787. For this it seems that considerable credit should go not only to men like Daniel Carroll and Thomas Fitzsimmons in their attitudes and personal contacts in the Constitutional Convention, but to two other great leaders of the day, Bishop John Carroll and George Washington. (See pp. 15–16.)

In the discussion of the ratification of the Constitution in the various states, the opposition voiced to ratification of the Constitution was not voiced by Catholics. Obviously, there were so few Catholics in most of the colonies that one could hardly expect to find Catholics commonly in positions of important legislative leadership. In these young states they were everywhere a distinct minority, and usually victims of discriminatory measures. Reliable estimates indicate that there were about 16,000 Catholics in Maryland; about 1,500 in Pennsylvania, and not so many as one thousand in any other state at this time. Various forces operated to discourage a rapid growth of the Catholic population. The total number of Catholic priests, according to Father Carroll in 1785,[3] was nineteen in Maryland and five in Pennsylvania, and these were the two states with the largest Catholic populations.

There are two or three interesting items reported from the Constitutional Convention which touch upon the subject of religion. Charles Pinckney, of South Carolina, gave what was doubtless the first statement in a formal consideration of federal constitutional provisions, of the thought which was rather common at the time and which later found expression in the first clause in the Bill of Rights, when he proposed that the legislature of the United States shall pass no law on the subject of religion. Shea,[4] relying on Yates,[5] remarks that, while it was omitted in the final Constitution, there was no objection to the doctrine raised in the Constitutional Convention. Such matters were left

[4] *Ibid.*, Vol. 2, p. 345.

[5] *Secret Proceedings of the Convention,* Albany, 1821, p. 217.

[3] Shea, *History of the Catholic Church in the United States,* Vol. 2, p. 259.

for future action, which resulted in the Bill of Rights. Charles Pinckney also made the proposal that resulted in the last clause of Article VI of the Constitution: "but no religious Test shall ever be required as a qualification for any Office or public Trust under the United States."

Thomas Fitzsimmons[6] (1741–1811), one of the two Catholic signers of the Constitution, was born in Ireland, and came to this country sometime before 1760. In 1770 he joined the shipping firm of George Mead and Company, in Philadelphia. In 1774, following the Boston Tea Party, he was made a member of the Committee of Correspondence to keep in communication with the men of other colonies concerning the growing crisis. He was the first Catholic to attain a municipal office in Pennsylvania. In 1776 he was elected to membership in the Council of Safety and in 1777 a member of the Navy Board created by the legislature of Pennsylvania. He served in the Revolutionary War under George Washington, and was chosen a delegate to the Constitutional Convention on December 30, 1786, with Benjamin Franklin, Robert Morris, George Clymer, Jared Ingersoll, James Wilson, and Gouverneur Morris. In 1787 he was a member of the Board of Pennsylvania Hospital. He was an incorporator and trustee of the College of Pennsylvania, and served in that capacity when the College of Pennsylvania was consolidated with the University of Pennsylvania. He was a member of the Committee on Consolidation with the University, and a trustee of the University of Pennsylvania until his death in 1811. He was also a member of the first Congress of the United States, in the House of Representatives from 1789 to 1795.

Daniel Carroll[7] (1730–1796) was educated at home as a small boy and from the age of twelve to eighteen at the English Jesuit College of St. Omer in French Flanders. Education of Catholic youth in

---

[6] The material in this paragraph is taken from *Thomas Fitzsimmons, Signer of the Constitution,* by the Rev. James A. Farrell, A.B., M.A., *Records of* American Catholic Historical Society of Philadelphia, Vol. XXXIX, No. 3, Philadelphia, 1928.

[7] The data on Daniel Carroll is taken from *Daniel Carroll, a Framer of the Constitution* by Mary Virginia Geiger (Washington: Catholic University of America Press, 1943).

Maryland in Carroll's boyhood was difficult and even hazardous on account of the drastic English penal laws which were still in force in Maryland. When Daniel was twenty-one, his father died, leaving heavy responsibilities on him—as manager of large estates and the family mercantile business. His only brother, John, later the first Catholic bishop and archbishop in America, was in France preparing for the priesthood.

Daniel's public life began at the age of forty-seven, in 1777, when he was elected to the Council of State of the new state of Maryland. He was re-elected four times. He resigned on January 17, 1781, to accept a seat in the Continental Congress.

On November 24, 1781, he was elected to a five-year term as state senator, and was re-elected in 1786. During his years as a state senator he was also a member of the Continental Congress from 1781 until the work of the Congress was over. He served part of this time also as President of the Senate. Geiger [8] writes, footnotes in the original:

> One important item remains to be dealt with during the second term of Carroll's service as senator of Maryland. It was characteristic of Daniel Carroll to desire that aid be given to both Catholic and Protestant churches. To Carroll, it mattered little to what religion a person subscribed. His motive was more universal—he wished to ensure religious freedom to all religions. There may be cited two examples to illustrate this—one occurred during his first term and the second during his other term as senator.
>
> Daniel Carroll advocated the passage of an act providing for the relief of widows and children of the clergy of the Protestant churches. . . .[146]

The other example better illustrates the point. During his term as president of the Senate on December 23, 1788, Daniel Carroll introduced a bill to "incorporate certain persons in every christian church or congregation throughout this state."

> Whereas it is reasonable and proper that all denominations of christians within this state, whose members conduct themselves on a peaceable and orderly manner, should receive and enjoy equal rights and privileges, without partially, preference or distinction, in all things concerning the temporalities and government of their respective churches, congregations and

---

[8] *Ibid.,* pp. 83–84.

[146] *Votes and Proceedings of Senate,* Jan. 18, 1785 (in Geiger).

> societies . . . every christian church, society or congregation . . . shall at any time hereafter be known and acknowledged in this state, and protected in the free and full exercise of their religion, by the constitution and laws of the same.[147]

Daniel Carroll was one of the few signers of both the Articles of Confederation and the Constitution of the United States. In the Continental Congress Carroll was active on many matters, particularly with such colleagues as Madison and Hamilton on army supply and public finance.

On May 26, 1787, Daniel Carroll was chosen as one of Maryland's five delegates to the Constitutional Convention at Philadelphia. He took his seat there July 9, 1787, and remained to the final day, and the signing of the Constitution on September 17, 1787. Later he was ardent and active in securing Maryland's ratification: "Regarding it, then, from every point of view with a candid and disinterested mind. I am bold to assert, that it is the best formed government which has ever been offered to the world." [9]

On January 13, 1789, Daniel Carroll was elected to the House of Representatives in the First Congress, where he served through its three sessions—March 4, 1789, to March 4, 1791. He was particularly concerned with the First and Tenth Amendments. To quote Geiger again: [10]

> During the debates in the House regarding this first proposed amendment, there arose a question whether it would be better to insert in the first article of section nine "No religion shall be established by law, nor shall the equal rights of conscience be infringed." [98] Immediately a religious conflict ensued. Sylvester of New York thought it "had a tendency to abolish religion," [99] while Gerry of Massachusetts wanted to word it: "No religious doctrine shall be established by law." [100] Sherman of Connecticut held it "unnecessary . . . no power is delegated to us to make religion an established one." [101] Daniel Carroll realizing the confusion that prevailed in the people's

[147] *Ibid.*, Dec. 23, 1788 (in Geiger).
[9] *Maryland Journal*, Oct. 16, 1787.
[10] Pp. 163–165.
[98] *Annals*, I, 729.
[99] *Ibid.*
[100] *Ibid.*, 730 (in Geiger).
[101] *Ibid.* (in Geiger).

minds concerning the vagueness of the clause that had been inserted in the ratified constitution forthwith offered this suggestion:

> As the rights of conscience are, in their nature, of peculiar delicacy, and will little bear the gentlest touch of governmental hand; and as many sects have concurred in opinion that they are not well secured under the present Constitution, he said he was much in favor of adopting the words [first suggested above]. He thought it would tend more towards conciliating the minds of the people to the Government than almost any other amendment he had heard proposed. He would not contend with gentlemen about the phraseology, his object was to secure the substance in such a "manner as to satisfy the wishes of the honest part of the community." [102]

Although Madison felt that the provision was "neither important nor altogether useless and thought Carroll's motion well expressed, Livermore was still unsatisfied and found a better way of expressing it: "Congress shall make no laws touching religion." . . .[103]

It has often been asserted that Bishop John Carroll had been instrumental in bringing about the first amendment to the Constitution, but this is an erroneous assertion without a shadow of proof.[104] He may have expressed his sentiments on the question as a representative of the Church, but his influence would have had no weight in the debates of the Houses at that time in any case. Rather it was Daniel Carroll who ought to be recognized. . . .

It [the Tenth Amendment] originally read: "powers not delegated by the Constitution are reserved to the states respectively." Carroll, however, again expressing his conservatism and democratic view suggested that the clause "or to the people" be added.[107]

This addition was adopted and is a part of the Tenth Amendment to the Constitution. The record shows that Carroll played an active part in framing the religious clause of the First Amendment and the Tenth Amendment which reserves "to the people" of the states the authority to say what power over them shall be exercised by the federal government.

Daniel Carroll was one of the three commissioners appointed in 1791 by Washington to plan the permanent seat of the government in

---

[102] *Ibid.*

[103] *Ibid.*, 537, 730.

[104] Bertrand C. Conway, "John Carroll, First Archbishop of Baltimore," *Cath. World,* CXVI (1922), 583.

[107] *Annals,* I, 76.

the newly created District of Columbia. He resigned in 1795, and died on May 7, 1796.

By the time the Revolution and the work of the Constitutional Convention were over, there seemed to be evident in the debates over ratification a softening of the anti-Catholicism that was so prevalent before the war with England. Probably no colony had gone further in discrimination against Catholics than Massachusetts Bay. Because the change is so clear in the Massachusetts debates on the Constitution (and because Father Riley has done such a meticulous piece of work in investigating and reporting them) Massachusetts will serve as a good example.

Concerning the debates in Massachusetts on the acceptance of the new federal Constitution, Father Riley writes: [11]

> In the convention called for this purpose there was considerable discussion over the presence or absence of a religious test oath. Several favored its inclusion because to act otherwise would indicate "a departure from the principles of our forefathers, who came here for the preservation of their religion." In its absence, to "the general government" would be admitted deists, atheists, and others from whom would emanate a dissemination of their principles "and of course, a corruption of morals." Reverend Isaac Backus, one of the four delegates from Middleboro, stated that "some serious minds discover a concern lest, if all religious tests should be excluded, the Congress would here after establish Popery, or some other tyrannical way of worship." [12] William Jones, the only delegate from Bristol, favored a test because "it would be happy for the United States," in his opinion, "if our public men were to be of those who had a good standing in the church." According to him "a person could not be a good man withut being a good Christian." His principal objection to the adoption of the Federal Constitution was its omission of a religious test and accordingly he voted against it. Major Thomas Lusk, the only delegate from West Stockbridge, "shuddered at the idea that Roman Catholics, Papists, and Pagans might be introduced into office, and that Popery and the inquisition may be established

---

[11] *Catholicism in New England to 1788,* pp. 242–246.

[12] Backus did not agree: See below. And Shea remarks (*A History of the Catholic Church in the United States,* Vol. 2, pp. 346–347): "every Protestant minister in the Massachusetts legislature at the time voted for the Constitution as it stood, and the Rev. Isaac Backus, a Baptist leader, famous as a militant advocate of religious liberty, remarked that "the imposing of religious tests has been the greatest engine of tyranny in the world."

in America," because of the absence of a religious test. Because of this absence he voted against the acceptance of the Constitution. The Honorable Amos Singletary, one of the two delegates from Sutton, "thought we were giving up all our privileges, as there was no provision that men in power should have any religion." He explicitly stated that he hoped to see only Christians hold office, "yet, by the Constitution, a Papist, or an Infidel, was as eligible as they." For this reason and his fear that Congress would extend the power of taxation he voted against the acceptance of the Constitution. The ministers did not continue their tradition of theocratic control and three of them spoke in favor of the exclusion of a religious test.[13] The fear that "popery, or some other tyrannical way of worship" would be established was groundless if no religious test were allowed by the Constitution. Reverend Phillips Payson, the only delegate from Chelsea, had nothing else to say in the Convention except to favor the exclusion of the religious test in answer to Colonel Jones of Bristol. According to him "attempts to erect human tribunals for the consciences of men are impious encroachments upon the prerogatives of God." Hence "had there been a religious test as a qualification for office, it would, in my opinion, have been a great blemish" upon the Constitution. Reverend Daniel Shute, one of the two delegates from Hingham, declared in his only speech that "the exclusion of a religious test in the proposed Constitution, therefore, clearly appears to me, sir, to be in favor of its adoption." Although objection to such exclusion was known to be very popular, "for the most of men, somehow, are rigidly tenacious of their own sentiments in religion, and disposed them upon others as the standard of truth," yet he felt otherwise; "To establish a religious test as a qualification for offices in the proposed federal Constitution, it appears to me, sir, would be attended with injurious consequences to individuals, and with no advantage to the whole." Such a test would not exclude unprincipled men, who would subscribe to any oath, but would exclude the honest and worthy men who were to be found in all denominations, "The Quakers, the Baptists, the Church of England, the Papists." This exclusion would "be a privation of part of their civil rights." Theophilus Parsons, one of the four delegates from Newburyport, also favored the exclusion of the religious test. Such a

[13] Apparently the record of the voting was not clear. Shea said all ministers were for the Constitution. Riley says in part of a footnote: "Twenty ministers were delegates to the convention. Most of them were favorable to the Constitution. Madison to Washington, New York, Feb. 3, 1788, in Jared Sparks (ed.), *Correspondence of the American Revolution; being Letters of Eminent Men to George Washington* (Boston, 1853), IV, 207. According to the list in Elliot, *Debates,* II, 178–181, fifteen out of nineteen ministers voted in favor of its acceptance. Samuel Bannister Harding, *The Contest Over the Ratification of the Federal Constitution in Massachusetts* (New York, 1896), 76, stated that fourteen out of seventeen voted for ratification." Riley, *op. cit.,* pp. 244–245.

test would not exclude "unprincipled men, atheists and pagans," and there would be insuperable difficulties in determining what was Christianity. He would make the only test of sincerity a man's "good life" and acting "an honest part to his neighbor," which was the best guarantee of honorable conduct "towards the public."

With the ratification by New Hampshire on June 21, 1788, the Constitution became effective for nine states. The other four followed: Virginia, June 25; New York, July 26; North Carolina, November 21, 1788; Rhode Island, May 29, 1790.[14]

In the debates over ratification in a number of the states, one argument for winning over objectors was the assurance that an effort would be made to add a Bill of Rights to the Constitution. Many state legislatures passed memorials and resolutions asking for such action on the part of the Congress. "One of the very few specific recommendations made by President Washington in his inaugural address was that Congress should give careful attention to the demand for these amendments."[15]

The fear that the federal government would impose a national religion on the whole country was widespread. The desire to have the new Constitution explicitly state that the federal government could not do this was expressed in a number of state resolutions.[16]

The language of the First Amendment is not a careless or casual formulation, nor phrases borrowed from documents designed for a situation other than the one which confronted the first Congress (as were Jefferson's "Wall of Separation" letter and Jefferson and Madison's writings concerning state laws in Virginia). The First Amendment was carefully phrased to meet a situation presented by resolutions and petitions from various states asking for a Bill of Rights. These petitions and resolutions came out of the discussions in the various states as they were considering the original Constitution. Several of these conventions accompanied ratification with a request for specific amendments or with resolutions setting forth declarations of principle

---

[14] Warren, Charles, *The Making of the Constitution* (Boston: Little, Brown and Co., 1928), p. 810.

[15] Kelly and Harbison, *op. cit.*, p. 174.

[16] For the action of various states, see O'Neill, J. M., *Religion and Education Under the Constitution* (New York: Harper & Brothers, 1949), pp. 112–114.

which are relevant here. Other amendments were proposed and discussed but not formally adopted.

It is a fact of first importance that most of the states that phrased resolutions or petitions dealing with religion in regard to the desired Bill of Rights dealt specifically with a religious provision which would prevent Congress from making it possible for *one religion nationally to be preferred over all others.* In other words, what the states asked Congress to provide was a constitutional amendment which would prevent a national "establishment of religion" in the age-old, strict, literal sense of a union between the government and a single religion.[17]

All the discussions about religion under the federal Constitution showed simply a desire that "no religious sect or society be favored or established by law in preference to others." No prohibition of equal aid to all religions, financial or otherwise, was mentioned. There is no mention of public funds, government cooperation with religion, or religion in education.

As shown above (pp. 22–23), Daniel Carroll took an active part in forming the religious clause of the First Amendment in the House. His cousin, Charles Carroll of Carrollton, in supporting it in the Senate furthered his purpose in signing the Declaration of Independence (see p. 14).

The third Catholic member of the First Congress, Thomas Fitzsimmons of Pennsylvania, seemingly took no noticeable part in framing this legislation. Three Catholic members of this Congress out of ninety (the total membership), while not quite so out of proportion to the small number of Catholics in the population at the time, was still a tremendous overrepresentation, if one were to consider that it should be based on such a proportion. Certainly in the activity of Daniel and Charles Carroll Catholics played a due part in the formulation of the First Amendment, and they have supported the religious clause of the First Amendment without significant exception from 1791 to 1951. (See Chapter 3.) No group in the United States has a better record.

In September, 1789, Congress submitted twelve proposed amendments to the states. But before the required number of states ratified the amendments,

[17] *Ibid.*, pp. 111–112.

the number of states in the Union increased from eleven to fourteen through the ratification of the Constitution by North Carolina and Rhode Island and the admission into the Union of Vermont in 1791. Ratification by eleven states was therefore necessary. During the two years from 1789 to 1791 various states took favorable action on all or most of the amendments, and in November, 1791, Virginia's vote made ten of the amendments part of the Constitution. . . .

The ten amendments adopted worked no real alteration in federal power. They gave formal recognition to certain traditionally accepted "natural rights," hitherto incorporated in the great English charters, colonial grants, and state bills of rights. They took no substantive powers from Congress which could reasonably have been implied before the amendments had been passed, and most of the procedural limitations, trial by jury and the like, probably would have been taken for granted in any event.[18]

In summary, the purpose of the Bill of Rights was not to introduce any change of any kind, but simply to make explicit what was implicit in the two controlling facts. (1) The federal government was a government of *delegated powers only.* It could do *nothing* it was not authorized to do by the states in ratifying the provisions of the Constitution. (2) The original Constitution, as ratified, delegated to the federal government no authority over such domestic concerns as religion, education, morals, etc. Some leaders, particularly Alexander Hamilton, thought it better under these circumstances not to have a bill of rights in the federal Constitution. Jefferson wanted a bill of rights "as a text" by which to try future federal governments if they should attempt to invade the rights of the people of the states.[19] Madison thought it not necessary, but probably useful if carefully phrased.[20] Madison submitted a carefully phrased bill of rights to the First Congress, in the House of Representatives of which he was a member. Catholics participated in putting the Bill of Rights in its final form, and American Catholics have endorsed and observed its provisions at least as well as other American groups ever since.

---

[18] Kelly and Harbison, *op. cit.,* p. 176.

[19] See "Letter to Madison, March, 1789," in Padover, Saul K., *Complete Jefferson* (New York: Duell, Sloan and Pearce, 1943), p. 123.

[20] This matter is treated further in Chapter 4 on "The Separation of Church and State." See Madison's "Letter to Jefferson, October, 1788," in Hunt, Gaillard (ed.), *The Writings of James Madison* (New York: G. P. Putnam's Sons, 1904), Vol. V, p. 269. For a long and fully documented discussion, see O'Neill, *Religion and Education Under the Constitution,* Chapts. 5, 6, and 7.

3

CATHOLIC SUPPORT OF AMERICAN FREEDOM

IMMEDIATELY following the ratification in 1791 of the first ten amendments to the Constitution (the federal Bill of Rights) there began the consistent record of American Catholic endorsement of our total constitutional situation. This approval, lay and clerical, has been substantially unbroken for 160 years. Yet today it is asserted that fundamental Catholic doctrine prevents Catholics from being good citizens in a free, democratic society. Even more specifically, the charge is that Catholics cannot believe in religious freedom and in equality *before the law* of the Catholic Church with other religious denominations. The "Catholic people" are not held responsible, but "the hierarchy," it is asserted, will not allow them freedom of thought and action and are scheming to destroy religious liberty as soon as they have the "power."

In the 160 years since the ratification of the Bill of Rights there have been over five hundred members of the hierarchy (bishops) of the Catholic Church in America. It is obviously impossible to examine all the writings of each and every American Catholic bishop, and space limits the quotations that can be furnished from the works of a few of the leading bishops. These demonstrate how unvarying has been their endorsement of the American system, especially religious equality and freedom before the law, in sermons, public speeches, and official documents. Readers can balance these statements against the total absence of *any statement,* or the citing of any teaching or action, from *any member* of the American Catholic hierarchy which supports the contention that the Catholic hierarchy are, or ever were, opposed to or planning to defeat and destroy American democracy and religious freedom.

I trust I do not need to consider the propositions that the American Catholic bishops have never understood Catholic doctrine in this area or, understanding it, have throughout our history hypocritcally taught what they knew to be false.

This is not to say that there are not some American Catholics who do not agree with the bishops in these matters. In fact, I should be surprised if a *complete* search of all the speeches and papers of all Catholic bishops who have ever lived in America would not uncover some expressions that *might be interpreted* to the contrary. However, I have never seen one. Those who try to make a case against the American hierarchy have never, so far as I can discover, cited one. I have known of a few that are the expressions of individual laymen, a few priests, not bishops, and certainly not Catholic theologians. Assertions that Catholic Americans do not believe in democracy and civil liberties, at least as well as other Americans, in so far as they are honest, must, therefore, arise from an avoidance of information. Obviously if one wants to hunt up special phrases that *some* Catholics have written *somewhere* about *something* (and if one is not interested in the validity or relevancy of a phrase in proving what it is offered to prove), one can make a fraudulent case against the Catholic Church, or against any organization that has had many members and a long history. But such puerile "scholarship" proves nothing about Catholic "doctrine" or about the belief and practice of American Catholics.

The participation of leading Catholic laymen of the day in the writing, ratification, and the support of the original Constitution and the Bill of Rights has been shown in the preceding chapter. That this Catholic endorsement of our American system has been recognized by competent non-Catholic scholars can be fully demonstrated. Space allows a few quotations only. Professor Ralph Barton Perry of Harvard writes: [1]

---

[1] *Puritanism and Democracy* (New York: Vanguard Press, 1944), p. 188.

Catholics could and did rightly claim an affinity of doctrine with the age of enlightenment. The conception of natural law was a recognized part of scholastic teaching. Catholicism consistently refused to accept the supremacy of the state in matters of morals and conscience, so that there was an appeal from civil authority, which might, at least in principle, be invoked as a sanction of political revolution. Catholicism's conception of man was closer to the optimistic attitude of the enlightenment than was Protestantism's emphasis on human depravity, and Catholics, as a minority, were glad to avail themselves of the guarantees of religious liberty. On these and similar grounds leaders of Catholic thought in America repeatedly affirmed their accord both with the Declaration of Independence and with the Constitution.

Dr. Ray Allen Billington, Professor of History in Northwestern University, after referring to Charles Carroll's purpose in signing the Declaration of Independence, writes: [2]

> Later, in the drafting of the Constitution Catholics played a leading part in the debates on religious freedom and helped write those basic clauses which prohibited religious tests for officeholding and which denied Congress the right to make any law "respecting an establishment of religion, or prohibiting the free exercise thereof." These guarantees were enthusiastically acclaimed by all American Catholics. "Thanks to genuine spirit and Christianity," the Reverend John Carroll wrote in the *Columbian Magazine* for December, 1787, "the United States have banished intolerance from their system of government. . . . Freedom and independence, acquired by the united efforts, and cemented with the mingled blood of Protestant and Catholic fellow citizens, should be equally enjoyed by all."

Professor Billington sums up the long struggle for disestablishment in the following passage:

> Between 1786, when Virginia severed the political bond between religion and government, and 1833, when lagging Massachusetts finally fell into line, the battle for disestablishment went on in state after state. In each struggle a popular leader emerged to absorb most of the glory; but the real heroes were the rank and file of the Presbyterians, Baptists, Quakers and Catholics.

Madison testified as follows in regard to support of his *Memorial*

---

[2] "American Catholicism and the Church-State Issue," *Christendom,* Vol. V, No. 3, 1940, pp. 355–365.

and Remonstrance (his great argument against making Christianity the established religion of Virginia):[3]

> It met with the approbation of the Baptists, the Presbyterians, the Quakers, and the few Roman Catholics, universally; of the Methodists in part; and even of not a few of the Sect [Anglican] formerly established by law.

The position of the Catholic hierarchy of America has been open, emphatic, unequivocal, and consistent from John Carroll down to 1951. I shall quote from the easily available works of the outstanding leaders of the hierarchy for 160 years.

Bishop John England, of Charleston, South Carolina, from 1820 to 1842, usually considered the leader of the American hierarchy of his day, was one of the most frequent, vigorous, and unyielding defenders of American democracy and religious equality and freedom of any leader, lay or clerical, in the history of our country. His *Works* in five volumes contain ample evidence. I quote from one of his best known speeches delivered before Congress in the House of Representatives on January 8, 1826:[4]

> A political difficulty has been sometimes raised here. If this infallible tribunal, which you profess yourselves bound to obey, should command you to overturn our government, and tell you that it is the will of God to have it new modelled, will you be bound to obey it? And how then can we consider those men to be good citizens, who profess to owe obedience to a foreign authority,—to an authority not recognised in our constitution,—to an authority which has excommunicated and deposed sovereigns, and which has absolved subjects and citizens from their bond of allegiance.
>
> Our answer to this is extremely simple and very plain; it is, that we would not be bound to obey it,—that we recognise no such authority. I would not allow to the Pope, or to any bishop of our church, outside this Union, the smallest interference with the humblest vote at our most insignificant balloting box. He has no right to such interference. You must, from the view which I have taken, see the plain distinction between spiritual authority and a right to interfere in the regulation of human government or civil concerns.

---

[3] *The William and Mary Quarterly,* 3rd, Ser. III (October, 1946), pp. 555–556.

[4] *The Works of the Right Rev. John England,* arranged by the Rt. Rev. I. A. Reynolds (Baltimore: John Murphy and Co., 1849), Vol. IV, pp. 172–190, at pp. 184–185.

You have in your constitution wisely kept them distinct and separate. It will be wisdom, and prudence, and safety to continue the separation.

You have no power to interfere with my religious rights; the tribunal of the church has no power to interfere with my civil rights. It is a duty which every good man ought to discharge for his own, and for the public benefit, to resist any encroachment upon either. It must hence be apparent, that any idea of the Roman Catholics of these republics being in any way under the influence of any foreign ecclesiastical power, or indeed of any church authority in the exercise of their civil rights, is a serious mistake.

Cardinal Gibbons wrote:[5]

Sixteen millions of Catholics live their lives on our land with undisturbed belief in the perfect harmony existing between their religion and their duties as American citizens. . . . They prefer its form of government before any other. They admire its institutions and its laws. They accept the Constitution without reserve, with no desire, as Catholics, to see it changed in any feature.

The Separation of Church and State in this country seems to them the natural, inevitable and best conceivable plan, the one that would work best among us, both for the good of religion and of the State. Any change in their relations they would contemplate with dread. They are well aware, indeed, that the Church here enjoys a larger liberty and a more secure position than in any country today where Church and State are united.

No establishment of religion is being dreamed of here, of course, by anyone; but were it to be attempted, it would meet with united opposition from the Catholic people, priests and prelates.

Archbishop John Ireland, an influential spokesman for American Catholicism in his time, on October 18, 1892, said:[6]

The Church and the age are at war. I voice the fact with sorrow. Both Church and age are at fault. . . . I blame the age. . . . I blame the Church. I speak as a Catholic. I know the divine elements in the Church. . . . But I know that upon those human elements much of the Church's weal depends. . . .

I am not afraid to say that, during the century whose sun is now setting, many leaders of thought in the Church have made the mistake of being too

[5] Gibbons, James Cardinal, "The Church and the Republic," Reprinted from *The North American Review, in Retrospect of Fifty Years* (Baltimore: John Murphy and Co., 1916), pp. 210–214.

[6] *The Church and Modern Society,* by John Ireland, Archbishop of St. Paul (St. Paul, Chicago and New York: Pioneer Press, 1905), Vol. I, pp. 108–112.

slow to understand the new age and too slow to extend to it the conciliatory hand of friendship. They were not without their reasons. . . . The movements of the age were frequently ushered into existence under most repellent and inauspicious forms. The revolution of 1789 . . . was the loud signal of the new era. The standard-bearers of the age often raised aloft the insignia of impiety and of social anarchy. But with all these excuses, churchmen thought and acted too slowly. . . . There were a few Lacordaires, who recognized and proclaimed the duties of the hour: but timid companions abandoned them; reactionaries accused them of dangerous liberalism, of semi-heresy; and they were forced to be silent. The many saw but the vices of the age, which they readily anathematized; its good and noble tendencies they either ignored or denied. For them the age was the dark world against which Christ had warned His followers. . . .

It was a mistake and a misfortune. "Go, teach all nations," Christ had said once for all time. Even if our age had been radically evil and erring, the methods and the zeal of the early apostles would have won it to the Saviour. But, in veriest fact, the present age, pagan as it may be in its language and its extravagances, is, in its depths, instinct with Christian emotions; it worships unwittingly at Christian shrines.

Men must be taught that the Church and the age are not hopelessly separated.

The Most Rev. John T. McNicholas, Archbishop of Cincinnati and Chairman of the Administration Board of the National Catholic Welfare Conference, spoke for the American hierarchy in 1948: [7]

The Manifesto recently issued by the organization, "Protestants and Other Americans United for the Separation of Church and State," is a strange document. . . . Every informed person—Protestant, Jew, and Catholic—must deny that the American Bishops have ever committed themselves "to a policy plainly subversive of religious liberty as guaranteed by the Constitution," and that the Catholic Church has ever sought "a position of special privilege in relation to the state," or that the Bishops have attempted "to fracture the constitutional principle at one point after another where the action can be minimized as trivial or disguised as falling within some other category than that of its ultimate intent," and likewise, "to breach the wall that sharply separates church and state in this country." These same informed persons must regard the Manifesto as an outrageous indictment,

[7] "The Catholic Church in American Democracy," Press release, Jan. 26, 1948, N.C.W.C., Office of Information, 1312 Massachusetts Avenue, N.W., Washington 5, D.C.

charging the Catholic Bishops with "aggressive activities of those who would subvert the Constitution to their sectarian interest."

The signers of the Manifesto speak of the Bishops of "a powerful church, unaccustomed in its own history and tradition to the American ideal of separation of church and state . . ." and committing "itself in authoritative declarations and by positive acts to a policy plainly subversive of religious liberty as guaranteed by the Constitution. This church holds and maintains the theory of the relation of church and state which is incompatible with the American ideal."

. . . .

We deny absolutely and without any qualification that the Catholic Bishops of the United States are seeking a union of church and state by any endeavors whatsoever, either proximate or remote. If tomorrow Catholics constituted a majority in our country, they would not seek a union of church and state. . . . The signers of the Manifesto assume that their attempt to have the Supreme Court reverse its decisions is a patriotic virtue, but that it is criminal for others to seek an interpretation of an amendment of the Constitution. . . .

Finally I quote from the official statement of the American Catholic hierarchy, issued after the annual meeting of the Catholic bishops in Washington, in November 1948.[8] This should be wholly satisfactory to any fairminded scholar who is interested in the position of the American hierarchy in regard to their attitude toward our American system of religious equality before the law, and religious freedom for everyone, now and in the future.

In regard to the establishment of religion clause, there is no doubt of the intent of the legislator. It is clear in the record of the Congress that framed it and of the state legislatures that ratified it. To them it meant no official Church for the country as a whole, no preferment of one religion over another by the Federal Government—and at the same time no interference by the Federal Government in the Church-State relations of the individual states. The opinion of the Court advances no reason for disregarding the mind of the legislator. But that reason is discernible in a concurring opinion adhered to by four of the nine judges. There we see clearly the determining influence of secularist theories of public education—and possibly of law. One cannot but remark that if this secularist influence is to prevail in our Government and its institutions, such a result should in candor and logic and law be

[8] Washington, National Catholic Welfare Conference, 1948.

achieved by legislation adopted after full popular, ideological interpretation of our Constitution. We therefore, hope and pray that the novel interpretation of the First Amendment recently adopted by the Supreme Court will in due process be revised. We feel with deep conviction that for the sake of both good citizenship and religion there should be a reaffirmation of our original American tradition of free cooperation between government and religious bodies—*cooperation involving no special privilege to any group and no restriction on the religious liberty of any citizen. We solemnly disclaim any intent or desire to alter this prudent and fair American policy* of government in dealing with the delicate problems that have their source in the divided religious allegiance of our citizens. [Italics mine. J.M.O'N.]

It would be difficult to write in simple English a better brief, clear, unambiguous endorsement of the American doctrine of the relation of government to religion.

The position shown here as taken by the American hierarchy from 1791 to 1949 is the regular, standard, traditional, American position of the meaning of the religious clause of the First Amendment (as shown in detail in Chapter 4). To talk of an "American principle of the separation of church and state" in any other terms (as in the Rutledge doctrine in the Everson and McCollum cases) is either incompetent or dishonest. "No special privilege to any group and no restriction on the religious liberty of any citizen," in the words of the Catholic bishops, has been our traditional and constitutional system throughout our history. No informed person can honestly question that it has been the position of all the following: [9]

1. Madison and Jefferson, both in their writings and in their official actions as presidents of the United States, each for eight years. Neither ever used the expression "an establishment of religion" to mean anything other than special government favor for one religion or one religious group, and consequent discrimination against all outside the favored group. (O'Neill, Chapters 5 and 6.)
2. The first Congress in debating and framing the Bill of Rights and in other laws and resolutions. (O'Neill, Chapter 7.)
3. Every Congress in United States history, both before and after the McCollum decision. (O'Neill, Chapter 7.)

---

[9] For detailed and documented substantiation, see O'Neill, *Religion and Education Under the Constitution,* at point shown after each statement.

4. Every President of the United States from Washington to Truman, including both. (Two of them, Grant and Garfield, wanted the Constitution changed to include the essence of the Rutledge doctrine, but Congress would not allow it to go to the states for possible ratification.) (O'Neill, Chapter 7.)
5. Every administration of every state in the Union, both before and after the ratification of the Fourteenth Amendment (1868). All have throughout their whole history used state money and personnel to aid religion or religious education in various ways (but not in all possible ways). (O'Neill, Chapter 9.)
6. The pre-eminent scholars in constitutional law from Joseph Story to Edward S. Corwin, including both. (O'Neill, pp. 44–45.)
7. Every relevant Supreme Court decision prior to that in the McCollum case (1948). The Everson *decision* was consistent with the language and purpose of the First Amendment, and with all prior American history and practice. The *opinions,* however, both majority and minority, in that case contained many errors. The majority arrived strangely at the *right decision* after indulging in inaccurate history, language, law, and logic. (O'Neill, Chapter 8.)

There is no opposition between American constitutional provisions and American traditional practice, on the one hand, and Catholic doctrine and American Catholic practice and objective, on the other hand. Differences of belief or statement on this matter do not represent a clash between Catholics and non-Catholics, but only a clash between the informed and the uninformed.

II

Catholic Belief and Practice

4

THE SEPARATION OF CHURCH AND STATE

PROBABLY the most fundamental and widespread misrepresentation of the position of American Catholics is the charge that they do not sincerely believe in the American system of the relationship of government to religion. This distortion usually misrepresents *both* the American traditional and constitutional system, and the attitude of American Catholics toward it. The *official* American expression of relation of government to religion is found in the Constitution of the United States, and in the various state constitutions. The American *tradition* in regard to the relation of government to religion, ambiguously called the "separation of church and state," must necessarily be found in American practice during the history of this republic as an independent nation.

We get the clearest and most important example of the falsification of both the American system of the relation of religion and government (church and state) and of the position of American Catholics in regard to it in statements in and about the so-called Rutledge doctrine. This was first expressed in any important setting or context by Mr. Justice Rutledge in the dissenting opinion in the Everson bus case.[1] In this case the court decided that the transportation of pupils to Catholic schools in New Jersey at public expense did not create "an establishment of religion" in violation of the federal Constitution. The *decision* is the only possible one that squares with history, tradition, legislative and executive practice, and previous Supreme Court decisions, but the

[1] 330 U.S. 1 (1947).

language of the opinion of the court by Mr. Justice Black contains historical and linguistic errors.[2] The Rutledge *dissenting* opinion has little relation to the realities of language, history, biography, or law.[3] The *dicta* in this dissenting opinion, however, and some of the careless language in the majority opinion in this case, concerning the purpose and meaning of the First Amendment, was the basis (in so far as there was a basis) for the McCollum decision [4] which outlawed "released time" in the public schools of Champaign, Illinois.

Here the court decided that voluntary religious education, in which all religious groups had equal opportunities, in public school buildings, in school hours, taught by representatives of the participating religious groups (Protestant, Catholic, and Jewish) constituted "an establishment of religion" in violation of the First and Fourteenth Amendments. This *decision* (the first in Supreme Court history so to treat the First Amendment, 157 years after it became part of the Constitution) is now the official expression of the Rutledge doctrine.

This is the essence of the Rutledge doctrine as expressed in the Everson and McCollum cases (italics mine):

> The Amendment's *purpose* was not to strike merely at the official establishment of a single sect, creed or religion, outlawing only a formal relation such as had prevailed in England and some of the colonies. Necessarily it was to uproot all such relationships. The object was broader than separating church and state in this narrow sense. It was to create *a complete and permanent separation of the spheres of religious activity and Civil authority* by comprehensively *forbidding every form of public aid or support for religion. . . .* The prohibition broadly *forbids state support, financial or other of religion in any guise, form or degree.* It *outlaws all use of public funds for religious purposes.*[5]

This statement is nonsense. The language of the First Amendment, which Justice Rutledge was discussing, is: "Congress shall make no law respecting an establishment of religion." Anyone who knows the meaning of these English words knows that the Rutledge statement is

---

[2] O'Neill, *Religion and Education Under the Constitution,* pp. 189–218.
[3] *Ibid.,* pp. 201–211.
[4] 333 U.S. 203 (1948).
[5] 330 U.S. 1, pp. 31–33.

absurd. Considering (1) that we had in America at the time the First Amendment was adopted and ratified five established Protestant churches in five of the states, and (2) that the Constitution was so drawn at Philadelphia as to make the federal government a government of delegated powers only, and (3) that no authority had been delegated to the federal government over any such matters as the relation of government to religion, and (4) that some of the established churches in the various states continued for a number of decades after the ratification of the First Amendment,[6] it seems to me that the statement of the justices in the Rutledge doctrine that the Amendment's purpose was to uproot all such relationships is a textbook example of "nonsense"—a mixture of the false and the silly. *Prohibitions of action* do not *uproot* either laws or weeds in the garden.

Anyone who knows the most elementary facts of relevant American history knows that the First Amendment was not designed to, *and did not,* uproot any establishment of religion anywhere, or *prevent* the constant use of federal funds to aid religion on a nondiscriminatory basis from 1791 to the present day.

We should keep in mind in this discussion of the Rutledge doctrine that the positions of the justices in the Everson and McCollum opinions was explicitly based on their assertions as to the *purpose* of the First Amendment. Such questions as the validity of educational theories, the *wisdom* of certain state laws, the merits of secularism or atheism, or the truth of any doctrine of any positive religion were not before the justices for decision. Their basic questions were: Does transportation of pupils to denominational (in this case Catholic) schools at public expense (Everson case) and does "released time" for voluntary religious education, not at public expense, in school buildings in school hours (McCollum case), constitute in each case "an establishment of religion" within the meaning of the First Amendment? The court said "No" to the first and "Yes" to the second. Four justices, dissenting, in the Everson case enunciated the Rutledge doctrine, and eight accepted it in the McCollum case.

The purpose of such a statement as "Congress shall make no law

[6] The last one (Massachusetts) disappeared in 1833.

respecting an establishment of religion," if it is not clear, should be sought by anyone, regardless of his religious convictions, in the dictionaries, encyclopedias, histories, biographies, and government records, relevant to the time and the men responsible for the use of the sentence in question. Competence in the use of the English language and in the techniques of scholarship are the requirements for such an investigation. Any differences of opinion in regard to the purpose of that statement in the First Amendment must result from inadequate scholarship on the part of someone, and that here, as elsewhere, the cure for inadequate scholarship is more and better scholarship, not assumptions and assertions based upon irrelevant emotions or theories of religion and education.

If the First Amendment had a purpose, the men of the First Congress who wrote and adopted it had to have that purpose in their minds. The purpose of any language that has a purpose, used anywhere, by anyone, must exist in the minds of the persons using the language. The *purpose* can be nowhere else. But these men of the First Congress, just after expressing their purpose in the language of the First Amendment, went on almost immediately [7] (1) to set up chaplaincies for Congress and in the army, (2) to initiate the proceedings, under Washington's recommendation, to spend government funds for the spread of Christianity among the Indians, and (3) to ask the President to call a day of prayer and thanksgiving to Almighty God for His blessing on the young republic. One must have small respect for the men of the First Congress of the United States to believe that they expressed the purpose ascribed to them by the justices of the Supreme Court in the Everson and McCollum cases, and then immediately started various undertakings to spend government money in aid of religious activity.

These ways of spending government money to promote religious activity in the United States have been expanded and carried on *without interruption* (but with some changes from time to time) from 1790 to 1951. All of them are being used today.

Further, we also have in the *Annals* of the First Congress Madison's

---

[7] O'Neill, *op. cit.*, pp. 110–111, 115–119.

clear statement as to what he considered to be the purpose of this language, viz.:

he apprehended the meaning of the words to be, that Congress should not establish a religion, and enforce the legal observation of it by law, nor compel men to worship God in any manner contrary to their conscience. Whether the words are necessary or not he did not mean to say, but they had been required by some of the State Conventions who seemed to fear that Congress might

> make laws of such a nature as might infringe the rights of conscience, and establish a national religion; to prevent these effects he presumed the amendment was intended, and he thought it as well expressed as the nature of the language would admit.[8]

The Federal Constitution provides, in the first place, that "Congress shall make no law respecting an establishment of religion." The questions may arise "What was the subject concerning which Congress was forbidden to legislate? What was meant by the men of the first Congress and the ratifying states by 'an establishment of religion'?" The answer is easy. They must have meant what the phrase had meant for centuries to historians, theologians, and other scholars, Catholic and Protestant, lay and religious, European and American, down to, and long after, the period in which the Bill of Rights was written, adopted, and ratified. "An establishment of religion," through all this time, meant (1) an *exclusive arrangement,* (2) created by government, (3) giving a preferential status *under the government* to one favored religion, and (4) a consequent discrimination against all other religions.

Neither the modern proponents of aggressive secularism nor the Supreme Court justices, in the current campaign to amend the Constitution by substituting the figurative "wall of separation between church and state" for the literal language of the First Amendment, have ever cited *a single instance* of a contrary use of the meaning of "an establishment of religion" by any historian, theologian, or other scholar of distinction, Catholic, Protestant, secularist, or atheist, European or American, in the whole sweep of time in which this phrase

---

[8] Benton, T. H. (Ed.), *Annals of Congress,* Abridged by J. C. Rives (New York: D. Appleton-Century Company, 1858), Vol. I, pp. 729–731. See also O'Neill, *op. cit.,* pp. 87–98.

has been dealt with innumerable times by such scholars. Specifically none of these propagandists has cited a single instance of any other use of the phrase by Jefferson, Madison, or other Founding Fathers.

The basic idea of the religious clause of the First Amendment was to express in words in the Constitution the situation which Alexander Hamilton, Thomas Jefferson, and James Madison all agreed was implicit in the constitutional situation expressed in the original Constitution as written and signed in Philadelphia in 1787, viz.: that the federal government had no authority in this area. Hamilton [9] thought this situation was so clear that the matter should not be mentioned in a Bill of Rights. Jefferson agreed fundamentally with this position, but he wanted, as he said, a Bill of Rights in order to have a text by which to try the actions of future federal governments if they should attempt to usurp the power of the state governments or of the people of various states.[10] A request for precisely this kind of expression in the Bill of Rights was expressed again and again in connection with the discussion of the original Constitution in the various states. Resolutions and petitions were passed which asked specifically for the inclusion in the Bill of Rights of a statement in agreement with the position that "no religious sect or society ought to be favored or established by law in preference to others." [11]

In other words, the *purpose* of the First Amendment was simply to make explicit what was implicit in the constitutional situation, viz.: that the state government, and not the federal government, should have exclusive governmental authority in the areas of what Jefferson called "their domestic concerns," such as religion and education. Language exactly expressing this much-desired situation, so that all in the future might read in the Constitution what the actual situation was, satisfied the widely prevalent desire of the people of the individual states to maintain their governmental authority in matters of religion. It had the secondary effect of making it impossible for the national government ever to create *"an establishment of religion,"* viz.: a single religion having under the national government a position of preference

[9] *Ibid.*, p. 92.

[10] "Letter to Madison, March, 1789," Padover, *The Complete Jefferson*, p. 123.

[11] O'Neill, *op. cit.*, pp. 112–114.

over all other religions. If Congress could never make a law on the subject, the federal government could never create such an establishment.

The state governments by the First Amendment, were given the desired constitutional statement to the effect that the federal government could not interfere with state action concerning "an establishment of religion," either *pro* or *con*. They proceeded eventually to disestablish the five established Protestant churches that were in existence at that time. In their complete freedom of action, they passed various laws and constitutional provisions concerning religion and religious education, *always* without the interference by the federal government and *always* without invoking the federal Constitution. This situation was accepted substantially without question for about a century and a half after the adoption of the First Amendment.

When the states ratified the first ten amendments (the Bill of Rights), they were not *giving themselves permission* to do anything; nor were the states giving Congress power to keep the states from doing anything. They were simply spelling out, so that men of the future might read, that certain powers then residing in the individual states were *not being transferred* to the Congress of the United States. It should be understood and remembered by those who think that all defense of freedom of any kind is a power conferred on the states by the federal Constitution that it was the *ratification* by the states which gave the Bill of Rights any legal status at all. The action of the First Congress of the United States in writing and adopting it was only a proposal to the states.

In ratifying the Fourteenth Amendment in 1868 the states surrendered some of their power to the federal government. How much, no one knows. The Supreme Court in dealing with the Fourteenth Amendment has rendered decisions that were not only inconsistent with each other, but also inconsistent with the language and purpose of the Fourteenth Amendment. The best sources of light on the purpose of this amendment (other than its words) are the statements of the men who adopted it.[12] There is also abundant confirmatory evi-

---

[12] *Congressional Globe, Thirty-ninth Congress,* Part 2 (Washington: Congressional Globe Office, 1866).

dence, gathered together in one place, and accurately quoted and documented.[13]

No person has an *intellectual* right to believe or to proclaim that the *intent or purpose* of the First Amendment was anything other than to prohibit *any federal law either for or against a national preference for one religion or one religious group*. Under the Constitution he doubtless has a *legal right,* and according to most codes of morality he has a *moral right* if his knowledge is sufficiently slight or his conscience not functioning.

If the Supreme Court justices are right in declaring that the "purpose" of the First Amendment was to prohibit any government aid, financial or other, to religion in any guise, form, or degree, we have never had a president of the United States who understood the purpose of the First Amendment and who had sufficient integrity to live up to his oath of office. This would mean that both Jefferson and Madison failed to understand the First Amendment or else were lacking in personal integrity. This would also be true of Washington, who as president was much interested in this action of the First Congress, of Monroe, who was a member of the First Congress (but not until after the Bill of Rights was adopted), of both the Adamses, of Lincoln, Garfield, and Woodrow Wilson, the historian and political scientist, of both Roosevelts—of all our presidents without exception. It would be interesting to read a tabulation by one of the Supreme Court justices, or by one of our militant secularists, listing our thirty-two presidents and indicating *in regard to each president* whether, in the opinion of the maker of the list, *each* president was lacking in an understanding of the First Amendment or in respect for his oath of office.

Not only have all our presidents acted upon the understanding that the First Amendment was not designed to prohibit impartial government aid to religion, but each Congress of the United States has done the same. Every Congress, without a single exception, has used public money in the promotion of religious activities.[14] Further, there have been some twenty attempts made to put into the Constitution the es-

[13] O'Neill, *op. cit.,* especially Chapts. 10 and 12.
[14] *Ibid.,* Chapt. 7.

sence of the so-called Rutledge doctrine, that no public money may be used to support religion or religious education "in any guise, form, or degree." Congress, acting for the American people, in the discharge of a responsibility placed upon it by the Constitution of the United States, has declined to adopt any of the various amendments introduced to express this doctrine. Eleven different attempts were defeated in Congress or died in Congressional committees between 1870 and 1888.[15]

The last such proposal, the Bryson bill, died in committee in the Eightieth Congress.

Not only have all presidents and all Congresses used public money in aid of religion and religious education, but every state in the Union, from the day of its beginning, has used state tax-supported facilities and personnel, cooperating with religion and religious education.[16]

No distinguished American scholar in the field of constitutional law has ever endorsed the Rutledge theory of the purpose and meaning of the First Amendment. From Joseph Story[17] to Edward S. Corwin[18] the line is unbroken. *The American Bar Journal*[19] also is opposed to the McCollum decision.

No relevant Supreme Court case prior to the McCollum decision has been cited or can be cited in support of the Rutledge doctrine. Justice Rutledge referred to previous "consistent utterances" of the court, but cited none, for the best of all possible reasons. He was also in error when he said the meaning of the phrase "an establishment of religion" was before the court for the first time in the Everson case. It was raised in much clearer fashion, and dealt with in conformity to

---

[15] *Ibid.*

[16] *Ibid.*, pp. 140–152, relying on N.E.A. *Research Bulletin,* Vol. XXIV, No. 1, p. 78.

[17] *Commentaries on the Constitution of the United States* (Boston: Hilliard and Co., 1833), 5th ed. (1891), Vol. II, sec. 1873. Quoted by O'Neill, *op. cit.,* pp. 63–64.

[18] *The Constitution—What It Means Today* (Princeton: Princeton University Press, 1947), 9th ed., pp. 154–156. Quoted by O'Neill, *op. cit.,* pp. 64–65.

[19] Vol. 34, No. 6 (June, 1948), pp. 482–484. See also Rev. Erwin L. Shaver, "Three Years after the Champaign case" (Oberlin). *Religious Education,* January-February 1951, pp. 33–38, and Robert F. Drinan, S.J., "The Novel 'Liberty' created by the McCollum decision," Washington, *The Georgetown Law Journal,* January, 1951, pp. 216–241.

over a century of history, tradition, and legal scholarship, in *Bradfield* v. *Roberts,* 1899.[20] In this case Justice Peckham, in an opinion delivered for a unanimous court, said that "a religious establishment" was "a phrase which is not synonymous with that used in the Constitution which prohibits the passage of a law 'respecting an establishment of religion.'" In other words, the First Amendment did not prohibit a law about a religious establishment, such as a hospital, church, school, orphan asylum conducted under religious auspices, but a law about a monopolistic position of favor to one religious group and so discriminating against all other religious groups. Used in the context of laws and constitutions, it could not have meant anything else to any competent lawmaker in 1789.

The position that this universally accepted American constitutional and traditional theory of the relation of religion to government is now simply *an un-American Catholic position* is a shameful and shabby pretense, unworthy of any scholar, any Christian, or any good American citizen.

The fact that some popes and other Catholics have condemned policies that were called "the separation of church and state" in other countries has been used by the unscholarly to support the false claim that the sort of separation we have in this country is contrary to Catholic doctrine. This claim can be true only on the assumption that substantially all American Catholics, bishops, priests, and laymen, for 160 years have been either ignorant of Catholic doctrine or universally and deliberately insincere. Fair-minded Americans ought to ask for some proof before accepting this assumption.

Anyone who either praises or condemns "the separation of church and state" without indicating (1) what kind or degree of *separation* he is talking about, (2) what kind of institution, organization, or influence he means by *church,* and (3) what sort of civic unit, form of government, or theory of politics he means by *state,* is either himself confused or is deliberately trying to confuse his readers, or both.

There is not, never has been, and cannot properly ever be, a single *Catholic position* on the *meaning* of the First Amendment. I wrote in 1949: [21]

---

[20] 175 U.S. 291.

[21] *Thought,* September, 1949, pp. 575–576.

I object to the idea . . . that informed American Catholics can and do properly take positions in regard to the First Amendment, or Supreme Court decisions concerning it, which are different from those of other understanding Americans who believe in constitutional democracy.

If the American people ever put into the Constitution a provision that is hostile to religion in general or to Catholicism in particular, I should expect every honest American Catholic to defend the Court for finding that provision in the Constitution, and to denounce the Court if it distorted the Constitution to make it say the opposite. To take any other position seems to me to qualify one for membership in Protestants and Other Americans United. There is not now any such provision in the Constitution. The best way to get such provision put into the Constitution is to take the position that there are Catholic interpretations, or special interpretations that are, or should be, favored in Catholic circles; in other words, that the Constitution properly means something to informed Catholics that it could not be expected to mean to informed non-Catholics. . . .

There is not, and cannot be in any proper sense of the phrase, a Catholic position, as distinct from a non-Catholic position, on an item dealing with the separation of powers between the states and the Federal government.

American Catholics are not, never have been, and cannot be, a group apart from other Americans who believe in the observance of all of the constitutional provisions the American people have adopted in both state and nation. Certainly anyone of any religion, or of none, is free to work for amendments which he would like to see ratified. But anyone who likes to see the Court subvert the Constitution, as it did in the McCollum case, to favor positions he favors, is an enemy of constitutional democracy, and as such is, in my opinion, an effective enemy of the political system most conducive to the development of religion, Catholicism, and civilization itself.

The men and women who have applauded the decision of the Supreme Court in the McCollum case as a defense of civil liberties in general and religious freedom in particular have apparently not realized how it creates a precedent for making "constitutional" the destruction of these very liberties. If the Supreme Court as constituted in 1948 can disregard the purpose and the language of the First Amendment (and one hundred and sixty years of federal and state, legislative, executive, and judicial interpretation of it), what can prevent a future Court with a different membership from doing the same thing? In the McCollum opinions the Justices did not even *discuss* the language of the First Amendment, or explain how they could "apply the 'wall-of-separation' metaphor" (Justice Frankfurter's words)[22] instead of the clause of the Constitution that was under dispute.

If they were justified in preferring to "apply" a figure of speech from the polite correspondence of Thomas Jefferson, why cannot their successors pick out a phrase they like from the letters of Franklin Roosevelt, Herbert Hoover, Woodrow Wilson, or Warren Harding, and be guided by that, instead of by the language that has been ratified by the American people as part of the Constitution? As a still more perfect parallel, take Jefferson's statement in an important document in which he was specifically and responsibly discussing *public education.* This was written thirty-one years after the ratification of the First Amendment and twenty years after the letter to the Baptists of Danbury in which he mentioned the "wall of separation."

> It was not, however, to be understood that *instruction in religious opinion and duties was meant to be precluded by the public authorities,* as indifferent to the interests of society. On the contrary, the relations which exist between Man and his Maker, and the duties resulting from those relations, *are the most interesting and important to every human being, and the most incumbent on his study and investigation.*[23] [Italics mine. J.M.O'N.]

Any future court can take this passage from Jefferson and, on the *assumption* that this necessarily expresses the purpose of the religious clause of the First Amendment, they can decide that this means that "the public authorities" (in the public schools) must require "instruction in religious opinions and duties" as "most incumbent on [the pupils'] study and investigation." They can then rule that instruction in religious *opinion* (belief) and religious *duties* must be included in the curriculum of every public school in the United States. Such an assumption and such a conclusion would do less violence to historical fact, language, logic, and the philosophy of Thomas Jefferson than was done in the McCollum case. And it would be in full accord with the tradition and practice of the American public school system for about its first seventy-five years.[24]

---

[22] 333 U.S. 203.

[23] "Freedom of Religion at the University of Virginia," Padover, *The Complete Jefferson,* p. 957.

[24] See Beale, Howard K., *History of Freedom of Teaching* (New York: Charles Scribner's Sons, 1941), Chapts. I–IV, and O'Neill, *op. cit.,* pp. 26–30.

Those who have applauded the McCollum decision either because they do not like religion or do not like it in the public schools are rocking the boat to get rid of some uncongenial traveling companions —only to find, perhaps, that the fellows they do not like are expert swimmers who will proceed to take over the boat.

Mrs. McCollum's victory has not accomplished much as a part of her campaign against religion.[25] It is being widely ignored in various states, including Virginia, which the justices used (inaccurately) as their Exhibit A. This ignoring of the McCollum decision may be of little importance so far as religion is concerned. It is, however, of primary importance in its unfortunate effect on the very idea of constitutional government. By substituting an edict of the Supreme Court for the provisions of the Constitution it cheapens both. It must be kept in mind that "substitution" not "interpretation" is the correct label for the court's activity. The justices did not even discuss the language of the Constitution or explain why they were free to ignore it.

The chief significance of the McCollum decision is the threat to constitutional democracy in the substitution of the "zeal and prepossessions" [26] of the justices for the language and purpose of the Constitution. This makes a breach in the wall of separation (which the Bill of Rights recognized but did not build) between the arbitrary decisions of government and the civil liberties of the people. This is the wall which should have been "kept high and impregnable." Now, however, through that breach some future court can go to get a better grounding than any the court had in 1948. On that precedent, if the future justices happen to like this sort of government, the court can proclaim that each state in its public schools should teach *religious opinions and duties* according to the tenets of Methodism, Catholicism, Mormonism, or some other religious creed, which each state may select by popular vote or act of the legislature. For my part I should rather have "released time" and constitutional government, or just constitutional government.

In spite of the constant agreement of the clear, official, unambigu-

---

[25] See Shaver, *op. cit.*, and Drinan, *op. cit.*

[26] Justice Jackson's statement of the only basis of the opinion in the McCollum case in which he *concurred*.

ous records of both the Catholic hierarchy and American government (both state and national) throughout our history, Mr. Blanshard tries to persuade his readers that there is a fundamental opposition between the Church and American democracy and freedom. His position is false and unproved. The central thesis of Mr. Blanshard's book is made up of his double misrepresentation of (1) the general principles of American freedom as expressed in the Constitution, and more particularly our traditional practice and our constitutional provisions in the area of government relations with religion, and (2) the American Catholic attitude toward these principles and traditions. Mr. Blanshard accepts, endorses, and assumes the validity of the Rutledge doctrine as expressing American tradition and constitutional provisions. He writes (p. 88): "The principle of the separation of church and state is not only one of the most fundamental principles of American life, but it expresses the determination of most Americans to avoid snobbishness and separatism in community affairs." He nowhere gives his meaning of "the separation of church and state," but assumes that the phrase means the Rutledge doctrine of no government aid to religion in any way. This is false, as has been shown earlier.

On the same page he writes: "The First Amendment to the United States Constitution forbade the establishment of any religion. . . ." This is inaccurate. The First Amendment only forbade *Congress* to make a law either for or against "*an* establishment of religion" and had nothing to do with a state establishment in any state. It said no United States (national) establishment could be created.

Mr. Blanshard endorses the statement of the Rutledge doctrine (p. 91), not mentioning its inaccuracies in history (particularly that of the First Congress), in the Supreme Court records, the record of the federal government for 160 years, and the consistent positions of Jefferson and Madison as shown by both their writings and their official actions.

Mr. Blanshard tried to spread the idea that criticism of the McCollum decision is a *Catholic attack* upon the Constitution. He remarked (p. 95), in reference to the McCollum decision, "The Catholic bishops of the United States, in solemn assembly at Washington, denounced the highest American court for paying 'scant attention to logic, history, or accepted norms of legal interpretation.' The bitter denunciations of this decision in the American Catholic press reinforced the conviction that it was one of the most important decisions in American legal history." He quotes the above fragment of a sentence *without any documentation.* A simple reference to its source would have enabled a reader more easily to get the whole statement from which this phrase is quoted. It is from the statement "The Christian in Action," issued by all the Catholic bishops of the United States.[27] The whole sentence from which this fragment is extracted reads as follows: "Lawyers trained in the American tradition of law will be amazed to find that in the McCollum case the majority opinions pay scant attention to logic, history, or accepted norms of legal interpretation." That is a mild and fairly accurate statement about the lapses from scholarship on the part of the justices in this case. Any inaccuracy ascribed to it should say that it is too complimentary in that it credits the justices with paying *some* attention to "history, logic, and the accepted norms of legal interpretation." More important, however, is the fact that just preceding this sentence from which Mr. Blanshard lifts a fragment the Catholic bishops refer to, and quote from, the statement of Protestant leaders in religion and education, which was released to the press in June, 1948. In other words, the Catholic bishops, in November, 1948, were stating (in some instances in phrases that are almost identical) the exact position taken in June of that year by leading Protestants. But Mr. Blanshard avoids any indication that the criticism of the McCollum decision has been indulged in by others than the Catholic hierarchy. The complete statement of these Protestant leaders was widely reported in the press. It is here reproduced from *Christianity and Crisis.*[28]

The press release was introduced by a statement, signed by the initials of Dr. J. C. Bennett, discussing "the New Conception of 'Separation' "

calling attention to the dangerous implications in the doctrine of separation of Church and State which is now being rapidly developed by the Supreme

[27] Washington, National Catholic Welfare Conference, November, 1948.
[28] July 5, 1948, pp. 89–90.

Court. . . . The signers of the statement are right in seeing that the Supreme Court extended the meaning of the original conception of "separation" in a most fateful way when it moved from the mere prohibition of an establishment of religion to the exclusion of all cooperation between the State and the various religious bodies even when such cooperation does not give any of them an advantage over others . . . The logic of this new position would destroy all types of cooperation between Church and State which the American people have long taken for granted from the military chaplaincy to tax exemption for church property. Each form of cooperation should be dealt with on its own merits and not eliminated in advance by an *a priori* dogma of separation. . . . This new form of the doctrine of separation tends in practice to give an advantage to aggressive secularism. . . .

STATEMENT ON CHURCH AND STATE

Recent decisions of the Supreme Court have extended the meaning of the constitutional prohibition of an establishment of religion so that any action by the State that is intended to benefit all religious bodies without discrimination is forbidden. This development of the conception of separation of Church and State seems to us to be unwarranted by the language of the First Amendment and to bring about a situation in which forms of cooperation between Church and State that have been taken for granted by the American people will be endangered. We believe that, whatever its intention may be, this hardening of the idea of "separation" by the Court will greatly accelerate the trend toward the secularization of our culture. We favor the separation of Church and State in the sense which we believe to have been intended in the first amendment. *This prohibited the State from giving any Church or religious body a favored position, and from controlling the religious institutions of the nation.* We contend that Jefferson's oft quoted words, "wall of separation," which are not in the Constitution but which are used by the Court in the interpretation of the Constitution, are a misleading metaphor. Cooperation, entered into freely by the State and Church and involving no special privilege to any Church and no threat to the religious liberty of any citizen, should be permitted. [See almost identical statement by the Catholic bishops, pp. 35–36.] As Protestants we desire to affirm this interpretation of the American doctrine of separation of Church and State, and to protest against the interpretation that has been formulated by the Supreme Court.

The situation created by these decisions of our highest Court makes clear that it is important for our great religious communions, without obscuring their differences of faith and policy, to explore the possibilities of working together. Only as we realize such possibilities shall we succeed in maintaining the religious foundations of our national life.

Signatories (to June 17, 1948):

Bishop James C. Baker	Rt. Rev. Angus Dun
Mr. Eugene E. Barnett	Dr. Harry Emerson Fosdick
Professor John Coleman Bennett	Dr. Charles W. Gilkey
Mr. John Crosby Brown	Dr. Douglas Horton
Professor Robert L. Calhoun	Professor Walter M. Horton
Dr. Lynn Harold Hough	Professor Justin Wroe Nixon
Dr. Henry Smith Leiper	Mr. Andrew H. Phelps
Dr. Benjamin E. Mays	Professor Liston Pope
Bishop Francis J. McConnell	Rt. Rev. Edward L. Parsons
Mr. Francis P. Miller	Rt. Rev. William Scarlett
Professor H. Richard Niebuhr	Professor H. Shelton Smith
Professor Reinhold Niebuhr	President Henry P. Van Dusen

Mr. Charles T. White

The Christian Century, June 30, 1948, in an editorial comment on this press release had the following to say under the heading "Protestants take Catholic Line":

> Claiming that the ruling forbids any action by the State that is intended to benefit all religious bodies without discrimination, the statement commits its signers to a position virtually identical with that of the Roman Catholic Church, which contends that tax funds and the civil law may be used to aid churches provided that the aid is available to all churches alike.

It seems to me pitiful that a religious journal can be so distressed by Protestants "taking a position" that is also that of the Roman Catholic Church. I have always supposed that Protestant Christians have been taking for the past few centuries some basic positions which the Catholic Church has taken for the past twenty centuries and still takes. However, the Catholic Church takes no position on the meaning of a phrase in the Constitution. Individual Catholics do; not all the same position. Doubtless the majority of those who are well informed take the same position as informed non-Catholics.

In one of the rare instances in which Mr. Blanshard quotes from a member of the American hierarchy (although he said [p. 6], "Wherever possible I have let the Catholic hierarchy speak for itself") he took (p. 49) one sentence from Archbishop McNicholas' statement (see pp. 34–35), as follows "We deny absolutely and without any qualification that the Catholic bishops of the United States are seeking a union of church and state by any endeavors whatsoever, either proximate or remote."

His comment on this clear and accurate statement of the well-known position of the Catholic bishops since 1791 on this question is simply this: "In the same statement Archbishop McNicholas indicated his belief in government support for Catholic parochial schools and described the Pope as 'the ruler of a sovereign state.' In the mind of Archbishop McNicholas this was not ecclesiastical double-talk, although it conveyed the false impression that the Catholic Church actually believes in the separation of church and state." Thus Mr. Blanshard seeks to convey the impression that American Catholics do not believe in the American plan of "the separation of church and state."

5

DEMOCRACY

IRRESPONSIBLE enemies of religion in general and of Catholicism in particular have been profitably busy recently in spreading false statements concerning the relation of Catholicism to democracy. Especially is an attempt being made currently to persuade non-Catholic Americans that American Catholics do not and cannot sincerely believe in our American democracy.

Anyone who has read the preceding three chapters should know that American Catholics have always believed in and supported the democracy of the United States. However, some people still seem to believe that Catholic support of democracy in our country is a temporary expedient, or a pretense, that is not in accord with fundamental Catholic doctrine.

Among the many publications that refute the contention that *the doctrine of the Church* is incompatible with democracy, there is one that should settle the doubts of anyone who is willing to learn. That is Sheppard's *Religion and the Concept of Democracy*.[1] I select this book not only for its content, which is excellent, but also because of its specific *sponsorship*. It is a Ph.D. dissertation at the Catholic University of America, which is conducted under the supervision and authority of the American hierarchy. This dissertation was directed by the Very

[1] Sheppard, Rev. Vincent F., *Religion and the Concept of Democracy*, A Thomistic Study in Social Philosophy, The Catholic University of America Philosophical Series, Vol. No. 107 (Washington, D.C.: Catholic University of America Press, 1949).

Rev. Ignatius Smith, O.P.,[2] Dean of the School of Philosophy at the Catholic University. At the time this book was published Dean Smith was also *Censor Deputatus* of the diocese of Washington. A *Censor Deputatus* is the official who examines manuscripts submitted for publication by priests and sisters to the bishop of a diocese. The censor grants the *Nihil Obstat* [3] if he finds in the material submitted nothing contrary to Catholic doctrines in faith or morals. Following such certification the bishop grants the *Imprimatur*. Further, this volume carries the *Imprimatur* of Archbishop O'Boyle of Washington. This is one book in which the *Imprimatur* should be of significance to those who wish to learn the relation of democracy to fundamental Catholic *doctrine*. While it is not *a guarantee* that any particular Catholic *agrees* with Father Sheppard, no one who will read this book should contend that Father Sheppard's position on democracy is *contrary* to the doctrine of the Catholic Church.

Father Sheppard wrote:

> Democracy stands midway between individualism and collectivism. Man is neither totally independent of society, as the former view implies; nor is he totally subordinated to it like a brick in a wall, as the latter would have him. . . . The mistake every anti-democratic philosophy commits is to oppose person and society. The individualists and the collectivists alike labor under the illusion that they are dealing with the person *versus* the group. The one champions private selfishness; the other, public voracity.[4]
>
> A truly human society must liberate man. It can do this negatively by not hindering him from pursuing the goal of his life. This amounts to holding sacred his basic rights. A truly human society makes no discrimination here, for rights spring out of man's very essence, which is absolutely equal in all. Society can also liberate man positively by providing a milieu which will give him some appreciable help in his struggle for self-realization. . . . For these reasons, we say that a truly human society must be democratic, for a democracy is a community of the equal, a community of the free.[5]

---

[2] O.P. means the Order of Preachers, commonly called *The Dominicans.* This order was founded in 1216 by St. Dominic. The Dominicans have been known for centuries as scholars in the fields of theology and philosophy.

[3] Attwater, Donald, *A Catholic Dictionary* (New York: Macmillan Company, 1943), p. 363. "Latin. Nothing hinders [it from being printed]. The words by which the censor of books certifies that he has inspected a given work and finds therein nothing contrary to faith or good morals."

[4] *Op. cit.*, p. 26.

[5] *Ibid.*, p. 37.

Archbishop John Ireland of St. Paul, an eloquent exponent of democracy, wrote:[6]

> . . . The Church is at home under all forms of government. The one condition of the legitimacy of a form of government, in the eyes of the Church, is that it be accepted by the people. The Church has never said that she prefers one form of government above another. But, so far as I may from my own thoughts interpret the principles of the Church, I say that the government of the people, by the people, and for the people, is, more than any other, the polity under which the Catholic Church, the church of the people, breathes air most congenial to her mind and heart.

No Catholic scholar pretends that there have not been in the past powerful antidemocratic voices in the Church.

Dr. Rommen, one of the outstanding Catholic scholars of our time, has an illuminating passage on this point—and a footnote that must not be overlooked:

> We think that Lacordaire, Ozanam, and Montalembert, who acknowledged the inevitable trend of modern civilization toward more freedom, were more right than their Catholic adversaries like Veuillot. Historical honesty demands also that we concede that certain popes (e.g., Gregory XVI and Pius IX, in the latter part of his pontificate) did not always show an appreciation of this trend. According to Schmidlin,[10a] a great drawback in Pius IX's ponticate was that his methods and maxims were often mistaken and ill-advised; that his political views and ecclesiastical policy, after the terrible disappointment of the revolution of 1848, turned from excessive enthusiasm for liberty to the opposite pole of rigid conservatism, so that, however fruitful his pontificate was for the spiritual well being of the Church he almost failed in all that had to do with material culture.[7]

---

[6] Ireland, John, *The Church and Modern Society* (St. Paul: Pioneer Press, 1905), pp. 117–118.

[10a] [Note in the original]

Schmidlin, Joseph, *Geschichte der Päpste* (Freiburg, 1933–1938) II, 109. In his memoires, Cardinal Ferrata notes that Pius was aware of these shortcomings; "My system and my policy have had their time; but I am too old to change. My successor will have to do it." (Ferrata, *Memoires,* 1920, I, 32.) Whoever studies the pontificate of Leo XIII will see how excellently and successfully the successor changed that course."

[7] Rommen, Heinrich A., *The State in Catholic Thought* (St. Louis: Herder Book Co., 1947), p. 597. (Imprimatur, Archbishop [later Cardinal] Glennon.)

No one should expect those whose only experience with political democracy was with a kind of democracy that was well mixed with atheism or some form of extreme opposition to religion to accept quickly and wholeheartedly this particular form of government. Doubts of democracy should be expected from those who never lived in a genuine democracy—which is necessarily true of most Catholics (and most non-Catholics) in the whole Christian period. Professor W. E. Garrison, no apologist for Catholicism, wrote: [8]

> The conclusion I wish to draw from these notes on the history of the "democracy" is that we must not expect to find it attached to affirmations of the rights of man before the eighteenth century. The medieval Christian tradition contained some democratic values, but they did not bear that label. For a period of fifteen centuries or more, covering the greater part of history of the Roman Catholic Church and the first two centuries of Protestantism, nobody believed in political democracy—except a few prophetic and adventurous souls.

Dr. Rommen, writing of the historical growth of democracy, sums up the situation:

> Historical study will show that, at the rise of modern democracy and its institutions in consequence of the bourgeois revolutions and the violent overthrow of the ancient regime, the great majority of Catholic writers in political philosophy were by no means friendly to democracy or liberal democracy. Furthermore, the famous encyclicals *Mirari vos arbitramur* of Gregory XVI (August 15, 1832) against De Lammenais and *Quanta cura* of Pius IX (December 8, 1864) together with the *Syllabus* published under the same date seemed to reject the new forms of government as a necessary outgrowth of the philosophical and theological errors so vehemently condemned in the encyclicals just mentioned. There were enough hotheads, such as Veuillot and his Univers, who propagated this theory. Actually the question of forms of government, of monarchy or democracy, are never mentioned in the encyclicals which are neither antidemocratic nor promonarchical, as any careful reader can easily find out.[9]

The distinguished Catholic scholar, Dr. Francis McMahon, for-

---

[8] Garrison, W. E., *Religion and Civil Liberty in the Roman Catholic Tradition* (Chicago: Willet, Clark and Co., 1946), pp. 5–6.

[9] *Op. cit.*, p. 481.

merly of the faculties of Notre Dame and the University of Chicago, writes:

> If many Catholics in Spain and Latin America showed hostility to progressive ideas, it is also true that the Catholics of Belgium for over a century have backed a democratic regime. The strongest opposition to Mussolini came from the Popular Party in Italy led by Don Sturzo.[10] Despite the spasms of fear that periodically afflicted many non-Catholics in the United States concerning the designs of Rome, the American Catholics have a record surpassed by no other group for loyalty to their country. These are historical facts. They do not prove that Christianity and democracy have been going in identically the same direction everywhere, but they do suggest that there is no intrinsic incompatibility between the two.
>
> . . . What was called for in South America was Christian democracy. By and large, the only democracy that Christians saw was agnostic or atheistic, and the only Christianity the defenders of democracy saw was one tied up with social reaction. What the Lord had meant to be joined together had been torn apart by the blindness and folly of men.[11]

Pope Leo XIII wrote: "Catholics, like all other citizens, are free to prefer one form of government to another precisely because no one of these social forms is, in itself, opposed to the principles of sound reason nor to the maxims of Christian doctrine." [12]

Finally, Professor McMahon [13] gives a sound Catholic (and sound American) answer to the position of the modern propagandists for the omnipotent state that the *absolute sovereignty of the people* is only democracy and not totalitaranism.

> If democracy means the *absolute* sovereignty of the people, without subjection to God and the laws of justice, if it means that the supreme criterion of truth and goodness is the sentiment of the majority; if it means *unlimited* freedom of speech and writing; if democracy means a religious way of life (the signers of the manifesto, *The City of Man,* speak of the "religion of democracy")—then it is repugnant to the Catholic faith, and not only to the Catholic faith but also to sound reason.
>
> One need not ignore the eternal standards of morality in order to be a

[10] Catholic priest well known in America as in Italy.

[11] McMahon, Francis, *A Catholic Looks at the World* (New York: Vanguard Press, 1945), pp. 167–169.

[12] Wynne, John J., *The Great Encyclical Letters of Pope Leo XIII.* (New York: Benziger Bros. 1903), p. 255.

[13] McMahon, *op. cit.,* pp. 170–171.

defender of democracy. One need not embrace the democratic faith at the expense of supernatural faith. One need not prostrate oneself before the common man as one prostrates oneself before His God in order to be a democrat.

The Catholic Church lays stress upon the way a government acts, not upon the type of political form it constitutes. The main requirement it lays down is that any regime, whatever its character, conform to the standards of law and justice, and respect as well the rights of the Church to bring her doctrine of eternal salvation to the people.

Mr. Blanshard's chapter on "Church, State and Democracy" goes to the very heart of his central thesis—that the Church is the enemy of American democracy and freedom. Misstatements and unsupported, undocumented attacks in that chapter repeat this thesis in various ways.

Mr. Blanshard writes (pp. 47–48) ". . . you cannot find in the entire literature of Catholicism a single unequivocal endorsement by any Pope of democracy as a superior form of government." True but irrelevant; you cannot find a similar statement about any other form of government. The Catholic Church does not teach that Christ proclaimed the superiority of any one form of political government, but Catholic scholars teach (as shown above) that democracy is consistent with Catholic doctrine.

Mr. Blanshard wants his readers to believe that Catholic Americans are not freely participating citizens in our democracy, but subjects of a "foreign power," bound to accept and vote for "policies" on orders from Rome. He writes (p. 44): "In fact, the philosophy of church and state espoused by the Vatican is the most important thing in the whole Catholic system because it determines the political and social policies which the bishops and priests will pursue throughout the world." . . . "The whole Catholic system of global discipline rests fundamentally on its great army of priests. The parish priest is the contact man between the hierarchy and the people, and the agent for Roman spiritual and political goods" (p. 34). Neither of these statements has any documentation or substantiation of any kind. If there is one thing a Catholic priest is *not,* it is an agent for political goods.

The contention that American Catholics do not, and cannot, participate freely in our democracy, because they must accept economic, social, and political policies dictated from Rome, is false, fatuous and incapable of proof. Overwhelming proof to the contrary is abundantly available to anyone who wants the truth.

The Church has no machinery by which this program could be accomplished, and if it were improperly tried, no machinery by which anyone could tell to what extent, if any, it had succeeded. Political and economic questions, the topics of the day, are not discussed in the Catholic pulpit. During the Smith-Hoover campaign when the political issue of Prohibition (not the virtue of temperance) was discussed in a number of Protestant pulpits, I was interested to find out if the regular rule of "no politics in the Catholic pulpit" would be relaxed or violated. I was on the faculty of the University of Michigan at the time, and so had no opportunity to observe directly the practices in other parts of the country. However, I did not hear, nor hear of, a single reference to Al Smith or Prohibition, or any other political discussion in any Catholic church throughout that campaign.

In all my sixty years of listening to sermons in Catholic churches, I have heard from the Catholic pulpit just three remarks that could be called political. They are easy to remember because it is always startling to hear anything of the sort in a Catholic church. Once I heard an appeal to vote "no license" in a county liquor option campaign. Even parishioners who agreed completely with the pastor on the question of no license were emphatically of the opinion that it was improper to discuss it in a Catholic pulpit.

Once I heard an indirect reference to a strictly political issue which was quite anti-New Deal in a sermon in Brooklyn, and once I heard a direct appeal for a protest to Albany against the ratification of the child labor amendment. On this question, as on practically all other *political questions,* Catholic priests, bishops, and laymen were on both sides.[14] Msgr. John A. Ryan was one of the most prominent and vigorous supporters of this amendment, and Senator Thomas Walsh of Montana, a Catholic, was one of the leaders favoring it in the Senate.

---

[14] McQuade, V. A., *American Catholic Attitudes on the Child Labor Amendment since 1891* (Washington: Catholic University of America Press, 1938), pp. 130 ff.

But many Catholics, and many non-Catholics, opposed it, as should be expected in our society.

American Catholics differ among themselves on all conceivable specific questions of foreign policy also, as much as any other group of Americans. In fact it would probably be impossible to find a specific question of economics, politics, or American foreign policy on which even the members of the American hierarchy agree unanimously. Direction, dictation, infallible teaching on such matters are contrary to fundamental Catholic teaching.

Among the leading Catholic publications in New York City which have national circulation, *America, The Commonweal,* and *The Tablet,* Mr. Blanshard would have found with a limited amount of investigation about as emphatic differences of opinion on foreign policy (and on economic and political policy) as could be found in either the Protestant or secular press.

Mr. Blanshard repeats the following absurdity again and again throughout his book—with no attempt at proof: "The American Catholic people," he writes (p. 5), "are compelled by the very nature of their Church's authoritarian structures to accept non-religious as well as religious policies that have been imposed upon them from abroad." This is, in fact, one form of Mr. Blanshard's basic thesis. From sheer repetition of this false charge he seeks to get it accepted.

> Whenever any issue arises in Congress which may or might affect Catholic interests, a seasoned lobbyist in priestly garb is likely to appear in a Congressman's office, reminding the legislator that 26,000,000 Catholics in America feel such and so about this matter. Even when the legislator knows perfectly well that the opinion is actually that of a handful of top-ranking bishops, acting on orders from Rome, he may swallow his convictions and say "Yes, yes," because he knows that in American Catholicism the bishops speak for Catholic power. He knows also that Catholic pressure can be mortally effective in swinging any close election against him. (Blanshard, p. 29.)

This has no documentation of any kind.

No group in America is divided more fervently (not to say bitterly) than Catholics on New Deal-Fair Deal measures. Al Smith and General William J. (Wild Bill) Donovan were on opposite sides throughout most of Al Smith's career, not only in New York state politics, but in the Smith-Hoover campaign. Mr. Hoover was placed in nomination for the Presidency at the Republican National Convention of 1932 by Joseph Scott of Pasadena, California, one of the most distinguished Catholic laymen of the day.

"How far does the Church as a sovereign power extend its jurisdiction? Everywhere where there are Catholics. It claims that it is a supernatural institution with complete territorial jurisdiction" (p. 41). *No documentation.* The phrases "sovereign power," "with complete territorial jurisdiction" in the atmosphere of twentieth-century America can effectively mislead the uninformed.

"The concepts of the sovereignty of the Catholic Church and the sovereignty of the Pope are welded together so closely that the average Catholic can scarcely make a distinction between political and religious programs" (p. 43). This insulting reference to average Catholics is not explained *or documented* in any way.

"Nobody knows how much of the Pope's funds go to religious and how much to political purposes—the distinction would be futile in any case because political and religious activities in the Roman system are inextricably mixed" (p. 44).

"Because of its medieval traditions the Church still acts in the United States today as if it were protecting the Catholic people from their own government" (p. 47). This remark is not explained and not documented in any way. It is hard to know what Mr. Blanshard is trying to say here. It exemplifies Mr. Blanshard's use of the word "medieval" simply as a loaded word, a name-calling device.

Mr. Blanshard follows this sentence with the remark: "It [the Church] refuses to admit that the Church in the social field is simply one agency within the state, and that the state expresses the will of the people as a whole . . ." (p. 47). Whether the state (i.e., the government) expresses the will of the people as a whole in any particular instance is a matter of fact to be determined by adequate investigation. It may or may not be true. The Church does not have (and obviously cannot have) a *general doctrine* that what are alleged to be expressions of the will of the people are necessarily either true or false. This part of the sentence has nothing to do with the status of the Church as a social agency.

If by "simply one agency within the state" Mr. Blanshard means "simply one agency *of* the state," he should have said, not that the Church refuses to *admit* that it is such an agency but that the Church *refuses to be such an agency.* And if he were scholarly and fair he would have included the statement that the same is true of Protestantism and Judaism as well as Catholicism. No positive religion ever "admits" in any field that it is "simply an agency of the state." Such a concept is contrary to the basic idea of both a free society and positive religion. It is the basis of the totalitarian philosophy of the omnipotent state. If, on the other hand, Mr. Blanshard does not mean "an agency of the state" (like the state department of education), but rather that the Church ought to "admit" that it is simply a private organization trying to do some good which is agreeable to the "will of the people as a whole" (like the American Civil Liberties Union, the League of Women Voters, or the Grange), the same comment applies. The Church could not possibly "admit" anything so untrue. Neither could (or would) Protestantism, Judaism, or any other positive religion.

"Catholics are taught to offer no resistance to the American policy of freedom at the present time but to take advantage of this freedom while working to destroy it—through the setting up of a state which will prevent the dissemination of non-Catholic views and limit the public activities of non-Catholic sects" (p. 53). This is "documented" only by a quotation from the familiar passage from Msgr. John A. Ryan's *The State and the Church.* This passage has been objected to and refused acceptance again and again by Catholic scholars—as a bit of scholarship would have discovered. (See pp. 84, 89.) Even the Ryan passage does not prove the charge of the teaching of hypocrisy.

Mr. Blanshard's misrepresentation of the relation of American Catholics to American democracy and American concepts of freedom is further expressed in his many references to the Church as a "foreign power" and to American Catholics as "subjects" of this foreign power.

The following are examples. He refers to the Catholic Church as "a political power whose seat of government is located outside the

United States" (p. 56), and to the Catholics throughout the world as "subjects" of a foreign power (p. 40), and to the Pope as a "European ruler" (p. 9), as an "absolute monarch" (p. 19). The *only fact* which he presents in all this is the fact that Vatican City is an independent country. This is true, but inadequate to carry the load Mr. Blanshard puts on it.

Vatican City is a small sovereign state because it has an area, a population, and an effective government, and is independent of any other country. These are the only four tests of statehood recognized in international law. However, the country of Vatican City is not the Catholic Church, though the Pope is the head of both, as the King of England is the head of both the country and the Church of England. Vatican City has no army, navy, or air force. Neither the Catholic Church nor Vatican City has any *force* of any kind with which to threaten or punish any nation or any person (except the citizens of Vatican City). The Church has, of course, the "force" of teaching and persuasion.

The idea that American Catholics (or English, German, African, Russian, or Chinese Catholics) are, in addition to their open citizenship in their various countries, subjects of a "foreign power," one would have thought too absurd to be taken seriously. But he (p. 259) and one of his most enthusiastic reviewers, Professor Boas of Johns Hopkins University (see p. 228) take the position that American Catholics are subservient to a *totalitarian* foreign power, and Blanshard recommends (p. 305) that the Catholic bishops of America be required to register as the "agents of a foreign power."

Mr. Blanshard refers to the Pope as "the absolute monarch of the Catholic world" and "the Commander-in-Chief of the Catholic army" (p. 19). This language is inaccurate, unscholarly, and loaded with irrelevant emotional connotation. That specific "orders" constantly flow from the Pope to American or other Catholic priests and nuns, directing them how to conduct themselves in their complex daily activities, should not be credited in the absence of abundant proof. Blanshard offers *none*. Obedience of this sort is not the relationship of anyone to the Pope. As Father Dunne remarked in his pamphlet, *Re-*

ligion in American Democracy (p. 8), "I do not agree with all the policies of every Pope, or of any Pope, much less of every or of any bishop, nor is there anying in my faith which obligates me to do so."

Perhaps Mr. Blanshard's low point as a scholar is his treatment of the heresy of "Americanism." In discussing Pope Leo XIII's condemnation of the heresy of "Americanism" in a letter to Cardinal Gibbons in 1899 (pp. 26–27), he failed to tell his readers what Leo XIII condemned; he gave the word a misleading interpretation. And *he gave no reference* to a source in which his readers could find the letter.

The philosophy that was unfortunately labeled "Americanism" was a group of doctrines that had been given some expression *in France*—not in America. These doctrines had been inaccurately ascribed to American Catholics. All this was briefly but clearly set forth in at least two books which Mr. Blanshard mentions, Corrigan and Maynard.[15] The doctrines are summarized by both. Anyone who was interested in having his readers know what it was the Pope wrote about to Cardinal Gibbons would have quoted from the letter itself, or at least have given an accurate reference to a place in which it could be found. Wynne publishes the letter in full.[16]

But Mr. Blanshard's discussion of "Americanism" has *no footnote or documentation of any kind.*

In a few minutes anyone could have found out that what the Pope condemned was (briefly summarized):

> 1—overemphasis on the influence of the Holy Ghost as against spiritual direction; 2—putting natural virtues above the supernatural; 3—overemphasis of active virtues to the exclusion of humility, charity, and obedience; 4—rejection of religious vows; 5—untried methods of attracting non-Catholics to the faith.

---

[15] Corrigan, Raymond, S.J., *The Church and the Nineteenth Century* (Milwaukee: Bruce Publishing Co., 1938), pp. 276–277, and Maynard, Theodore, *The Story of American Catholicism* (New York: The Macmillan Co., 1948), pp. 498 ff. A third scholarly treatise which Mr. Blanshard could easily have consulted tells the same story—Curran, Francis X., S.J., *Major Trends in American Church History* (New York: America Press, 1946), pp. 139–140.

[16] Wynne, *op. cit.*, pp. 441–453.

Father Curran puts it thus: [17]

While American Catholics were engrossed with the problems facing the Church in the United States, they were suddenly startled by accusations emanating from Europe. A mistranslated life of Isaac Hecker, the convert who had founded the Paulist Fathers, was the source whence some French priests deduced the existence of tendencies in the American Church to minimize essentials of faith and obedience in order to bring the Church into step with the modern world. The furor caused by these accusations, and possibly the existence of such tendencies in European branches of the Church, influenced the Holy See to issue a letter condemning such trends, which were grouped under the title of "False Americanism." The surprised leaders of the American Hierarchy immediately acceded to the condemnation, but denied that this "Americanism" existed in America. Cardinal Gibbons' reaction was typical: "I sent the Holy Father a reply to his letter received February 17 on the subject of Americanism. After thanking His Holiness for dispelling the cloud of misunderstanding, I assured him that the false conceptions of Americanism emanating from Europe have no existence among the prelates, priests and Catholic laity of our country." [18]

Dr. Maynard writes: [19]

. . . none of these things . . . had ever been proposed by any responsible leader of American Catholicism. Obviously what was condemned constituted heresy; only it did not exist in America. "Americanism" was merely the label which became accidentally attached to it.

Its condemnation, however, was hardly more than hypothetical. "Americanism" had never existed as a precisely formulated doctrine anywhere, and had hardly any disciples. Of these there were none in America.

Father Corrigan says:

Doctrinaire Royalists in France had a low opinion of American Democracy; conservatives generally disliked our modern ways; pious souls thought our religion was entirely on the surface; rigid Catholics were sure we must be half Protestant. Add to this the expressed conviction of Liberals abroad that American Catholics would not long sacrifice their independence to the

---

[17] Curran, *op. cit.,* pp. 139–140 ff.

[18] Will, Allen S., *The Life of Cardinal Gibbons* (New York: E. P. Dutton, 1922), Vol. I, p. 557 f.

[19] Maynard, *op. cit.,* pp. 500, 516.

"dictatorship of the Vatican," and we have a sufficient explanation of the flare-up when a mistranslated *Life of Father Hecker* appeared in Paris, in 1898.[20]

Both Dr. Maynard[21] and Father Curran[22] quote from a letter which Archbishop Ireland wrote from Rome in 1900:[23] "The Pope told me to forget the letter on Americanism, which has no application except in a few dioceses in France."

Clearly the Pope's letter to Cardinal Gibbons had nothing to do with American democracy and patriotism or even philosophical or religious doctrines advocated by American Catholics. Had Mr. Blanshard read with care the Pope's letter to the Cardinal, he would have known just what it was that the Pope actually condemned. Particularly he would have learned that the Pope specifically *excluded from his disapproval the very things Blanshard says the Pope condemned:* "the characteristic qualities" that are "special" to America, "the condition of your [the American] commonwealths, or the laws and customs which prevail in them."[24]

The Blanshard comment is contained in two paragraphs (pp. 26–27) from which I quote:

> The Popes have been apprehensive about American Catholicism for many years, and they have watched its growth in power with great anxiety, being fully aware of the dangerous influence of liberalism under religious freedom. This fear reached its climax with the transmission by Leo XIII in 1899 of a special letter to Cardinal Gibbons condemning the "heresy" of Americanism. Every move by the American Church toward "Americanism" has been scrutinized and double-checked to avoid the possibility of a drift toward national independence. . . . Leo XIII, instead of creating an American primate whose viewpoint and background might be fundamentally American, created an Apostolic Delegacy at Washington. . . . Since the Pope's appointee is always an Italian, whose line of promotion runs toward Rome instead of the United States, there is little danger that he will become infected with the "heresy" of Americanism.

---

[20] Corrigan, *op. cit.,* p. 276.

[21] *Op. cit.,* p. 516.

[22] *Op. cit.,* p. 140.

[23] Storer, Mrs. Bellamy, *In Memoriam Bellamy Storer,* (Privately Printed, 1923), p. 46.

[24] Wynne, *op. cit.,* p. 452.

This complex of misstatement and insinuation against Catholic support of "national independence," of economic, political or social *liberalism* and *religious freedom* in America is without foundation, and is presented without any proof or documentation of any kind, not even one footnote.

These two paragraphs on "Americanism" are to me the nadir in scholarly discussion for this book. The constantly reiterated theme is that the power of the Catholic Church in America, directed from Rome, is a threat to American freedom—to American democracy, to the American way of life, in short, *to Americanism.* In his search for something to substantiate this charge, Mr. Blanshard found that, in a letter to Cardinal Gibbons, Pope Leo XIII condemned something that was, *in France,* labeled "Americanism." Mr. Blanshard thereupon discussed a bundle of straw men of his own invention, *unaided by any statement by any Catholic to which he referred his readers.* Anyone who accepts anything in these paragraphs on Americanism as being true or dependable in any way must accept it simply on the unsupported assertion of Paul Blanshard. Obviously this passage tends to make readers believe that the Church in general, and Leo XIII in particular, was opposed to Americanism, to American liberty, to the characteristics of the American way of life in this Republic. This is not true.

6

RELIGIOUS FREEDOM

ONE of the chief elements in attacks on Catholicism in America is the claim that Catholics are a constant and growing threat to religious freedom in our country. Since religious freedom is a basic tenet of American freedom, this specific charge (if believed) arouses maximum suspicion against American Catholics. Even though it plays a large part in all anti-Catholic campaigns, it is false. Probably the most useful tactic in the false propaganda is to refer to conditions in Spain (often inaccurately) and to *assume* that these are approved by American Catholics, are dictated by Catholic *doctrine,* and are what American Catholics will enforce in America if ever they get the power. To the Catholic (or the non-Catholic) who has investigated conditions in Spain, and American Catholic attitudes toward them, this complex of assumptions is clearly erroneous. However, many such Americans who have no ill will against their Catholic fellow citizens lack sufficient information to recognize the false assumptions for what they are. And a few are profitably engaged in distributing prejudice and misinformation.

The Catholic Church is the established church in Spain, as the Lutheran Church is the established church of Sweden (and Denmark, Norway, and Finland), and Judaism is the established religion of Israel. These establishments of religion (as all others) are necessarily created by the governments of the various countries. These establishments probably seem to most people to be the business of the people and governments concerned, and not matters that should be charged to American Catholics, Lutherans, or Jews.

It is possible to have at the same time an establishment of religion (governmental favor granted to one religion only) and substantially all that is usually meant by "freedom of religion." Historically an establishment of religion and freedom of religion have been treated as two separate concepts—as in the First Amendment of our Bill of Rights. The latter concept has usually been taken to mean freedom of doctrine, of worship, of preaching and teaching. These matters are not necessarily restricted by governmental favor in officeholding, taxes, voting, jury service, giving testimony in court, or financial support of ministers. In conformity to the general use of the terms, including the constant use by Jefferson and Madison, the two ideas of establishment and freedom of religion have been kept separate in state constitutions and Supreme Court cases. As of today, however, it is frequently found that an establishment of one religion means some restrictions of the freedom of other religions, as in Spain and Sweden. American Catholics are, and always have been, against an establishment of any religion and in favor of religious freedom for all religions, as the term is used in the United States.

Professor M. Searle Bates, formerly Vice-President of Nanking University, China, and now Professor of Missions at Union Theological Seminary, New York, published in 1945 (on data assembled about 1938) a long and detailed study of religious liberty.[1] Professor Bates has two classifications. The first (pp. 504–526) is based on constitutional provisions concerning religious liberty, and has five classes:

1. *Regimes Indicating Essentially Full and Equal Religious Liberty.* The United States is listed here, in a total of 34, including such extremes in religious preferences of the populations as Belgium and North Ireland.
2. *Regimes Recognizing the Preponderance of One Religion but in Principle Assuring Satisfactory Liberty for Others.* Total, 9. This list runs from Eire and Portugal to Syria and Yugoslavia.
3. *Regimes With an Established Religion but Assuring Liberty for Other Religions without Serious Discrimination.* England and Argentina are among the 12 in this list.

[1] Bates, M. Searle, *Religious Liberty: An Inquiry.* Accomplished under the auspices of a Joint Committee appointed by the Foreign Missions Conference of North America and the Federal Council of the Churches of Christ in America (New York: Harper & Brothers, 1945).

4. *Regimes with an Established Religion Accompanied by Important Privileges and Discriminations.* This group has 15 members, including Spain, Sweden, Norway, Denmark, and Finland.
5. *Regimes Opposing or Restricting Religion in General.* Only two countries are listed in this last place: Mexico and Russia.

Here are Dr. Bates' results in tabular form.

Number of countries predominantly, significantly, or characteristically in

	Catholic	*Protestant*	*Orthodox*	*Moslem*	*Other*	*Totals*
Class 1 "Essentially full and equal religious liberty"	15	12	0	3	4	34
Class 2 "Preponderance of One Religion but Satisfactory Liberty for others"	6	0	2	1	0	9
Class 3 An established religion, but no serious discrimination	7	2	0	2	1	12
x — *x*						
Class 4 An established religion, important privileges and discriminations	3	4	3	4	1	15
Class 5 Opposing or restricting religion in general	1	0	1	0	0	2
	32	18	6	10	6	72

The slightly better showing in the percentage of Catholic countries, as compared to Protestant countries, above the line *x* of "important privileges and discriminations," should not lead anyone to think that this is proof that Catholic countries are *in fact* any better. This table deals with constitutional language, not actual practice, and in addition lines cannot be drawn here with a high degree of exactness. The table is significant *evidence* that roughly the record of Catholic and Protestant civic units in the matter of granting religious liberty is about equal—which is, in my opinion, what anyone acquainted with relevant history ought to expect.

Professor Bates' second classification[2] deals with "conditions of religious liberty"—not constitutional phrases. Concerning this classification of seventy-nine of the "principal states and areas of the world," Dr. Bates writes as follows:

> The conditions of religious liberty involve so many different elements and are so difficult of just measurement that only a tentative listing can be made, with wide varieties in each group. Nevertheless, it appears worth the effort to attempt a summary sketch of the entire situation throughout the world, imperfect though the lines must be, rather than to leave this inquiry without such a conspectus. The sketch is in general as of 1938, excluding acute disturbances of war.
>
> The two types of listing vary both in categories and in the placing of individual countries. This list endeavors to consider political and social practice rather than constitutional measures as such. Discrimination is taken as an important criterion but without undue emphasis, it is hoped. The necessary relativity of the listing must be continually recalled. One might readily reassign a certain state to an adjacent category but hardly to a greater distance from the listed position.

Class I. *A High Degree of Freedom from Preference and Discrimination.* [Total 30, including: Belgium, Brazil, Canada, England, Ireland (both North and South), Scotland, and the United States.]

Class II. *Preferences and Discriminations, relatively minor, not generally acute.*
[Total 18, including: Argentina, Bolivia, Sweden, Norway, Denmark, and Finland.]

Class III. *Freedom limited; pressures, controls, preferences and discriminations.*
[Total 16, including: Burma, India, Austria, Peru, Portugal.]

Class IV. *Freedom severely limited, state restrictions or socio-religious pressures.*
[Total 12, including: Greece, Palestine, Russia, Spain.

Class V. *Repressive Uniformity with death or utter ostracism for apostasy.* [Total 3: Afghanistan, Arabia, Tibet.]

---

[2] *Ibid.*, pp. 546–548.
[3] *Ibid.*, pp. 547–548.

Professor Bates' summary in words [3] is transposed here to a tabular form:

	Countries predominantly "by tradition or by present fact"					
	Catholic	*Protestant*	*Orthodox*	*Moslem*	*Other*	*Total*
Class I	16	13	0	0	0	29
Class II	9	7	0	0	0	16
Class III	9	1	0	0	0	10
Class IV	1	0	3	8	0	12
Class V	0	0	0	2	1	3
	35	21	3	10	1	70

Here there are more Catholic than Protestant countries in each of the two top categories; but a larger *percentage* of the Protestant countries than of the Catholic countries get this better rating.

Dr. Bates' study demonstrates the untruth of the pretense that the denial of religious liberty is a Catholic phenomenon, a doctrinal necessity, an inevitable result of "Catholic domination."

Since 1938 the *policies and practices* of either Catholic or Protestant countries may well have changed. But Catholic *doctrine* (which I wish all commentators could keep separate from the policies of certain governments) has not changed. It seems probable that as of 1950 the grouping together (in class 2) of Spain, Norway, Denmark, Finland, and Sweden, in Dr. Bates' classification on *constitutions,* should be repeated in his second classification, on the political and social practice of religious freedom.

Considering the somewhat fluid state of constitutional arrangements in Israel, it seems hardly worth while to discuss that situation. However, Judaism is the established religion of Israel,[4] and, exactly like all Catholic and Protestant establishments, it prescribes special advantages for members of that religion, and necessarily certain disadvantages for all who do not belong to that faith.

Again, just as many American Catholics object to restrictions on

[4] See two articles: "Religion by Fiat in Israel," by Hal Lehman, *Commentary,* August, 1949, pp. 110–117; "A Plea for Religious Freedom in Israel," by Milton R. Konvitz, *Commentary,* September, 1949, pp. 220–226.

Protestants in Catholic Spain, many American Jews object to the restrictions on others than members of the government-favored faith in Israel. I am confident also that there are many American Protestants, and specifically many American Lutherans, who object to the restrictions on others than Lutherans in Sweden, and the other countries in which any Protestant church is established.

Spain and Sweden, however, seem excellent current examples of the essential similarity of the working of Catholic and Protestant establishments. My information on Spain is taken from reports by Dr. W. E. Garrison in a series of articles recently published.[5]

These were not written for the purpose of exhibiting the Spanish government or the Catholic Church in Spain in a favorable light. Dr. Garrison is an ardent Protestant who labors under serious misconceptions of Catholic doctrine in regard to the relations of government and religion (see pp. 226–227). But here he was not discussing Catholic doctrine; he was reporting on conditions as he found them in Spain. From his point of view (and mine) he found them pretty bad. I submit that any dispassionate reader who will compare his findings with the Swedish constitution and laws on conditions in Sweden will find that, despite some differences, the restrictions on Catholics in Sweden and on Protestants in Spain add up to about equal lists of disadvantages for those outside the established church in each country.

My information on Sweden is taken almost wholly from a copy of the Constitution of Sweden, in English, sent with a letter dated July 28, 1950, from Mr. Eric Boheman, of the Swedish Embassy, addressed to my friend, Senator Wayne Morse, in answer to an inquiry which Senator Morse made in my behalf. Mr. Boheman quoted from special decrees which supplement the Constitution.

The observance of the provisions in Sweden and the social atmosphere of restriction vs. freedom seem to parallel the conditions in Spain. Mr. Lawrence Peterson, an American student in Sweden, completing a doctoral dissertation on a combined scholarship from Notre Dame University and the government of Sweden, writes:[6] "The

---

[5] "Religious Liberty in Spain," *The Christian Century,* particularly Nos. I and II, October 11 and 18, 1950.

[6] "Catholics in Sweden" *The Sign,* June, 1950, p. 15. See also in the same

nearest thing I know to illustrate how a fish must feel out of water is for a Catholic to live in Sweden. This is a Protestant country through and through. There is practically no Catholic life and absolutely no Catholic atmosphere."

Sweden has about 16,000 Catholics out of a population of about 17,000,000; Spain about 20,000 Protestants out of a population of 26,-000,000.

In the following tabulation of the situations in the two countries, I have used (with unimportant deletions) the exact language of Dr. Garrison's articles, with his quotations from Spanish documents, and from the Swedish Constitution and the decrees quoted by Mr. Boheman. In neither case, in the interest of clearness and space saving, have I attempted to keep separate the language of the articles, the Constitution, and the decrees.

In Spain

The profession and practice of the Catholic religion, which is that of the Spanish state, will have the benefit of official protection. No one shall be molested for his religious convictions or for the private exercise of his faith. Public ceremonies or manifestations other than those of the Roman Catholic religion are not allowed.

Protestants have liberty to be Protestants. There is no thought police.

Protestants can organize churches, these churches can hold property, and in these buildings they can assemble for Evangelical worship.

Protestant ministers seem to have complete freedom of utterance in their pulpits.

In Sweden

The Council of State must be composed of native Swedish subjects who profess the pure evangelical faith.

The head and spokesman of each department must profess the pure encyclic faith.

All the business of the government (except military matters) shall be submitted to the King in council of state and be decided there.

The King . . . shall not constrain or allow to be constrained the conscience of any person, but shall protect everyone in the free exercise of his religion, provided he does not thereby disturb public order or occasion general offense.

The King in council of state shall have power to appoint and promote

---

number Senator Brewster of Maine on "Protestants in Spain"; and *Stifled Liberties,* an article reporting an address by Bishop Ansgar Nelson of Sweden at St. Mary's Seminary, Baltimore, Nov. 28, 1950, *The Voice,* January, 1951.

In Spain

All Spaniards may be entrusted with public office and functions, according to their merits and abilities.

Every Spaniard may freely express his ideas, provided they do not attack the fundamental principles of the state and are allowed to meet and associate freely for lawful purposes and in accordance with the established laws.

Protestants cannot have a church building that looks like a church or have a church anywhere except on a narrow side street. This is not as bad as it sounds. Many narrow streets in Spanish cities are very nice streets.

They cannot lawfully do anything that would be regarded as the *public* practice of their religion or its promulgation and extension.

All Spaniards have the right to receive education and instruction and the obligation to acquire it, either within their family circle or in private or public centers, at their free choice.

Protestant churches are not allowed to make any public announcement of their services. No bulletin board is permitted.

They cannot really publish anything—that is, print it and offer it for general circulation outside of their own circle.

They cannot open a new church, or reopen an old one that has been closed, or hold services in a private house, without first securing specific permission from the authorities. . . .

An Evangelical seminary for the

In Sweden

native Swedes to all offices and posts, high and low. Only persons professing the pure evangelical faith may be appointed to offices involving the obligation to give instruction in the Christian religion or in theology; no person not belonging to the pure evangelical faith shall, however, take part, as judge or incumbent of any other office, in the discussion or decision of questions relating to divine worship or to religious instruction. Each head of a department [required to be a Lutheran] shall submit and deal with all business relative to the promotion, appointment, leave of absence, and discharge of all officials and employees in the offices and establishments under the department.

Other Christians than Lutherans may have a congregation recognized by the Swedish State, thus acquiring the right to practice their religion publicly, only if they comply with certain regulations.

Non-Lutheran churches cannot legally hold property without the permission of the Government.

Convents or monasteries may not be established in Sweden.

The non-Lutheran churches may not maintain parochial schools for children under 15 without special permission from the Government.

. . . there shall be no discrimination against religious dissenters in Sweden and no limitation of their rights and liabilities as Swedish citizens other than those provided by law.

In Spain

training of ministers is conducted openly. They cannot conduct schools, even for their own children. . . .

Protestants can and do give religious instruction to their own children. . . .

Protestants do some publishing, or at least some printing, for the information and edification of their own company. . . .

Protestants who received Catholic baptism in infancy (i.e., converts or the children of converts) are under the jurisdiction of the Roman Catholic Church in respect to marriage. They cannot have civil marriage without permission of the priest.

In Sweden

A member of a Lutheran congregation who wishes to leave must announce his intention to the pastor and state the denomination he wishes to join.

The marriage bans for all persons (for a civil marriage or in any church) are announced through the State Church. All marriages must be registered by an officer of the State Church.

The public registration of all Swedish citizens is performed by the pastors of the State Church.

Its ministers are government employees and have a number of functions to perform which are quite secular, including the collection of vital statistics of births, marriages, changes of residence, deaths, etc.

Catholic Churches have since 1895, however, by special statute enjoyed the right of registering the births, baptisms, deaths and funerals of Catholics.

A commission has been at work in Sweden recently on proposals for more religious freedom in that country. According to Mr. Boheman's letter, *if the recommendations of the committee are made law,* the restrictions will be *somewhat less* in the future: "It will be possible to establish convents and monasteries in Sweden *with the consent of the Government;* a non-Lutheran will be able to occupy any government position except that of (1) Minister of Education and Church Affairs, (2) Minister of Justice and a Minister without portfolio who substitutes for one of the two aforementioned ministers; the procedure of leaving the State Church will be *simplified.* In the future it will not be necessary for teachers of religion in the schools to belong to the Swedish Church if they do not profess a faith which *differs fundamentally* from that of the Lutheran Church." (Italics mine.)

The recent statement of Dr. D. W. Brogan [7] that these reforms have already been made is premature.

I am not presenting this report for the purpose of attacking Sweden or excusing Spain. I disapprove of the restrictions in both countries. In all countries which have an established religion restrictions or disadvantages (severe or slight) are *necessarily* the fortune of all who are not members of the state religion. Practically every civilized nation throughout history, Protestant, Catholic, and other, has had "an establishment of religion." Almost all of them have one today. The United States is the only predominantly Protestant country that has never had an establishment of some Protestant church. A number of the American states have, however, had Protestant established churches.

Doctrines, policies, practices, and historical facts concerning the relation of the temporal to the spiritual, the repression of heresy, dogmatic intolerance (the belief that one's own creed is true while creeds that differ are not true), and civil toleration (equal respect and equal freedom *before the law,* for men whose religious opinions and practices differ) are related topics that may be easily confused.

The Rev. Max Pribilla [8] makes the distinction quite clear between dogmatic intolerance and civil toleration. He writes:

> This dogmatic intolerance, which the Church by her very nature must maintain, has often been made a subject of reproach against her. But in fact every Church which takes itself seriously must assert dogmatic intolerance. Recent Protestant theologians have borne witness to this. Hans Liermann, for example, Professor of Canon Law at Erlangen, writes: "You cannot expect dogmatic toleration from any Church, because each Church believes she possesses a treasure of truth in her dogma which cannot be surrendered. If she yields on this point, she throws in her hand. Henceforth she can only claim to possess a relative truth, and this is not sufficient basis for a Church. A Church which suffers from this dogmatic softening of the bones must sooner or later perish, because she is disloyal to her real and

---

[7] *Harper's Magazine,* May, 1950, p. 49.

[8] Pribilla, Max, "Dogmatic Intolerance and Civil Toleration," *The Month* (conducted by the English Jesuits) (London: Longmans, Green and Co.), October, 1950, New Series Vol. 4, No. 4, pp. 252–260. A translation, in slightly adapted form, of an article which appeared in *Stimmen der Zeit* in April, 1949.

highest end. Consequently it is a fact which has to be recognized, that every Church must be dogmatically intolerant." . . . dogmatic intolerance belongs to the sphere of knowledge and, since it merely recognizes the primacy of truth and logic, injures no one's rights [p. 252].

There remains the objection that guaranteeing religious freedom gives the same rights to error as to truth, and thereby dogmatic intolerance is surrendered. The answer to this is that freedom of religion does not mean the protection of error . . . but protection of the erring man, who should not be hindered from serving God according to his conscience. Even an erroneous conscience imposes duties and confers corresponding rights.[1] The protection granted to a man in error in the exercise of his duty is something good. . . . Hence the establishment of religious freedom does not mean that true and false beliefs are put on the same level. But as long as men differ as to what constitutes the true faith, they must respect one another's opinions and exercise toleration [p. 258].

Concerning the ancient Catholic doctrine of the priority of conscience, mentioned above by Pribilla with a reference to St. Thomas Aquinas, Cardinal Newman, in answer to a statement by Gladstone, marshalled the theologians in 1874 in a statement[9] that should satisfy sincere scholars:

I shall end this part of the subject . . . by appealing to various of our theologians in evidence that, in what I have been saying, I have not misrepresented Catholic doctrine on these important points.

That is, on the duty of obeying our conscience at all hazards.

I have already quoted the words which Cardinal Gousset has adduced from the Fourth Lateran; that "He who acts against his conscience loses his soul." This *dictum* is brought out with singular fulness and force in the moral treatises of theologians. The celebrated school, known as the Salmanticenses, or Carmelites of Salamanca, lays down the broad proposition, that conscience is ever to be obeyed whether it tells truly or erroneously, and that, whether the error is the fault of the person thus erring or not. They say that this opinion is certain, and refer, as agreeing with them, to St. Thomas, St. Bonaventura, Caietan, Vasquez, Durandus, Navarrus, Corduba, Layman, Escobar, and fourteen others. Two of them even say this opinion is *de fide*. Of course, if a man is culpable in being in error, which he might have

---

[1] [Note in the original]

Summa Theologica, I-2, q. 19, a. 5.

[9] *Letter to the Duke of Norfolk* (London: Longmans, Green and Company, 1874—New Impression 1907), pp. 259–260.

escaped, had he been more in earnest, for that error he is answerable to God, but still he must act according to that error, while he is in it, because he in full sincerity thinks the error to be truth.

Thus, if the Pope told the English Bishops to order their priests to stir themselves energetically in favor of teetotalism, and a particular priest was fully persuaded that abstinence from wine, etc., was practically a Gnostic error, and therefore he felt he could not so exert himself without sin; or suppose there was a Papal order to hold lotteries in each mission for some religious object, and a priest could say in God's sight that he believed lotteries to be morally wrong, that priest in either of these cases would commit a sin *hic et nunc* if he obeyed the Pope, whether he was right or wrong in his opinion, and, if wrong, although he had not taken proper pains to get at the truth of the matter.

Monsignor John A. Ryan (to add a distinguished American voice) writes,[10] concerning

. . . the question whether a civil enactment is contrary to good morals. In these contingencies, the Catholic citizen is not in an essentially different position from the non-Catholic who rejects the principle that the state can do no wrong. *In both cases the decision will finally be made by the citizen's conscience.* In forming his conscience, that is, in considering what decision a right conscience ought to make, the non-Catholic citizen will pursue a somewhat different course from the Catholic. He will consult the minister of his denomination, perhaps, or his Bible or some other person or book. The good Catholic will consult his bishop or priest, or authoritative works on ethics. *In the end each will be compelled to decide the question for himself in the light of what helps he has received and according to his own best judgment, that is, according to his conscience.* [Italics mine. J.M.O'N.]

The Syllabus of Errors, issued by Pius IX in 1864, is simply a listing of a number of "Erroneous Propositions," which had been discussed at length earlier by him and Gregory XVI. These condemned propositions, when misunderstood, quite naturally make non-Catholics suspicious of the abiding loyalty to American freedom of the Catholics of America. Unscholarly or unscrupulous propagandists have frequently relied on the *Syllabus* as a handy arsenal for ammunition against the Church and Catholic citizens. No sincere scholar, how-

[10] Ryan, *The Catholic Church and the Citizen* (New York: Macmillan Co., 1928), pp. 41–42.

ever, has any excuse for misunderstanding it; it has been expounded and discussed by responsible scholars for nearly a century. One hour in any library with only a modest collection of books referring to Catholicism should be enough.

The *Syllabus* is only a list of titles, an index, like a table of contents. The *Syllabus* is not an *ex-cathedra* pronouncement; the doctrine of infallibility does not apply to it.[11] It should be used in exactly the way in which an interested reader would use any listing of topics. To understand what the Pope was writing about, and what he meant by what he wrote, one should read the document in which the condemned proposition was originally discussed—not just the frequently condensed and always unexplained propositions in the *Syllabus*. Moreover, when the letter, bull, allocution, encyclical, or other document referred to is located, it should be read with two thoughts in mind. *First,* in all probability the document is not an *ex-cathedra infallible* statement. The reader should know the necessary conditions which must be met by any statement to which the doctrine of infallibility applies (see ch. 11). Any delver into such documents should be able to distinguish among: (*a*) statements of universal doctrine (*b*) reports of historical events, with or without commentary on them (*c*) declarations of policy, with or without exposition or argument and (*d*) perhaps a few more types of subject matter that might be found in papal writings.

Second, one who is reading an English translation of an original Latin or Italian script may wonder why the English language is written that way. It should be remembered that the document is not only this type of translation, but also that it is designed primarily for scholars familiar with the subject matter discussed and also with Latin and in many cases with Italian. The layman who is not a linguist nor a philosopher may need the help of such a scholar in order to get the exact meaning of the papal treatise.

There are certain propositions in the *Syllabus* that have most bothered Americans. I shall quote concerning these again from Cardinal Newman and Monsignor John A. Ryan.

---

[11] See Corrigan, *The Church and the Nineteenth Century,* pp. 175–183.

Msgr. Ryan wrote: [12]

The authority attaching to the condemnation of these eighty propositions, together with the sense in which the condemnation is to be accepted, can be accurately ascertained only by consulting each proposition in the papal document from which it was drawn. . . . For example, the seventy-seventh proposition reads: "It is no longer expedient that the Catholic religion should be established to the exclusion of all others." When we turn to the Allocution from which this is taken, we find, to quote Cardinal Newman, that "the Pope was speaking not of states universally but of one particular state, Spain" . . . and that "he was protesting against the breach in many ways of the Concordat on the part of the Spanish government.[3] . . ."

Another great mistake is to assume that the condemnation of an erroneous proposition implies the assertion of the contrary proposition. In many cases it is not the contrary but the *contradictory* of a condemned proposition which is to be accepted as true. The difference can be readily illustrated. "Every Irishman has red hair" is a universal proposition. When I assert that it is false I do not imply the truth of the contrary. I do not mean to say that no Irishman has red hair. Obviously my meaning is that not every Irishman has red hair. It is in this sense that we are to understand the condemnation of propositions fifty-five and seventy-seven. The former declares that "The Church must be separated from the state and the state from the Church," while the latter reads, "It is no longer expedient that the Catholic religion should be established to the exclusion of all others." The contrary of these propositions would be, respectively, that the Church must never be separated from the state and that the Catholic religion must *always* be the only one permitted by the state; contradictory propositions would be, respectively, that the state must not *always* be separated from the Church and that the Catholic religion *may sometimes* be protected by the state to the exclusion of all others. It is in this sense that the two erroneous propositions were condemned. Only he could logically object to the condemnation of these propositions in this sense who believes that the union of Church and state should under no circumstances, nor in any society, not even in a community exclusively Catholic, be maintained. This is pure and simple nonsense.

---

[12] Ryan, *op. cit.*, pp. 36–39.

[3] [Note in the original]

Letter to the Duke of Norfolk, ch. vii. This chapter, entitled "The Syllabus," is undoubtedly the ablest, the most comprehensive and the most convincing refutation of objections against the Syllabus on the score of civic loyalty that has ever been written. While it has direct application to Great Britain, being a reply to an attack made by Hon. William Ewart Gladstone, it is fully applicable to conditions and controversies in the United States.

Cardinal Newman testifies on two more propositions from the *Syllabus:*

"In countries called Catholic the public exercise of other religions may laudably be allowed." The men who were forbidden the public exercise of their religion were foreigners, who had no right to be in a country not their own at all, and might fairly have conditions imposed upon them during their stay there, nevertheless Mr. Gladstone (apparently through haste) has left out the words "hominibus illuc immigrantibus," on which so much turns. Next, as I have observed above, it was only the sufferance of their public worship, and again of all worships whatsoever, however many and various, which the Pope blamed; and further, the Pope's words do not apply to all States, but specially, and, as far as the Allocution goes, definitely, to New Granada. . . . There was in this case no condemned proposition at all, but it was merely, as in the case of Spain, an act of the Government which the Pope protested against [p. 287].

But now let us see, on the other hand, what the proposition really is, the condemnation of which leads him [Gladstone] to say, that the Pope has unrestrictedly "condemned those who maintain *the* liberty of the Press, the liberty of conscience and of worship, and the liberty of speech,"—has "condemned free speech, free writing, and a free press." The condemned proposition speaks as follows:—

1. Liberty of conscience and worship, is the inherent right of all men. 2. It ought to be proclaimed in every rightly constituted society. 3. It is a right to all sorts of liberty (omnimodam libertatem) such, that it ought not be restrained by any authority, ecclesiastical or civil, as far as public speaking, printing, or any other public manifestation of opinions is concerned.

Now is there any government on earth that could stand the strain of such a doctrine as this . . . ? [p. 273].

It is the liberty of *every one* to give public utterance, in *every* possible shape, by *every* possible channel, without *any* let or hindrance from God or man, to *all* his notions *whatsoever*. . . . All that the Pope has done is to deny a universal, and what a universal! a universal liberty to all men to say out whatever doctrines they may hold by preaching, or by the press, uncurbed by church or civil power. Does not this bear out what I said in the foregoing section of the sense in which Pope Gregory denied a "liberty of conscience"? It is a liberty of self-will. What if a man's conscience embraces the duty of regicide? or infanticide? or free love? You may say that in England the good sense of the nation would stifle and extinguish such atrocities. True, but the proposition says that it is the very right of every one, by nature, in *every* well constituted society. If so, why have we gagged the Press in Ireland on the ground of its being seditious? Why is not India brought within the British constitution? It seems a light epithet for the Pope to use, when he calls such a doctrine of conscience *deliramentum:* of all conceivable absurdities it is the wildest and most stupid [pp. 274–275].

A thorough and scholarly discussion of fundamental Catholic doctrine in regard to the relation of church to state is *Governmental Repression of Heresy,*[13] by the Rev. John Courtney Murray, S.J., of Woodstock College:

The question of the right of civil government to repress heretical opinions or modes of worship is a minor and peripheral aspect of the general problem of relationships between Church and state. However, I have chosen to deal with it for the initial reason that it is the neuralgic point on a contemporary controversy. The controversy centers largely about a certain famous paragraph in an essay on *Immortale Dei* by the late Msgr. John A. Ryan. . . . [p. 3].

This statement, and others similar to it, have been widely understood to mean that the principle of civil intolerance is inherent in the Catholic doctrine of the Church and the State; that it is inhibited from operation only by lack of political power on the part of Catholics to enforce it; and that the limiting measure of its operation is simply the necessity of avoiding the evil of serious social disturbance. In a word, with us civil intolerance in greater or less measure is "the principle," matter of right and duty; and civil tolerance in greater or less measure is opportunism, a matter of political expediency [pp. 3–4].

. . . statements of Catholic doctrine that lead to the understanding stated above cannot but generate suspicion, prejudice and hostility. These feelings are indeed widely active, and are a serious obstacle to the work of the Church [p. 4].

. . . the discussion of the Church and state must proceed from an historical point of view. Nothing is more unhelpful than an abstract starting point. Such, for instance, is the position of the generality, "error has no rights." As it stands the statement is meaningless; for rights are predicated only of persons (or of institutions). If it means anything, it means that error is error; but this is hardly a "principle" from which to draw any conclusions with regard to the powers of the state. . . . The doctrine of the two powers (the spiritual and the temporary) has had a long history and has seen much development; and there is no reason to suppose that the development is entirely ended [pp. 10–11].

---

[13] Reprint from the *Proceedings* of the Catholic Theological Society of America following its presentation at a meeting of the Society in Chicago in June, 1948. (Page numbers attached to specific quotations.)

. . . But if it is meant that any particular form of socio-religious organization, whether of the past, present or future, constitutes the Catholic ideal, it is false. It is doubly false if it implies any nostalgic yearnings to reinstate medieval juridical and political conceptions. . . . There was a Christendom once; in fact, there have been several Christendoms, and a variety of "Catholic states." But all of them were highly imperfect, not ideal [pp. 14–15].

I should perhaps point out that one need not see error in the *acts* of the medieval papacy that were an exercise of immediate temporal jurisdiction, the most dramatic instance being the deposition of princes. These acts have adequate explanation. The error was in the *theory* that pretended on theological grounds to make this immediate temporal jurisdiction a permanent and necessary attribute of papal sovereignty. The Popes were on sound ground, having their feet in their own times; the theologians, thinking themselves to be on the footing of eternal principles, were actually in the air [pp. 16–17].

Many passages in Mr. Blanshard's book and in this one touch on religious freedom. Since his fundamental position is that the Catholic Church is a menace to American freedom, and since religious freedom is a basic tenet of American freedom, his whole book is largely an attempt to get his readers to believe that American Catholics are a constant and growing threat to religious freedom in our country. His technique is assumption plus repetition. Ostensible substantiation, where he offers any, consists mainly of one or more of the following more specific false assumptions: (*a*) any passage from a publication with an *Imprimatur* necessarily expresses fundamental Catholic *doctrine,* which all Catholics are supposed to believe and obey; (*b*) any phrase from a papal encyclical is held by Catholics as an *ex-cathedra* infallible statement of doctrine (even if the encyclical is not discussing *doctrine*); (*c*) any passage from a document of a government in the hands of Catholics must also represent fundamental Catholic doctrine.

Summarized thus, this complex of assumptions seems too silly to be used by a mature and literate American. These exact assumptions, however, plus the avoidance of information available in almost any good library, or on request from any informed American Catholic, and his misinterpretation of many of the phrases used constitute Mr.

Blanshard's attack on Catholic Americans in regard to their support of religious freedom. Mr. Blanshard made no use of Dr. Bates' copious information on this subject, nor did he list the book in his bibliography. Perhaps a glance at Dr. Bates' listing of the countries of the world according to the status of religious liberty will suggest the reason for this omission.

One of his constantly recurring assumptions is that the restrictions on religious freedom in Spain and Latin America (whatever they are or whatever he assumes them to be) show what conditions in the United States will be if American Catholics ever get control of the government. He writes: "When an American Catholic bishop says fervently that he accepts the doctrine of the separation of church and state, the skeptical inquirer may turn his eyes southward and see what the bishop means by this profession of an American doctrine." He offers no evidence, no documentation to support this. By frequent references to Spain and Latin America thrown in here and there, particularly in his Chapter 11, "Fascism, Communism and Labor," he uses the device of sheer repetition to impress upon his readers that restrictions on religious freedom are a Catholic phenomenon, and freedom of religion a Protestant phenomenon. He refers to the "astounding claim . . . that the Vatican is not fascist" (p. 240). He quotes (p. 251), from an American Catholic,[14] passages from a Spanish "manual for religious instruction" material that is contrary to the belief and practice of substantially all American Catholics and the specific teaching of the Catholic hierarchy throughout our history —as I have already shown. He does not name or refer to a single American Catholic who ever believed in or taught anything of the kind.

There were undoubtedly some Catholics, as there were some non-Catholics, in America who approved of Mussolini, Hitler, and other totalitarians. But Mr. Blanshard's assumption that this is the Catholic position, dictated by Catholic doctrine, is a clear instance of not using easily available information.

Mr. Blanshard writes (p. 244):

[14] Hughes, Emmet J., *Report from Spain* (New York: Henry Holt and Co., 1947).

The noted Catholic scholar, Professor D. A. Binchy of University College, Dublin, in his *Church and State in Fascist Italy,* says of Pius XI: "He believed that democracy was too feeble and incoherent to serve as a dam against the Communist tide, and a strange irony made him turn to the new form of authoritarian government as offering the only hope of successful resistance."

This sentence is taken from near the middle of a long paragraph, the whole point of which is to explain the Pope's *temporary* distrust of "existing Catholic parliamentary parties, nearly all of which had strong democratic leanings" and his *temporary* identification of "democracy with [a] particular brand of secularist liberalism." The whole paragraph is a defense of Pius XI against the exact charge in substantiation of which Mr. Blanshard quotes one sentence out of context. Dr. Binchy's paragraph closes:

> . . . he was to learn by bitter experience that the totalitarian State, with its claim to control the whole spiritual life of its subjects, is far more dangerous to religion than the most "indifferent" or secularist democracy. And it is characteristic of his integrity that the most uncompromising and inspiring formulation of the rights of the human spirit against the totalitarian monster should have come from the pen of a man who had been so glibly accused of Fascist sympathies. It was no mere coincidence that the two great Encyclicals, *Divini Redemptoris* and *Mit brennender Sorge,* should have appeared within a week of one another, the first directed against the tyranny of atheistic Communism, the second against the neo-paganism of the Nazis. Rarely has a juxtaposition been so fully vindicated by events.[15]

[15] Binchy, D. A., *Church and State in Fascist Italy* (New York: Oxford University Press, 1941), pp. 84–86.

7

CATHOLIC EDUCATION

PROBABLY the most common and most effective argument against any auxiliary services at public expense to children in Catholic schools—such as transportation, nonreligious textbooks, or any official recognition of them as a part of the American system of education—is one that is fundamentally an argument against the *existence* of such schools. This is that they are "divisive," promote "hostility and suspicion" between Catholic and non-Catholic children, and that the cure for these conditions is universal public education. I have examined many articles, speeches, and letters to the press containing this "argument" against parochial schools and against "released time" for religious education in public schools. I have never seen any evidence to support it. The assumption that students in public schools do not know who is Protestant, who Catholic, who Jewish, seems possible to intelligent people only if they have had little or no contact with public schools. If the knowing of these differences means hostility and suspicion among the pupils, then homes and schools seem obviously to be failing in ways that would not be cured by eliminating parochial schools or released time.

So long as America remains a free society we are going to have such differences, not only in religion but also in regard to politics, economics, and the other major influences in our complex national life. The way to stop religious differences developing into suspicion, hostility, anti-Semitism, anti-Protestantism, anti-Catholicism, and other "divisive" and evil attitudes is to stop the assumption that these things necessarily *have to result* from the inevitable choices in a free America.

The only visible alternative is the omnipotent state which will tell all parents what training their children must have, and at whose hands, in what schools, and by what methods in what subjects. Uniformity can come only through dictatorship—whether of the proletariat or of some well-armed conqueror makes little difference. The whole history of the United States proves that unity does not require uniformity. Unity in patriotism, in devotion to freedom, in basic concepts of social justice and morality, can be achieved in a diverse society, so long as freedom and the rights of minorities are maintained. After all, every American who ever lived is (or was) a member of a minority—probably of five or six different minorities at the same time. America has never had a unified, integrated, dominant majority in control of our pattern of life. In religion, politics, economic interests, regional loyalty, racial background, social status and convention, we are all members of various minorities. Once the militant statists have succeeded in wiping out minority rights, they will have wiped out the essence of "the American way of life," the traditional and constitutional "right to be different" which is the principal distinction between the American way of life and the ways of various other countries of the world.

The fear is sometimes expressed that Catholic parochial schools *may* inculcate anti-Semitic, anti-democratic, or other subversive doctrines. True, such doctrines *may* be taught anywhere. I have never seen or heard of any *evidence* that such doctrines ever were taught in American Catholic schools. However, anyone who has had much experience with public education in America, or who has even investigated this matter in the public press, knows that these doctrines not only can be, but have been, spread in American public schools. Not often, not generally, but sometimes.

I submit that it is impossible for anyone accurately to rate any schools in the United States as superior and inferior through a process of deduction from the nature of the authority which conducts the school and without a definition of the schools' objective. Educators of experience know that the two most important factors affecting the quality of any school are the kind of teachers and the kind of students.

Some teachers in parochial schools are quite inferior regardless of their piety; and some are superlative teachers. And some teachers in public schools are as bad as any that can be found in parochial schools, and some are as good as the human race ever produced. My whole life in education, as well as my experience with six children, all of whom attended at times both types of schools, convinces me of these facts. Sometimes Mrs. O'Neill and I had to correct the doctrinal positions our children learned in parochial schools. Whether the teachers tried to teach doctrine they did not understand correctly or whether they were simply incompetent expositors is beside the point. The result was deplorable. The easy answer is not to take the child out of the parochial school and send him to the public school. From the frying pan into the fire routine offered no relief. Sometimes we had to correct more, and more difficult, matters than Catholic doctrine that the children brought home from the public schools.

There is one indisputable fact which—while certainly inconclusive and perhaps not even persuasive to many Americans—ought not to be lost sight of by educators. Catholic schools conducted by the American Catholic clergy are necessarily always conducted by educated men; no one can deny that this is not always true of American public schools, which are in many important ways in the hands of elected school boards. If anyone doubts this remark about the control of public schools, I suggest that he investigate the files of the American Civil Liberties Union, the Association of American University Professors, and the committees on education in various state legislatures.

The majority of American Catholic children attend the public schools, and the majority of parishes (or missions) have no parochial schools. Millions of American Catholics are students, and thousands are teachers and administrators in American public education. In spite of these facts we are frequently told that American Catholics are bound to follow the leadership of an embittered hierarchy, which is violently opposed to public schools.

The facts, as anyone can easily find out, are to the contrary. American Catholics are in favor of the American public schools, support them with some criticism as others do, and frequently wish that they were very much better than they are. An attitude of less than complete satisfaction is fairly common among people who are acquainted with public schools, parochial schools, or any other kind of schools.

No attempt seems ever to be made to reconcile the statement that Catholic parents are "forced" to send their children to Catholic schools with the above facts. I have never heard of such a case or seen one cited by the opponents of Catholic schools. Anyone who has read and thought a bit about this situation, knows that no Catholic priest or bishop can *force* anyone to go to school at all—to any school. The only authority that can force children to go to school is governmental authority. The state exercises its force through compulsory attendance laws, which, in all states, apply *equally* to private and public, religious and secular schools.

Any Catholic parent who accepts the teaching of a priest or bishop in preference to his own initial opinion must, in the nature of things, decide that, all things considered, the priest or the bishop knows best. If our hypothetical parent happens to be one who does not accept the Church and the clergy as dependable teachers in this area, he will disregard their advice or teaching. And neither bishop nor priest can do anything about it, except, *perhaps,* exclude such a parent from the sacraments of the Catholic Church. But one should assume that the reception of the sacraments of the Catholic Church would be a matter of no importance to anyone who did not believe in the teachings of the Catholic Church. The Church's doctrine of the primacy of parental authority in the education of children (as against public authority) is generally the doctrine of the whole civilized world (outside of totalitarian countries) and is specifically implicit in the Constitution of the United States according to a unanimous Supreme Court in 1925 [1] in the Oregon case.

In many parochial schools there is not room enough for all the Catholic children who wish to attend. In the large cities most of these schools (like most of the public schools) are greatly overcrowded. It is not therefore necessarily a preference of the parents that sends many Catholic children to public schools. Also in many parts of the country, where there is room in the Catholic schools, non-Catholic parents send

[1] *Pierce v. The Society of Sisters,* 268 U.S. 510.

their children to Catholic schools in preference to the public schools. No informed person can deny that in some places the Catholic schools (measured by standards that appeal to some people) are better than the public schools; and in some places (measured by certain standards) the public schools are better than the parochial schools; and the attitudes in both of these positions do not follow religious lines.

So long as we remain a free society there will be denominational schools in this country—Catholic, Protestant, Jewish, or other. In the past decade all such schools have been on the increase; and they will probably continue to increase for years to come. Pontiac, Michigan, has recently added a Baptist parochial school to its list of Catholic, Lutheran, and Jewish religious full time day schools. What should be the chief concern of all who are interested in the education of American youth is that all these schools be as good as possible, all be treated fairly by state and federal governments, and that all religious schools of every denomination have identical status before the law. This is the only educational creed that squares with the best of American tradition, with our federal Constitution, and with Catholic teaching and practice in our whole history.

In discussing Catholic teaching and practice we should remember that in the matter of education, as in many other matters, the Catholic Church is a teacher. The Church has no police force, no sheriffs, no army, or navy, to force anyone to do anything. The Church teaches. Anyone who accepts its teaching does just that. Anyone who refuses to accept its teaching naturally ceases to be a Catholic—and takes the consequences, which are, of course, substantially nil if the Church is not a dependable teacher.

Anyone who is capable of thinking necessarily has to decide for himself whether or not he accepts the Church as the true teacher in the realm of faith and morals. No power on earth, ecclesiastical or governmental, can prevent any person capable of thinking from thinking whatever he chooses on this subject (or on any other) and coming to whatever decision his thoughts lead him to. In other words, in the realm of mature, sane, reasonably intelligent human beings, "thought control" is a contradiction in terms. In most of its current use against the Catholic Church, or against the United States government by the

Communists, or against the Communists by anyone, the phrase "thought control" is a cheap slogan, capable of influencing only people who are essentially incapable of serious thought.

The suppression of information, as in government censorship, and the spread (or distortion or suppression) of information in schools, colleges, churches, the press, and innumerable other agencies of a complex society, obviously *affects* thought. But no power on earth can exercise "thought control" or prevent anyone from holding any opinion on any subject. Obviously, people can get into trouble (with the secret police, the Gestapo, etc., in totalitarian dictatorships, or with district attorneys and policemen, in certain types of instances, such as libel, slander, incitement to riot, etc., in a free country) by *expressing* cetrain kinds of thoughts. However, the power that jails Jones for slandering his neighbor cannot *control* the thoughts of Jones concerning the neighbor even while Jones is in his cell.

Obviously, if any person wishes to receive the sacraments of the Catholic Church he has to receive them on the Church's conditions. Just so, if anyone wants to become a student and receive the privilege of membership in any college or university he has to accept such membership and privileges on the conditions laid down by the institution of his choice.

Anyone who has ever had any interest in finding the truth of the matter must know that a Catholic who is capable of thinking follows the teaching of the Church because he believes in it and is exercising his right to believe what he thinks is true and to do what he thinks is right.

If I, or any other Catholic, wanted to cut himself off from the Catholic Church and have nothing further to do with its teaching or its sacraments, what would happen? The hierarchy or the priests could not punish me. If one of them told me that I would be punished in the next world for this defection, it would not affect me *unless I believed that he was right,* in which case I would not have been following a good conscience when I severed my connection with the Catholic Church.

Only those who believe that the Catholic Church is a true and accurate teacher are under any intellectual or moral obligation to follow her teaching, and in this country *no one* is under any *legal* obligation to follow her teaching or under any *legal* obligation to refuse to follow her teaching.

The idea that only Catholics are opposed to the exclusion of religion from education cannot be honestly held by anyone who reads the Protestant religious press or even one who makes a competent survey of the secular press.

Recently Dr. Luther A. Weigle, retired Dean of the Yale Divinity School, wrote as follows in an article in *Christianity and Crisis* for July 24, 1950:

> But does it follow that the public school must "maintain a strict and lofty neutrality" as to God? . . . And the answer, in terms of history and principle, profession and practice, is clear. Such a neutrality is not maintained by either our state governments or by our national government. It is unthinkable that the United States government should be atheistic, as is the present government in Russia. And as the government, so the schools. They may be neutral as to the strife of sects; but they cannot be neutral as to God. Yet that is demanded of them, not only by a mother in Illinois who was indoctrinated in atheism from early childhood, but by a group of leaders in public education. One of the new elements in the situation is the determined effort on the part of this group to eliminate God from education. Their line of attack shifts from time to time—that belief in God is necessarily and wrongfully authoritarian in character, that there is no absolute truth or value or obligation, that in matters of faith good teaching is always neutral, that God is irrelevant to the real crises and decisions of human life and history, that belief in God is an actual hindrance to human idealism. Boyd Bode denounces "the theory that moral values require cosmic endorsement"; and John Dewey maintains that belief in God detracts from devotion to ideals, impedes one's service to his fellowmen, and is in reality a subtle form of unbelief or lack of moral faith.

Dr. Charles Clayton Morrison, former Editor of the Protestant journal *The Christian Century,* recently wrote: [2]

> Protestantism has been greatly weakened in its inner character by this kind of education. Unlike Catholicism, the Protestant churches . . . have given

[2] "Protestantism and the Public School," in *The Christian Century,* April 17, 1946. Quoted by the Rev. Robert C. Hartnett, S.J., in a pamphlet *Equal Rights for Children* (New York: America Press, 1948), pp. 31–32.

to the public school their consistent and unreserved devotion. The result is that their own children have been delivered back to their churches with a mentality which is not only unintelligent about religion but relatively incapacitated even to ask the questions out of which religion arises, to say nothing of answering them the way religion answers them. This result must not be thought of in terms of children only. For these children have become the adult membership of Protestant churches. The mentality of the entire body of American Protestantism has thus been fashioned under the influence of the secularized public school.

The request by Catholic school authorities for recognition as American schools that perform a service to the public and specifically for auxiliary services for their pupils is sometimes referred to as a "demand" for full support of parochial schools by public funds. There is no such demand, and it is extremely doubtful if "full support" would be accepted if offered. Further, the implication that there is only *one Catholic position* in regard to federal aid to education is ridiculous. American Catholics, like other Americans, take a number of different attitudes toward federal aid to education. Just how many of them on a plebiscite would line up for any one position neither I, nor anyone else knows. The fact that many Catholics opposed the passage of the recent Barden bill because they honestly believed it contained improper discrimination against Catholic children and Negro children, and improperly aided areas that should not be aided by federal funds, or for some other reason, does not constitute proof that there is any such thing as a *Catholic position* on federal aid. Every informed person knows that many non-Catholics also, both in and out of Congress, opposed this bill for various reasons.

The following six positions are held by regular, orthodox, practicing American Catholics. Anyone who proclaims that there is anything in fundamental Catholic *doctrine* that makes it a violation of Catholic teaching to hold any one of these positions on such a question as federal aid to education is either misinformed or deliberately dishonest.

1. Opposed to any federal aid to education as a threat of federal control.
2. Approve it if limited only to "areas of need."
3. Approve it if given without discrimination, as partial support only, to all

schools that educate American children in accordance with the educational standards of the individual states.

4. Approve it only for schools under *public* control—i.e., oppose it in any form (even health and safety measures) for children attending Catholic schools, as endangering specifically Catholic education.
5. Approve it, on condition that it would aid particularly American Negro children, as the most educationally neglected and discriminated against of all American children, if administered by religious schools (Protestant and Catholic on equal terms, especially in the South) as of more assistance to the Negro children than if administered by white southern politicians (educational or of any other type).
6. Approve it if it covers "auxiliary services" (transportation, nonreligious textbooks, health, etc.) for all types of schools.

An explicit demonstration that there is no one Catholic position that is imposed on Catholics either by the American hierarchy or by the Pope is furnished by the official record of the Catholic members of the House Committee on Education and Labor in the Eighty-first Congress. When they came to a vote on the Federal Aid to Education measure which had passed the Senate as S-246, commonly called the Taft bill, the *six Catholics on the committee voted three for and three against.*

All informed persons, Catholic and non-Catholic, know that the affairs of the twenty-odd million American Catholics are not perfectly conducted in all areas and in all situations, especially in education. No informed commentator will object to the statement that precisely the same remark can be made in regard to Protestant and Jewish education, public education, and private nonsectarian education.

There are inevitable difficulties in the adjustment of the ideals of any ancient faith, as Catholicism, Judaism, or Protestantism, to a country and an age that is far removed from the period of the formulation of the doctrines and procedures of the faith. None of them is pure "American," as Mr. Blanshard uses the term.

Even Protestantism, which has much less deep and elaborate roots in far-off times and places than has Catholicism or Judaism, and which has always been the majority among the religious groups in this country, has had, and still has, some difficulties of adjustment to the atmosphere of the America of today. This has been particularly true in the past century, as shown by the weakness of Protestant resistance to the rapid spread of secularism, the "fifth column" of atheism, and as such the essential enemy of all religious influence in American life.

The most effective criticism of Catholics and Catholicism is to be found in Catholic publications, and is usually written by Catholics. The assumption that everything Catholic is beyond criticism is found only among poorly informed Catholics, and is attributed to Catholics in general only by willfully uninformed or dishonest commentators. Catholic discussion, both exposing the defects and suggesting remedies in Catholic education, are common and widely published. Just so are the criticisms of Protestant education by well informed and sincere Protestants, of labor unions by members of unions, of public education by leaders in public education, and of Congressional government by members of Congress.

Turning to the field of higher education, there obviously are many poor, badly equipped, inadequately staffed small Catholic colleges in this country. There are too many of them, according to some standards and to certain specific objectives for such institutions. The same is true of Protestant colleges. In my twenty-two years of service on the faculties of the University of Wisconsin and the University of Michigan, and in fact on many occasions since that time I have visited, on various errands, literally dozens of small Protestant colleges of the Middle West. I know them pretty well. I have had their graduates in my courses, in the graduate schools of both these state universities and of Northwestern University. I know their faculties, a good deal about their equipment, and I know well many of their graduates. Everything that can be said about the inadequacy of the staff, equipment, libraries, laboratories (as measured by certain standards for certain objectives) of small Catholic colleges can be said about these small Protestant colleges.

In spite of all this, anyone who knows these institutions knows that they are doing an admirable job for their students. Their faculties are, by and large, devoted, self-sacrificing men and women, who seem to me to be working for the same kind of satisfactions and rewards that impel Catholics to enter the priesthood or the teaching sisterhoods. They are not working for either money or fame. They are working to make better men and women, better citizens, better Christians, of the young men and women who are their students. All such colleges are now in danger. Through hostile legislation (and court decisions that are "judicial legislation"), as a result of the onward sweep of secularism and atheism, or from misguided public largess to public education in such astronomical amounts that the small private colleges will find it impossible to compete against the equipment, the highly paid staff, the fabulous libraries and laboratories of the tax-supported public institutions, these small Protestant colleges may all disappear. If this happens, education in America will have lost many of its best and most irreplaceable instruments.

Public education in America today is, on the whole, as good as it is largely because of the pace that has been set by the private institutions. Like private education, public education is, in many places, very good indeed; and again, like private education, it is, in many places, very bad indeed; and in general it would be much worse if it were not trying to keep up with the private schools and colleges.

I believe that freedom of religion and freedom of education will live or die together in America as in Russia. "The true danger to liberty is a ministry of public worship and popular enlightenment with too complete a control over education. The mere existence of free schools of the Church has done more to protect the liberty of education than all the oratory for freedom." [3]

I submit, further, that any person who considers the relevant facts of history and the current situation will agree that if ever the national catastrophe of the substantial extinction of the small private, religious colleges comes to this country the first group to submit and die will be the Protestant colleges, and the last group to go under, if they ever go under (which is doubtful so long as we remain a free society) will be the Catholic colleges. As a Catholic who has spent forty-five years in education (thirty-nine in public education) in various states in the Union, I want to testify that in my opinion the dying out of the small Protestant denominational colleges would be a tragedy for this country. It would be a benefit to no phase of American life which should

---

[3] Rommen, *The State in Catholic Thought,* p. 361.

be endorsed by anyone who believes in personal freedom, democracy, or positive religion of any kind whatever.

How does Mr. Blanshard treat the facts of Catholic education? He introduces his Chapter 4 (pp. 59–78) entitled "Education and the Catholic Mind" with the statement that "a tremendous revival of anti-Catholic feeling is taking place in the United States" and that this "anti-Catholic sentiment is not an offensive against the Church so much as a broad defensive [*sic*] movement against a new educational aggressiveness on the part of the hierarchy." Then with an advance alibi disclaiming bigotry as the basis of the current anti-Catholicism and a presentation to himself and his coworkers of the honorary citation of "liberals who have always stood most courageously for personal tolerance," Mr. Blanshard proceeds to write twenty pages exhibiting, in the words of Mr. Will Herberg (see p. 237), "vulgar anti-Catholicism on almost every page."

Mr. Blanshard asks four questions: "Are the Catholic schools worthy of national support? Are they democratic? Do they teach responsible freedom? Do they teach tolerance and national solidarity? Non-Catholics have a right to ask these questions not only because the Catholic schools are training nearly 3,000,000 future citizens in more than 8,000 tax-exempt institutions, but also because the people have accepted the Catholic schools as substitutes for public education under the state compulsory-education laws." Note that he does not say what sort of aid, or how much, he means by national support—or what kind or how much any Catholic spokesmen are asking for, or would accept if it were offered to them. By "democratic" and by "responsible freedom" we can, I suppose, infer from his position given throughout Chapter 4 that he means such freedom as is "responsible" to whatever rules or principles have been established by those chosen by a vote of the "peoples government." If Mr. Blanshard is familiar with education, public or private, in this country, he knows that there is not a professionally respectable faculty in any school, college, or university in America that will submit to serving such an objective. They all owe first loyalty to truth, *as they see it,* and to honesty and other types of morality, according to proper professional standards as educators and the dictates of the *individual conscience,* and not to the school board's ideas, the legislature's decisions, the politicians' needs, or the orders of a secret police.

In the chapter on "Education and the Catholic Mind" there are the usual large number of footnotes attached to the paragraphs in which Mr. Blanshard makes his sweeping charges against Catholic education, but they document chiefly only two kinds of statements: (1) Catholic criticism of Catholic education, informed and constructive if reported in context, and (2) such colorless statements as those on the number of pupils in Catholic schools, the value of school property, etc. This technique of proving that which needs no proof and assuming that which should be proved is one of Mr. Blanshard's basic argumentative methods.

He writes (p. 60) ". . . dividing the children into competing and even hostile groups, conscious of their own differences and suspicious of each other's way of life. . . . This divisive pattern . . . this separatism is particularly harmful." None of the implications of all this harsh language is supported by evidence or citations.

Mr. Blanshard quotes (p. 62) the ancient Canon law and the decrees of the Council of Baltimore to the effect that all Catholic children *must* be educated in Catholic schools. He makes no attempt to explain how these statements are interpreted and applied by responsible Catholic authorities in America. But he writes (p. 101): "The majority of American Catholics have always voted against segregated schools in the only way in which they could vote, by sending their children to the public schools." This assumes inaccurately that all Catholic children in public schools are there by the refusal of the parents to send them to the parochial schools—which contradicts his position (p. 67): "No Catholic parent, as we have seen, is allowed freely to choose a non-Catholic school for his children. In practice it is clear that the doctrine of the primacy of parents is simply a device for asserting the supremacy of the priest as against the power of a democratic government."

In this area Mr. Blanshard seems to be disturbed by the fact that many millions of his fellow citizens believe things that he does not believe and practice things of which he does not approve. He would like to have the Catholic parents of America forced by the government to have the *freedom* to send their children *only* to the public schools.

Mr. Blanshard's paragraphs (p. 64) discussing the development of the public school system have just one footnote attached. That note refers the reader to seven books. There is no specific reference which backs up anything contained in these paragraphs. He closes with these two sentences:

> Most American Protestants recognized the necessity for compromise and agreed to support the public schools as secular institutions divorced from distinctively religious teaching. It was a decision in keeping with the spirit and letter of the Constitution, since the First Amendment had declared against any "establishment of religion."

This passage is totally misleading. Protestantism was an integral part of the American public school system for about a century. The change to straight secularism was brought about by state constitutional arrangements, by state action only, unaffected by the First Amendment. This action was occasioned by the Catholic-Protestant controversy in the first half of the last century.[4] Protestantism in the public schools continued in some places in spite of the constitutions for about another fifty years. The Catholics in the main objected to compulsory Protestantism in public schools supported by public money, and Protestants in the main objected to any public money for Catholic schools. Professor Howard K. Beale,[5] of the University of North Carolina, sums up the situation thus:

> While sectarianism was increasingly discouraged, practically all schools still included religion in their curricula. School opened with prayer. The Bible was read and portions of it memorized. Hymns were sung. The principles of Protestant Christianity, so far as they were accepted by all Trinitarian sects, were instilled into the children . . . they [the Catholics] contributed in taxes to the support of schools in which their teachers were not allowed to teach and could not have taught the required subjects anyway without violating their own consciences. Furthermore, the Catholics were

[4] O'Neill, *Religion and Education Under the Constitution,* pp. 24–30, 140–152.

[5] Beale, *A History of Freedom of Teaching in American Schools,* p. 98.

not satisfied to have religion excluded from the schools. Like the Protestants, they wanted to teach religion to children, but again like the Protestants, they wanted to teach their own religion.

For copious and accurately documented information on this educational controversy see also another excellent book by another non-Catholic historian, Professor Ray A. Billington, of Northwestern University.[6]

The provisions of the various states outlawing religion in the public schools and state support for religious schools were in no way brought about by the First Amendment. That amendment applied *only* to the actions of Congress. The specific purpose of it was to leave the states free to do as they pleased in legislation affecting religion. The Fourteenth Amendment (1868) was recognized by the Supreme Court (in 1925) as having only a possible, vague, and as yet unmeasured effect on state responsibility in the area of civil liberties. Long before that time practically every state had taken the action Mr. Blanshard was (or should have been) referring to. Further, the First Amendment had *not* declared against "any establishment of religion," but only against *any law by Congress* about *"an establishment* of religion," either pro or con. This was a bar against an establishment of religion by Congress—a national religion for the United States. State establishments continued undisturbed long after the First Amendment was ratified, until 1833 in Massachusetts.

Discussing the Catholic school system, Mr. Blanshard reports (p. 72), with no evidence or documentation, "Very few non-Catholics know anything about it and Catholic laymen get their overall picture from the self-serving declarations of their hierarchy." How is it possible for Catholic parents not to know about the schools their children attend? What the "self-serving declarations" of the hierarchy are, Mr. Blanshard does not tell us.

Mr. Blanshard disapproves of the teaching sisterhoods. He feels sorry for them, and seems almost to assume that they are prisoners, unwillingly doing slave labor:

---

[6] Billington, Ray A., *The Protestant Crusade* (New York: The Macmillan Co., 1938). This book is about to be reissued by Rinehart and Co., New York.

When American newspapers talk about teachers' wages and teachers' incentives, these 80,000 nuns are not included. National labor unions make no attempt to organize them, although the Church favors unionization for almost everybody else [p. 67].

They [the nuns] belong to an age when women allegedly enjoyed subjection and reveled in self-abasement. Their unhygienic costumes and their medieval rules of conduct establish a barrier between themselves and the outside world . . . [p. 67].

Even the names of the 259 religious orders for women in the United States reflect a medieval attitude of piety and feminine subordination that seems utterly alien to the typically robust and independent spirit of American womanhood [p. 67].

Their personal lives are carefully segregated from free males and free thinkers [p. 69].

. . . they do not acquire occupational tenure within the school system [p. 69].

. . . they are compelled to live in convents . . . [p. 71].

Almost any sincere non-Catholic can find out anything he wants to know about Catholic schools. Mr. Blanshard cites no cases of any inquirer who was not courteously received, in fact welcomed, and given any information he sought about the school. His statements about unions, tenure, salaries, romance, free males, and free thinkers were well commented upon by Father Dunne: [7]

The total incomprehension of things Catholic which disqualifies Blanshard as an objective critic is nowhere more in evidence than in his description of Catholic teaching nuns. Sometimes this lack of comprehension is merely funny; sometimes it is insulting. . . .

Blanshard seems unable to understand that nuns are not paid wages because they do not want wages. They have freely and deliberately embraced a life of religious poverty in which everything is owned in common and nothing is owned personally. The nuns have entered religious orders because they desired to follow this rule of life. It is one of his curious blind spots that Blanshard, who apparently has considerable sympathy for the idea of socialism, is totally unable to understand people *voluntarily* embracing the ideal of communal living from motives of Christian idealism.

The weaknesses of Mr. Blanshard's discussion of Catholic education have been recognized by others than Catholics:

[7] Dunne, *Religion and American Democrary* (New York: America Press, 1949), p. 23.

He maintains that the parochial school is a divisive influence under the thumb of the hierarchy, and therefore deserves no support whatsoever, not even bus transportation. Catholic methods of teaching are too authoritarian to his taste and the instructional content is overloaded with religous symbolism and doctrines. . . . However, his dice are overloaded, in education at least. Without questioning the assumption that Catholics do exercise influence in the public schools, one might inquire why Blanshard does not also mention in passing that Protestants enjoy some measure of control over secular schools and colleges. But, if it should be objected that Blanshard is writing about Catholics solely, then it would seem that his study is being conducted in a socio-cultural vacuum. It does not take the objective critic long to discern that Blanshard is employing the double standard of criticism and the technique of imparting partial truths by withholding evidence contrary to his opinions. Thus, he does not state anywhere that numerous Catholics approve and employ Progressive teaching methods, even if they do disapprove of the underlying educational philosophy.[34] He upbraids the Mother Seton Arithmetics for inserting drawings of saints and angels, but fails to mention that the same books also indoctrinate pupils with the intergroup idea by depicting Negro children on a plane of equality with white children. Further, he complains that the Catholic members of the President's Commission on Higher Education dissented when financial support was recommended for public colleges only, but he neglects to say that they did not dissent from the proposal to end Negro discrimination, as did four Southern leaders (Report, Part II, p. 29 n.). There are more instances of misinterpretation, fragmentary information, and one-sided criticism, but it would be tedious to multiply instances. If the rest of the volume is as vulnerable as the chapters on education, then Blanshard may be charged with shoddy scholarship, if not indeed with outright religious bias.[8]

Mr. Blanshard writes (p. 65): "Most Americans assume that education is primarily the business of the whole community and that the people's government is the logical agency to educate the children of the people."

He does not say how he found out what "most Americans assume."

---

[34] [Note in the original]

W. J. McGucken, "The Catholic Way in Education" (Milwaukee: Bruce, 1934), pp. xiii–xiv. Blanshard quotes McGucken, but has overlooked the Catholic educator's remarks about modern methodology. He would have been shocked if he had consulted L. J. O'Connell's "Are Catholic Schools Progressive?" (St. Louis: Herder, 1946).

[8] Brickman, William W., "The School and the Church-State Question," *School and Society,* May 6, 1950, pp. 279–280.

Education laws in the various states are, as a matter of fact, based on the assumption that it is for the parents to choose the type of school to which their children will be sent. The state does not accept the parochial school as a *substitute* for the public school (as he says, pp. 60, 73) any more than it accepts the public school as a substitute for the parochial school. The schools are equal in the eyes of the attendance laws. It is for the parents to decide which their children will attend.

Mr. Blanshard offers no proof of the validity of the statements (p. 263) concerning the refusal of the Church to admit the socialist view of "the supreme power of the democratic state over all aspects of secular life" and "the superior claim of the public schools in the education of the people." Clearly the Catholic Church (in common with all other positive religions, and all believers in human freedom) always has, and always will, deny that any state has *supreme* power over *all aspects* of secular life. Since some of the aspects of secular life have moral implications, no church, organization, or individual *having any moral code* can ever grant that any state has such power. Mr. Blanshard ought to know that Protestantism and Judaism are at one with Catholicism on this point. And clearly, also, neither the Church grants nor the American states assert "the superior claim of the public schools."

In one of the most vulnerable passages in his book, Mr. Blanshard writes (p. 66):

> Any law based upon the accepted American theory [*sic*] that education is primarily the function of the people encounters the opposition of the hierarchy. In March, 1947, liberal political forces in New York appeared to be on the verge of success in their long fight for a bill that would prevent racial and religious discrimination in the state. Suddenly Coadjutor Archbishop J. Francis A. McIntyre of the Archdiocese of New York, now Archbishop of Los Angeles, denounced the bill as one "formed after Communistic pattern," not acceptable to Catholics.

The implications that this bill expressed the desire of "the liberal political forces in New York" for "success in their long fight for a bill that would prevent racial and religious discrimination" and that it was killed because it was "not acceptable to Catholics" are both false. The bill's purpose was fine; its specific provisions outrageous and unworkable. It was opposed by substantially every college and university president in New York State. It was reliably reported that every president in the state was opposed. Certainly not one of them came out in public in favor of it. The Committee on Academic Freedom of the American Civil Liberties Union, of which I was chairman at the time, was unanimously in opposition. The bill was withdrawn by its sponsors in the legislature on account of the almost universal opposition of all informed and interested people. It was competently rewritten the next year, was passed, and has been working well, to the satisfaction of those who opposed it in its original form. But Mr. Blanshard singles out Archbishop McIntyre and "the Catholics" once again as the enemies of the "liberal forces" and the "accepted American theory of education."

In comparison with other religious groups in America, American Catholics have not achieved proportional distinction in scientific research and positions of prominence in education. This situation has, in recent years, been a matter of concern to Catholic leaders. Probably there is more reliable information in regard to this problem in a book by Father O'Brien, of Notre Dame University, than in any other one book.[9]

Mr. Blanshard and others who have been trying to make a case against the Catholic Church in America in recent years attribute this situation to the doctrines of the Church itself. This is done as a simple assumption. There is no evidence whatever to validate this as the explanation.

A careful consideration of all the relevant factors which apply to this problem should lead to the following:

1. There is evidence both in education and in publishing that the situation has been improving rapidly in the past decade.

2. The great majority of Catholic youth who have been in a position to go through colleges and universities in the past generation have been the descendants of relatively recent immigrants. As Dr. O'Brien expressed it: [10]

---

[9] John A. O'Brien, *Catholics and Scholarship* (Huntington, Ind.: Our Sunday Visitor, 1938).

[10] *Ibid.*, pp. 9–10.

. . . To devote one's life to scientific research normally requires a comfortable economic background, which renders possible the attainment of a University education and the further pursuit of graduate study.

Catholics on the whole have come from the poorer classes and until comparatively recently have been unable to provide such prolonged education for their children. They have been among the more recent immigrants and have been under the necessity of directing their children largely to the "bread and butter" courses rather than the purely cultural and rigorously scientific ones. . . .

. . . Even at the present time when Catholics are coming to the universities in larger numbers than ever before, they are going in chiefly for such professions as law, medicine, engineering, journalism and seldom for the career of a University teacher or scientific research worker. But this is of their own election and in no manner traceable to any pressure of their religious faith.

3. Most Catholic colleges and universities are *young* in comparison with the leading secular universities of America. They are also relatively *small* and, again in the same comparison, extremely *poor*. Their income is almost wholly from tuition and not from endowments and, of course, none of it from taxes. In these ways the Catholic colleges and universities are quite like many of the Protestant colleges and universities throughout the country. All denominational colleges are at a disadvantage when compared with private institutions like Harvard and Yale or with public institutions like the great state universities.

4. Most of the members on the faculties of Catholic colleges and universities are priests, brothers, and sisters; that is, they are men and women who have definitely accepted a life of sacrifice, personal poverty and obedience, whose primary object is to serve religion. The Catholic Church is a religious institution. Her mission is to save souls. She believes that the conduct of educational institutions is a necessary part of her program to carry out this mission. It will probably continue to be only the exceptionally talented and rarely fortunate religious teacher in a Catholic college or university who will attain great distinction as a scholar or creative artist in scientific or cultural fields. The majority of highly distinguished (in the eyes of the world in general) Catholic educators, scientists, scholars, writers will be Catholic laymen and, in so far as they have positions in educational

institutions, they will probably be on the faculties of public or well-endowed private non-Catholic colleges and universities.

5. In the past it was doubtless true that anti-Catholic prejudice prevented some people from gaining positions or promotions in some of the private, secular, and public institutions. There seems to be no valid evidence that this is an important part of the situation today. Of course, there is an occasional incompetent, prejudiced, or dishonest administrator in public or private education, just as there are similar men in every walk of life. However, the idea that the public colleges and universities, or even the great private institutions, are administered as anti-Catholic or pro-Protestant seems without foundation in fact. Of course, the public institutions are today rapidly becoming pronouncedly more and more secular. In the public colleges and universities, as in the public schools, it is becoming increasingly true that an aggressive secularism is becoming the "established religion" of the United States of America. But this movement, aided by the Supreme Court's edict in the McCollum case, is being opposed by both Catholics and Protestants.

6. Finally, anyone who wishes to explain the lack of large numbers of Catholics of high distinction in cultural and intellectual life should consider the great number of such potential leaders who enter the priesthood. The screening of candidates for the Catholic priesthood in America is very rigorous, and the years of education and training are such that normally only young men of superior mental and physical capacity and of great strength of character can survive. "Why, as priests, do they not go on to distinguish themselves as scholars and writers?" The answer must include the following:

a. What Dr. George N. Kramer (writing under the pen name of Justin E. West) in O'Brien[11] calls "this arid land of American Catholic complacency." Not yet do a sufficient number of Catholics seem to realize the harm done to the Church and to the legitimate interests of American Catholics by our failure in distinguished scholarship.

b. The burden of work on parish priests and priests teaching in schools and colleges.

[11] *Ibid.*, p. 51.

c. What Dr. O'Brien calls (p. 14): [12]

. . . The obstacles to developing a research program in our schools are two: one is the psychological attitude towards anything that does not come under the heading of what is now understood as "priestly work"; and the other is the terrific barrier of indifference on the part of superiors.

d. What the Rev. P. H. Yancey, S.J., of Spring Hill College refers to as the "closer affiliation with local research groups, state academies of science, and other organizations of scientists" . . .[13]

This is, in my opinion, the greatest obstacle in the list. Catholic scholarship is not so well known and so highly rated as it deserves to be because too many Catholic scholars do not follow Father Yancey's advice. They need to be affiliated and active in all the leading scholarly organizations of the country, prepared to be accepted (and to accept others) on the basis of scholarly achievement only. They should end "disastrous American Catholic complacency" and be deeply concerned with the standing they can earn in the opinion of other scholars.

---

[12] *Ibid.*, p. 14. Quoting *The Tabloid Scientist,* Feb. 1, 1935.
[13] O'Brien, *op. cit.* p. 14.

8

CATHOLIC "CENSORSHIP"

THE freedom of speech or of the press, to which all Americans owe allegiance and to which all Americans are legally entitled, is a constitutional freedom. Censorship that interferes with freedom of the press or freedom of speech in a way which violates the provisions of the Constitution of the United States, or the constitution of a state, or laws passed under the authority of the constitutions is always, without exception, a *governmental activity* behind which there is actual force. Sheriffs, police forces, and militia are agencies of government, not the agencies of private citizens or of nongovernment organizations.

None of our constitutional freedoms was designed to, or should be invoked to, protect anyone from the criticism or persuasion of other persons or groups.

No official, committee, or organization of the Catholic Church has any such force available. They are, therefore, wholly incapable of exercising censorship. They can do nothing which should be called censorship by well-informed people. They have, however, the same right to criticize, condemn, or endorse any book, play, or movie that the *New York Times* enjoys. To call such activity "censorship" when one does not agree with it, and freedom of press and speech when one does agree with it, is nonsense.

The Catholic Church is a teacher—a teacher speaking with effect *to those who accept its teaching*. The effectiveness of the Church in the area that is inaccurately called "censorship" depends wholly upon the *voluntary* acceptance of the Church's guidance by those who read or listen. The same thing is true of the effectiveness of the leadership of any religious, political, or economic group.

Anyone would have difficulty in making a clear and rational distinction between the activity of a Catholic agency which adversely criticizes or condemns a book or a movie and the activity of a secular magazine or newspaper which does the same thing. It may be claimed that the Catholic agency will be listened to, and the expressed opinions from these sources will be acted upon, by more people than will act upon the book reviews, the editorials, and the dramatic criticisms of the *New York Times, The New Yorker,* the *Herald Tribune,* and *The Saturday Review of Literature*. Such a remark, whether true or not, is irrelevant.

Anyone who wishes to see a play, regardless of what the dramatic critics think of it in New York, or who wishes to read a book, regardless of the reviews it gets at the hands of the leading journals, is free to read the book, and may see the play if he hurries before it goes off the boards. The play may disappear on account of having been condemned by a dozen private citizens (dramatic critics) expressing their private opinions. The person who reads or hears of the condemnation of a play, movie, or book by a Catholic priest, bishop, committee, or organization has precisely the same freedom. He may read the book, he may see the play or the movie, and neither bishop, priest, nor organization can *prevent* him from exercising his own judgment in this matter or can *punish* him for going against their advice, counsel, or direction.

When anyone says that the Catholic who goes to a movie, or a play, or reads a book so condemned will have a feeling of guilt, a "sense of sin," the answer is that that is the individual's private concern and is not a matter for public consideration or a threat to American freedom. Clearly there is no such thing as *punishment* that any agency or arm of the Church can inflict upon him. Many non-Catholics, as well as Catholics, would certainly feel a sense of guilt, of sin, of immorality, in going to see a play or in reading a novel denounced as indecent by any person or journal or other agency in whose standards they had confidence.

What any such person does to free himself from his sense of guilt or sin can only be decided by himself. Whether it leads him to the Catholic confessional, to a Protestant minister, a Jewish rabbi, a practicing psychiatrist, or to suicide must ultimately and inevitably be his own personal responsibility.

If one wishes to reply that "the hierarchy" or the Church claims to *punish in the next world* those who go against Catholic teaching, the answer is easy. Without going into the long, elaborate, *theological* answer that would perhaps in other circumstances be best, it should be enough for a layman who is not a theologian to say here that the threat of such punishment would be no threat at all to those who do not accept the Church as a true and responsible guide. If some Americans wish to be guided by the teachings of the Catholic Church, rather than by the teachings of Protestantism, Judaism, or some secular organization, others should accept that situation without rancor. They will have to accept it so long as they consent to live in the United States and the United States continues to maintain elementary personal freedom.

It may be argued that so many Catholics will follow the advice or direction of individuals or organizations in the Church that the condemned play or movie will be withdrawn, and the book will be hard to get, and that this interferes with the freedom of non-Catholics. This, again, is in essence in no way different from the situation we have when a play or movie is so roundly berated by the dramatic critics in a few New York publications that its career on the professional stage is ended for all time. Such are the hazards of living in a free country.

Anyone in a free society who expresses an opinion in public has to run the risk that a good many people may agree with him and act upon his advice. This horrible thought, however, seems not greatly to impede editors, dramatic critics, and book reviewers.

Mr. Blanshard is disturbed (p. 199) by "a considerable amount of internal Catholic influence [in Eric Johnston's office]. The industry's Production Code was written by one of the most aggressive Jesuit writers in the country, Father Daniel Lord, and the Production Administrator, Joseph I. Breen, is a Catholic." I suppose the movie industry, like the publishing industry, in our country is free to hire the advisers it wants, even Catholic advisers.

All the great publishing houses employ readers and editors who go over manuscripts submitted to the publisher and advise their employers on the advisability of publishing. All newspapers and magazines follow the same procedure. This is an essential feature of a free press. When the movie industry sets up an office and hires people (presumably rated competent by the movie companies) to advise their employers in regard to the propriety, and probable profit in producing a given movie they are doing in essence exactly what the publishing house does.

It would be interesting to see a proposed constitutional amendment for either the federal Constitution or for state constitutions which would make it impossible for the movie industry, or the Legion of Decency, or for individual Catholic, Protestant, and Jewish clergymen, or other private individuals, teachers, or publishers to do precisely what all of them are now doing. It would, it seems clear, be a provision which would eliminate freedom of speech and freedom of the press in this country. It would prohibit most editorials, dramatic criticism, movie criticism, and book reviews in the public press, and would almost inevitably eliminate editors and readers from publishing houses. Such a provision given constitutional status would stop the radio, the movie industry, most of the publishing business of America, and would effectively write *finis* to our attempt to function as a free democratic society. The only way in which such a measure could stop what is foolishly called the "censorship" of the Catholic Church, and leave some freedoms to some Americans would be to limit its application strictly to Catholic officials and agencies.

Mr. Blanshard's attack *on the Catholic religion* is responsible for having started a chain of circumstances which gave us probably the only attempt ever made by a supposedly responsible journal to persuade the public that the Bill of Rights prohibits a subscriber to that journal from dropping his subscription. This is the crux of the protest of *The Nation* to the fact that the Board of Superintendents of the Public Schools of New York City declined to renew the school subscriptions to *The Nation* on account of Mr. Blanshard's articles in that journal attacking American Catholics and the Catholic religion.

Since this case has had tremendous publicity containing gross misrepresentation of American Catholics and the Catholic Church as promoters of censorship and the violation of American constitutional rights, it seems appropriate to give the case some attention. It is "Exhibit A" of those who currently accuse the Church of censorship.

In June of 1948 the Board of Superintendents of the New York Public Schools, in making up its list of subscriptions to periodicals for the coming school year, decided not to resubscribe to *The Nation.* Dr. William Jansen, Superintendent of Schools, said that the failure to resubscribe was due to the articles by Paul Blanshard published recently by *The Nation* attacking the Catholic religion.[1]

When the decision not to renew the subscriptions became known, *The Nation* started a campaign of protest. Paul Blanshard charged that the decision of the Board of Superintendents was an instance of *censorship by the Roman Catholic hierarchy,* and Dr. Jansen (a Lutheran) said Mr. Blanshard's charge was "sheer nonsense" and twice in the daily press denied this explicitly.[2] He stated (what should have been assumed in the absence of evidence to the contrary) that no request or pressure of any kind came from any Catholic source.

In August "a group of writers and publishers" (who of all people should have known that freedom to subscribe or buy or to refuse to subscribe or buy is a vital aspect of freedom of the press) sent a telegram to Maximilian Moss, Acting President of the Board of Education, from which I quote: "When the Board of Education [it was not the lay Board of Education, but the professional Board of Superintendents, that refused to resubscribe] banned the magazine, *The Nation,* from the public school libraries it assumed censorship powers [*sic*] which place in jeopardy publishing, education, the press, and all freedom of thought . . . to proscribe students' intellectual inquiry is to proscribe the potentials of tomorrow." [3] This irresponsible

[1] *New York Times,* June 24, p. 1.
[2] *Ibid.,* July 20 and Oct. 12, 1948.
[3] *Ibid.,* Aug. 26, 1948.

rhetoric is a sample of the nonsense written by mature people in the heat of *The Nation*'s campaign.

So long as we can keep America a free country, Mr. Blanshard will have the legal right to offer such pieces for publication, and *The Nation* will have the legal right to publish them, according to its editorial taste. Clearly the rights of freedom of speech and press were in no way involved in this situation. So long as we have civil liberties in America any board, group, library, or person will be wholly free to subscribe, or to refuse to subscribe, to *The Nation* or any other publication that keeps within the law.

The editor of *The Nation,* Miss Freda Kirchwey, contended, shortly after the most bitterly anti-Catholic of the articles (see Dr. Jansen's report below) appeared in her journal, "that the Blanshard articles were not attacks upon faith." She declared that the articles were "sober" and "carefully documented" and that they were written "by a man of the highest integrity." [4] Bishop Oxnam joined in with a resounding proclamation which annexed all the adjacent territory in religion, education, and patriotism. He declared that the affair was "an affront to all whose religious principles demand loyalty to truth, to all educators who believe in discovering the truth and communicating it to the student, and to all patriotic Americans who know that democracy must rest upon the free expression of truth." [5]

If a school system is not free to refuse to subscribe to *The Nation,* what freedom may it have in making up the list of its periodicals? As Dr. Willard Johnson, National Program Director of the National Conference of Christians and Jews, put it: "Does a school system not have the right to choose with care the teaching and learning materials for its students? Must it buy every book and magazine published so as not to violate freedom of the press?" [6]

At the beginning of the controversy Superintendent Jansen issued a statement explaining why the action was taken. In it he said: "The Blanshard articles have contributed to religious animosity by going into matters of faith and out of the realm of politics or social con-

---

[4] *Ibid.,* July 24, 1948.
[5] *Ibid.*
[6] A press release of July 14, 1948.

troversy. The series of articles by Mr. Blanshard are definitely anti-Catholic." [7]

The Rev. Dr. F. Ernest Johnson, of the Department of Research and Education of the Federal Council of Churches of Christ in America,[8] endorses the position that Mr. Blanshard did *attack religion* in the articles in *The Nation.* Dr. Johnson referred to Blanshard's many plunges into theology, said he attacked "plainly religious doctrine" and some that was "by no means exclusively Roman Catholic."

In July the Board of Education held an open meeting on the subject of dropping the subscriptions to *The Nation.* When the allegation of Catholic pressure came up, Dr. Jansen asked each member of the board individually about it. Each testified that there had been no Catholic pressure whatever.[9] In the official report Dr. Jansen wrote: "Finally, the allegation has been made that our decision was based upon pressure from various people. This allegation is completely false and groundless. No member of the Board received a request from any group, or from any individual representing any group, asking that the subscriptions to the magazine be discontinued. The only pressure has been from groups opposing our action." [10]

The following phrases are taken from *The Nation*'s full-page advertisement [11] appealing for funds "toward expenses of the campaign":

> You have seen how liberty dies in the modern world . . . a publication is banned. . . . We published articles displeasing to the officials of the Roman Catholic Church. . . . It is not *The Nation* that is under attack. . . . It is the right to information, the right to opinion, the right of the American mind to be free from control by any power group—whether clerical, political or economic—that are under attack. . . . This conspiracy against thought . . . to mobilize public opinion against the growing menace of thought control . . . a Constitutional right is at stake. . . . Contribute what you can. . . . Talk to people. Write to officials. Stand up for freedom. . . . For when the bell tolls for *The Nation,* it tolls for thee.

[7] *New York Times,* June 24, 1948.

[8] *Weekly Information Service,* 297 Fourth Ave., New York 10, N. Y., Nov. 27, 1948.

[9] *The Tablet,* Brooklyn, N.Y., Aug. 28, 1948.

[10] Pamphlet issued by the Board of Superintendents, Oct. 1, 1948.

[11] *The New Republic,* Aug. 9, 1948.

These phrases were widely distributed by a once distinguished journal because in a supposedly free country some people chose not to continue to subscribe to *The Nation*.

The most deeply disturbing aspect of this whole affair, however, is the way in which distinguished, literate, thoughtful, unprejudiced people swallowed whole the attempt to inflame the public against American Catholics and to make this failure to renew subscriptions appear as a violation of civil liberties, of constitutional rights.

In October, months after Dr. Jansen's explanation of the board's action, with a specific denial of the charge of censorship by the Catholic Church, over one hundred persons, some of them of great and deserved influence, signed "An Appeal to Reason and Conscience in Defense of the *Right of Freedom of Inquiry in the United States*" (italics mine). This document claimed that *The Nation* had been "suppressed" and implied that "one of the churches of the country" had exercised in this case a "simple veto" on material for the public schools.

Probably many of the signers lent their names to this grossly inaccurate statement in a belief in the truth of the wholly false claims that the Blanshard articles did not attack the Catholic religion, and that the failure to subscribe was due to action by the *Catholic Church*. However, accepting such a claim without proof is a serious lapse in the responsibility of influential citizens.

In his reply to the statement *"in Defense of the Right of Inquiry"* [*sic*], Dr. Jansen said: "The Constitution of this State forbids religious instruction in our classrooms. Should then the attacks on religion be tolerated?"

Dr. Francis T. Spaulding, State Commissioner of Education, in dismissing the appeal of *The Nation* from the superintendents' decision, said that "no question of the freedom of the press is involved." The attorney for *The Nation* had argued that the refusal to resubscribe was "in violation of constitutional guarantees of the freedom of the press." Dr. Spaulding went on to say that the board "has not merely the right to determine the periodicals to which it wished to subscribe, or which it will accept for deposit in its school libraries, but a fundamental responsibility so to determine, in accordance with its best judgment of the educational welfare of its pupils." [12]

To have this situation in which an educational administrative board exercised its routine authority, either wisely or unwisely, in conformity to its professional and legal responsibility and to the principles of academic freedom, grossly misrepresented to the public over the signatures of distinguished men and women, is a severe blow to civil liberties in general, and to academic freedom in particular.

Had *The Nation*'s uproar remained only a private enterprise in the interests of its circulation and of Mr. Blanshard's book, no great harm would have resulted. However, the names of men, women, and organizations of distinction and influence gave weight to this campaign of misrepresentation. This greatly magnified the danger of spreading suspicion and intolerance among Americans and of injury to the cause of civil liberties in America.

The activity of these persons and organizations is directly contrary to the position in regard to academic freedom and responsibility taken consistently for years by the American Association of University Professors and the American Civil Liberties Union. While I was chairman of the Committee on Academic Freedom of the American Civil Liberties Union we had some cases that almost exactly parallel the New York *Nation* case. In these the committee, acting for the Civil Liberties Union, and carrying out the Union's unvarying policy up to that time, defended *the sole right of the educational authority to make such decisions* and the concomitant duty to take the *sole responsibility* for the merits of the decisions.[11a]

Academic freedom means, among other things, that the academic person or group has the freedom, the right, and the responsibility to make professional decisions in regard to such matters as educational methods and materials. The right to make a decision means *the right to be wrong in the opinion of some other person or group.*

Outsiders have a perfect right, of course, to criticize any decision as unwise, bad educational planning, or stupid for various reasons. No

---

[11a] This committee, however, supported *The Nation* in this case.

[12] *New York Times,* May 28, 1949.

literate and informed person has an intellectual right to call any such decision *censorship* or the violation of anyone's constitutional rights—however bad he may think the decision to be. The Constitution of the United States does not require anyone to subscribe to *The Nation.*

A parallel case will illustrate the standard practice of responsible organizations in the area of academic freedom. The Committee on Academic Freedom of the Civil Liberties Union under my chairmanship was concerned with a case from the University of Texas. The Board of Regents of that university attempted to dictate concerning specific reading matter in the English Department. For a lay body, such as the Regents, to dictate to professional educators in such a detail has universally been held by professional bodies to be a clear infraction of the principle of academic freedom. A fair parallel offense would be for the lay trustees of a hospital to dictate to the professional staff of physicians and surgeons on how to treat the patients. This was the position taken unanimously by the committee and with the warm approval of the Civil Liberties Union, expressed to me by Mr. Roger Baldwin, then Director of the Union, and by others.

The attempt to appeal from the Board of Superintendents to Mayor O'Dwyer or the State Commissioner of Education, made in *The Nation* case, was similarly a clear violation of the age-old principles of academic freedom. The freedom of the schools would be gone if any mayor could dictate the books or periodicals to be supplied to the school libraries. Likewise, if a state commissioner could and should force the New York City schools to subscribe to *The Nation* he would, in the interests of the most elementary justice, have to force all other state school systems to do the same. Then where would he stop in prescribing magazines for all the state schools? Which ones would be in and which out? Then whose civil liberties would be violated and who would protest against what "censorship"?

These questions should have been faced before leaders of deserved reputation and influence joined the cries of censorship, conspiracy against thought, a church veto, violation of constitutional rights, the freedom of inquiry, and the right to information and opinion—all because some subscriptions to a weekly magazine had not been renewed! Unless civil liberties can get better support from such leaders, they will probably dwindle and disappear from American life. Who subscribes to *The Nation,* and if not, why not, is a matter of trifling importance compared to the importance of maintaining the civil liberties which are now rather precariously the heart of the American way of life.

Concerning this situation, Mr. Blanshard writes (p. 7): "Some portions of this book, now completely revised and re-written, appeared in *The Nation* in twelve installments, ending on June 4, 1948. They provoked an instant and fiery response from the Catholic hierarchy throughout the United States, and an equally ardent defense in liberal and academic circles. I salute *The Nation* and its gallant editor, Freda Kirchwey, for meeting the attack with unfailing courage; and I salute the distinguished Americans, headed by Archibald MacLeish, who publicly supported *The Nation* in asserting its right to discuss a fundamental social issue."

These are the facts:

1. Not a single response, fiery or frigid, by even one member of the Catholic hierarchy is quoted or referred to in Mr. Blanshard's book. Nor have I been able to find even one anywhere else.

2. The "attack" which Miss Kirchwey met with "unfailing courage" and which Mr. MacLeish's committee opposed, was a *failure* by the Board of Superintendents of New York City Public Schools to resubscribe to *The Nation.*

3. The Catholic hierarchy had *nothing* to do with this matter.

4. *The Nation*'s right to discuss anything under the sun was in no way involved.

"The censorship system of the Roman Catholic Church in the United States is," writes Mr. Blanshard (pp. 180–182), "a highly organized system of cultural and moral *controls* that applies not only to books, plays, magazines, and motion pictures, but to persons and places. In a sense *the Catholicism that the hierarchy imposes* upon its people is itself *a great system of censorship,* a *system of condemnations and taboos. . . .* The extreme rule against mixed marriage with Jews is in a sense *a censorship of all Jews as Jews,*[13] a form of discrimina-

---

[13] The Church takes no such position. See pp. 251–252.

tion based upon a condemnation of their religious ideas. . . . It would be fortunate if the effects of censorship could be limited to Catholics, but in real life Catholics, Protestants, Jews, and unbelievers are exposed to the same plays, books, magazines and films. The *strictures* of the Catholic hierarchy upon its own people cannot be isolated from the life of the rest of the community. . . . Catholic censorship, therefore, cannot be considered in isolation. It is an important factor in American social policy, and it cannot *hide behind the protective screen* of a single faith. Since it affects the lives of so many non-Catholics *it must be submitted to non-Catholic analysis and judgment.* The question then that will concern us in this chapter is not whether Catholic censorship is a good thing for Catholics but whether it is a good thing for the American people."

After quoting what he says is "the general rule" (without any indication as to whom or what he is quoting from), Mr. Blanshard writes (p. 183): "In practice this rule means that no Catholic is *allowed* to read knowingly and without special permission any book attacking any fundamental doctrine of the Catholic Church." (All italics are mine. Note the biased and inaccurate use of the italicized words.)

"No book favoring sterilization of the feeble minded, birth control, euthanasia, artificial insemination, therapeutic abortion, cremation, humanism, state operation of all colleges, divorce, complete separation of church and state, and other subjects, can be deliberately and knowingly read by a good Catholic" (p. 185).

"It [the Church] teaches that a Catholic sins who reads the side of a public discussion that contains direct attacks upon the Catholic position" (p. 185).

These statements in so far as they are specific enough to be clearly understood are all *false* and are all given *without documentation of any kind,* not even one of Mr. Blanshard's peculiar footnotes. And none of them deals with censorship. Any well-informed person should know on reading the above that they are nonsense. Uninformed readers who accept them as truth must do so as a simple act of faith in the private revelations of Paul Blanshard.

Mr. Blanshard has, indeed, found a number of passages which

indicate that (*a*) *some Catholics, have* (*b*) *written some things, that are* (*c*) *more or less in agreement with,* (*d*) *some of his statements.* But certainly they are not expressions of fundamental Catholic doctrine which all Catholics are expected to believe. Even the *Imprimatur* on some of them means to the informed, not that the doctrines or policies expressed are *authentic Catholic* positions, not even that the official giving the *Imprimatur* agrees with the statements (see pp. 195–196), but only that in the opinion of the official they are not directly contrary to fundamental Catholic doctrine. In other words, they seem to the giver of the *Imprimatur,* at most, as something that a Catholic *might believe.* Granted. What some Catholics, some Protestants, some Jews, and some atheists believe is likely to strike the well informed in various areas as weird and wonderful. And I am afraid that there is nothing much that Mr. Blanshard or I can do about it.

Mr. Blanshard's chapter on "Censorship and Boycott" has thirty-two footnotes attached to its thirty-one pages. None of them proves his case as expressed in the passages quoted above. Most of them are bibliographical references attached to unimportant quotations from private individuals. Their status as "authentic Catholic statements" is only that of a book review by a Protestant as an "authentic Protestant statement." A number of them are quotations from Catholic priests and laymen, expressing severe criticism of the writings and actions of *other Catholics.* In other words, here as in other parts of his book considerable parts of Mr. Blanshard's material consists of quotations from the constant and searching self-criticism of Catholics by Catholics. Mr. Blanshard seems not to realize that these passages refute his basic contention that all Catholics have to think alike as directed by the hierarchy.

The manuscript of Mr. Blanshard's book was submitted to various New York publishers who did not care to publish it. Was this censorship? If it was, and Mr. Blanshard would like to have a situation in which the publisher could not refuse to publish his book, he would have a situation in which a publisher would be compelled to publish whatever was submitted to him, and that would doubtless mean that we would not have any publishers.

Mr. Blanshard writes in *The Atlantic Monthly, February, 1950* (see my Chapter 15), that several of the publishers who refused to publish his book did so because they were afraid of Catholic reprisals. He offers nothing whatever in substantiation of this charge. Certainly if any publisher to whom Mr. Blanshard submitted the book gave it to an editor who had even an elementary acquaintance with the material Mr. Blanshard was treating, the editor would not have to read more than a few pages to have ample reason for refusing to publish.

But suppose, sometime, a publisher should actually find out and should say frankly and truthfully that if he published a certain book his publishing house would probably be boycotted by American Catholics, or American Protestants, or American Jews, or labor unionists, or public school teachers, or any other group—what is Mr. Blanshard going to do about it? What can anyone do about it? One can, it seems to me, cite it as a proof that we are still a free society in which publishers can either publish books or refuse to publish them, and take the consequences of either course.

Such a situation would demonstrate further that members of the American public, Catholics, Protestants, Jews, secularists, agnostics, and atheists, are free to buy or to refuse to buy books or magazines; to go to plays or movies, or to stay away. Those who do not like this situation will have to put up with it as long as we remain a free society. Or, perhaps they can migrate to Russia, or other Iron Curtain countries. If they can take their dictation somewhat diluted, they might find an atmosphere more agreeable to their tastes in Yugoslavia, Spain, or Argentina. But if this situation, which they call "censorship," makes them unhappy they will never be happy in America so long as America maintains the principles of the Bill of Rights.

9

CATHOLICS AND SOCIAL POLICIES

MANY Americans assume that "the Catholic vote" exists, that it includes most Catholics and is controlled by the hierarchy, that this vote is essentially conservative or reactionary, that Catholic doctrine opposes liberal social policies, and that consequently Catholics refuse to cooperate with non-Catholics in the promotion of desirable social movements and the adoption of needed social reforms. This whole aggregation of assumptions is contrary to fact. The record of Catholics in Congress is adequate proof.

For some time now tables have been published showing the "liberal" or "progressive," as against "conservative" or "antiprogressive," attitude of Catholics in Congress as compared to that of the whole membership of the Congress of the United States.

Father Edward S. Dunn, S.J., reports as follows on the record of Catholics in the Seventy-ninth Congress: [1]

There were eleven senators and seventy-seven representatives in the 79th Congress who are, or claim to be, Catholics. How did the Catholic members of the House vote on important issues? To determine that, a selection was made from among the fifteen recorded roll calls used by the *New Republic* in their "Facts for November" supplement for September 23, 1946, and the twelve issues listed by the *CIO News* for August 19, 1946. Ten issues were selected, six that were common to both lists, two used only by the *New Republic* and two only by the CIO. Five of the measures concerned labor relations, three price control and the remaining two might be regarded

[1] Reprint from *American Catholic Sociological Review* (Chicago: Loyola University, December, 1946), pp. 259–266.

as miscellaneous. All are fair criteria of a liberal or progressive attitude toward the vital issues in domestic affairs. Thus a vote on what was the progressive side was marked by a plus and an anti-progressive vote by a minus sign. Absences were not counted in any way.

On the ten measures chosen, the members of the House cast 1540 progressive votes against 2050 anti-progressive votes, for a liberal average of about 43 percent of the total votes cast. But, the seventy-seven Catholic members cast 582 progressive votes against 122 non-progressive votes, so that almost 83 percent of all the votes they registered were on the liberal side.

The voting charts of the *CIO News* and the *New Republic* show that good or excellent records on the progressive issues were made by Senators Chavez, McMahon, Mead, Murray, Myers, and Wagner. Senators Ellender, O'Mahoney, and Walsh voted for only about half on the liberal issues. Senators Carville and McCarran, both from Nevada, did not often vote for progressive measures.

Apparently the Catholic hierarchy did not compel these Catholic representatives and senators to vote all one way, and that way on the nonliberal, antiprogressive side.

Bill No.	Liberal vote of Whole Senate (On 15 bills)	Liberal Vote of Catholic Senators	House Whole (On 14 bills)	House Catholics
1	65%	81%	83%	85%
2	37%	90%	38%	72%
3	46%	90%	13%	69%
4	27%	72%	20%	70%
5	26%	72%	33%	65%
6	38%	88%	48%	90%
7	30%	60%	22%	60%
8	11%	40%	25%	63%
9	28%	63%	40%	84%
10	73%	81%	48%	79%
11	64%	77%	15%	63%
12	59%	81%	72%	88%
13	15%	50%	15%	61%
14	54%	90%	9%	40%
15	50%	42%		

Senate voted liberal 33% of the time. Catholic Senators voted liberal 71% of the time.

Whole House voted liberal 34% of the time; Catholics in the House, 71%.

Mr. Dale Francis, of Notre Dame University, has given us [2] a similar report on the Eightieth Congress. On fifteen bills rated "progressive" or "antiprogressive," according to the approval or disapproval of *The New Republic,* here is the voting record in percentages. The separate bills and the voting records of the individual Catholic members of the Congress are shown in the tables given below.

The individual voting records of the eleven Catholic senators in the Eightieth Congress, on the fifteen bills reported on in the above table, are shown here. While heavily progressive as a group, the Catholic senators in their personal records range from almost completely progressive to almost completely antiprogressive. No control by the hierarchy here.

SENATE

Senate	Cut ERP Funds	Admit Jewish DPs	Extend Reciprocal Trade	Portal-to-Portal Pay	Over-ride T-H Veto	Anti-Inflation Amendment	Revive Excess Profits Tax	Override Tax Cut Veto	Exempt RRs from Anti-Trust	Federal Aid to Education	Weaken Rent Control	Kill Public Housing	Restrict Social Security	Funds for TVA Steam Plant	Segregated School Plan
	1	2	3	4	5	6	7	8	9	10	11	12	13	14	15
McMahon (L) Conn.	+	+	+	+	+	+	—	—	—	+	+	+	+	+	+
Ellender (D) La.	+	—	+	—	—	+	—	—	—	+	O	+	—	+	—
O'Conor (D) Md.	+	+	+	—	—	+	—	—	—	—	+	—	—	+	—
Murray (D) Mont.	+	+	+	+	+	+	+	O	+	+	+	+	O	+	O
McCarran (D) Nev.	+	O	+	+	+	O	+	—	—	+	—	+	O	+	O
Chavez (D) N. Mex.	—	+	+	+	+	O	O	—	—	+	+	+	O	+	O
Wagner (D) N. Y.	+	+	+	+	+	+	+	+	+	+	+	+	+	+	+
Myers (D) Pa.	+	+	+	+	+	+	+	+	—	+	+	+	—	+	+
McGrath (D) R. I.	+	+	+	+	+	+	+	+	+	+	+	+	+	+	—
McCarthy (R) Wis.	—	+	—	—	—	—	—	—	—	—	—	—	—	—	O
O'Mahoney (D) Wyo.	+	+	+	+	+	+	+	+	+	+	O	+	+	+	—

The symbol (+) indicates, in the opinion of the *New Republic,* a progressive vote. Symbol (—) indicates antiprogressive. Symbol (O) indicates absent or not voting.

[2] *The Commonweal,* Jan. 14, 1949, pp. 342–345.

The voting records of the forty-five Catholic representatives in the House in the Eightieth Congress are given in this table. It shows that the Catholic representatives, like the Catholic senators, are as a group overwhelmingly progressive, but the range is almost the full spectrum, from records that are one hundred per cent progressive to some that miss being one hundred per cent antiprogressive by just one vote. Again the hierarchy did not compel them all to vote one way.

HOUSE OF REPRESENTATIVES

House	Cut ERP Funds	Extend Reciprocal Trade	Portal-to-Portal Pay	Override T-H Veto	Admit Jewish DPs	Anti-Inflation Amendment	Overide Tax Cut Veto	Exempt RRs from Anti-Trust	Weaken Rent Control	Funds for TVA Steam Plan	Restrict Social Security	Anti-Poll Tax Bill	Mundt-Nixon Bill	Funds for Thomas Com.
	1	2	3	4	5	6	7	8	9	10	11	12	13	14
McDonough (R) Calif.	+	—	—	—	+	O	—	—	—	+	—	+	—	—
Gordon (D) Ill.	+	+	+	+	—	+	+	+	+	+	+	+	+	+
Gorski (D) Ill.	+	+	+	+	—	+	+	+	+	+	+	+	+	—
O'Brien (D) Ill.	+	+	+	+	+	+	+	+	+	+	+	+	+	—
Price (D) Ill.	+	+	+	+	+	+	+	+	+	+	+	+	+	+
Madden (D) Ind.	+	+	+	+	+	+	+	+	+	+	+	+	+	+
Boggs (D) La.	+	+	O	—	—	+	—	—	+	+	—	—	O	—
Domengeaux (D) La.	+	—	O	—	—	+	—	—	+	—	O	—	—	O
Hebert (D) La.	+	—	—	—	—	+	—	—	+	—	—	—	O	—
Larcade (D) La.	—	—	—	—	—	+	—	—	+	O	—	—	—	—
Meade (D) Md.	+	—	—	—	—	+	—	O	+	+	—	+	—	—
Donohue (D) Mass.	+	—	—	+	+	+	—	—	+	+	—	+	+	—
Kennedy (D) Mass.	+	+	+	+	+	+	+	+	+	+	O	+	O	—
Lane (D) Mass.	O	O	+	+	O	+	—	O	+	O	—	+	O	—
McCormack (D) Mass.	+	+	+	+	+	+	+	O	+	+	+	+	—	—
Bennett (R) Mich.	—	—	—	O	—	—	—	—	—	—	—	+	—	—
Dingell (D) Mich.	+	+	+	+	+	+	+	+	+	+	+	+	+	+
Lesinski (D) Mich.	+	+	+	+	—	+	+	+	+	+	+	+	+	+
Sadowski (D) Mich.	—	+	+	+	+	+	+	O	+	+	+	+	+	+
Blatnik (D) Minn.	+	+	+	+	+	+	+	O	+	+	+	+	+	+
Devitt (R) Minn.	+	—	—	—	+	—	—	—	+	—	—	+	—	—
O'Hara (R) Minn.	—	—	—	—	—	+	—	+	—	—	—	O	O	—
Hart (D) N. J.	+	+	+	+	—	+	—	+	+	+	+	+	—	—
Norton (D) N. J.	O	+	+	+	+	+	+	+	+	+	+	+	+	+
Buckley (D) N. Y.	O	+	+	+	+	O	+	—	+	+	+	+	+	—

HOUSE OF REPRESENTATIVES (*Cont.*)

House	Cut ERP Funds	Extend Reciprocal Trade	Portal-to-Portal Pay	Override T-H Veto	Admit Jewish DPs	Anti-Inflation Amendment	Override Tax Cut Veto	Exempt RRs from Anti-Trust	Weaken Rent Control	Funds for TVA Steam Plan	Restrict Social Security	Anti-Poll Tax Bill	Mundt-Nixon Bill	Funds for Thomas Com.
	1	2	3	4	5	6	7	8	9	10	11	12	13	14
Delaney (D) N. Y.	+	+	+	+	+	+	+	+	+	+	+	+	+	O
Heffernan (D) N. Y.	+	+	O	+	+	+	+	+	+	+	+	+	+	O
Kearney (R) N. Y.	+	—	—	—	+	—	—	—	—	—	—	+	O	—
Keogh (D) N. Y.	+	+	+	+	+	+	+	—	+	+	+	+	—	—
Lynch (D) N. Y.	+	+	+	+	+	+	+	O	+	+	+	+	+	—
Marcantonio (AL) N. Y.	—	+	+	+	+	+	+	+	+	+	+	+	+	+
O'Toole (D) N. Y.	+	+	+	+	+	+	+	O	+	+	+	+	—	O
Pfeifer (D) N. Y.	+	+	+	+	+	+	+	+	+	+	+	+	+	+
Rooney (D) N. Y.	+	+	+	+	+	+	+	+	+	+	+	+	—	O
Somers (D) N. Y.	+	+	+	+	+	O	+	+	+	+	+	+	+	+
Feighan (D) Ohio	+	+	+	+	+	+	+	+	+	+	+	+	+	—
Kirwan (D) Ohio	+	+	—	+	+	+	+	+	+	+	+	+	+	+
Eberharter (D) Pa.	+	+	+	+	+	+	+	+	+	+	+	+	+	+
Kelley (D) Pa.	+	+	+	O	+	+	—	+	+	+	+	+	+	+
McGarvey (R) Pa.	O	—	—	—	—	—	—	—	—	—	—	+	—	—
Fogarty (D) R. I.	+	+	+	+	+	+	+	+	+	+	+	+	+	+
Forand (D) R. I.	+	+	+	+	+	+	+	+	+	+	+	+	+	+
Kilday (D) Tex.	+	O	—	—	—	+	—	+	—	+	—	—	—	—
Brophy (R) Wis.	+	—	+	+	—	+	—	—	—	—	—	+	—	—
O'Konski (R) Wis.	—	+	—	—	—	+	—	—	+	+	—	+	—	—

The symbol (+) indicates, in the opinion of the *New Republic*, a progressive vote. Symbol (—) indicates antiprogressive. Symbol (O) indicates absent or not voting.

Mr. Joseph L. Hansknecht, Jr. in a master's degree thesis at the Catholic University of America, 1951, analysed the voting records of fifty Catholic members of the House of Representatives in the 81st Congress in comparison with the voting records of a "comparable" group of fifty non-Catholic members. The members of each group were selected after an elaborate study of their backgrounds. The two groups were "comparable" in the following matters: length of service in Congress, occupations, education, military service, marital status, Congressional district control (by a dominant political party or shifting from one party to another), regional distribution, and concentration of population.

After the individuals had been selected to get two groups, one Catholic and one non-Catholic, that were as nearly as possible alike in the above mentioned factors, twenty roll call votes dealing with the following eleven issues were chosen for analysis: labor legislation, public housing and rent control, social security, minimum wages, civil rights, anti-trust and excess profits taxes, veterans' pensions, farm program, military aid to foreign nations, economic development of foreign nations, and export controls.

This thesis reveals that according to the official record: (1) there was no "Catholic vote" in the sense that Catholics follow a "line" of any kind, or the direction of any person or group. They do not vote as Catholics but primarily as Republicans or Democrats as others do; and (2) the large majority of them (over 80%) vote as liberals "unless one considers Americans for Democratic Action, the CIO, and the AF of L as reactionary."

Testimony in harmony with the detailed evidence given above is available from a non-Catholic who occupies a rather good "window" from which to view the passing political parade of liberal and non-liberal persons and groups. Mr. James Loeb, Jr., National Executive Secretary of Americans for Democratic Action, writes: [3] "If all Catholics in the United States abstained from a presidential or Congressional election, the result would undoubtedly be a swing further to the right than we have known in this country for generations. Similarly if all Congressional Catholics went on strike for a full session, the result would make the 80th Congress seem by comparison a high mark of liberalism."

In 1938 there was organized at the Catholic University of America a Commission on American Citizenship. This was done at the instance of the members of the American Catholic hierarchy who constitute the trustees of the university. The activities of this commission are not

[3] *The Commonweal,* June 16, 1950, p. 239.

secret and its purposes and "philosophy" have been clearly stated in a booklet of 125 pages, published in 1943 and reprinted frequently since then: *Better Men for Better Times.*[4] Anyone genuinely interested in discovering important Catholic programs and objectives in American social policy could hardly have avoided contact with this document. It obviously cannot be reprinted in full in this book, but some extended quotations from it seem to be well in order, both on account of its sponsorship and because the quoted passages refute so completely the common false assumptions in regard to Catholic doctrine and teaching in the field of social policy. If there is such a thing as an official, authentic statement of Catholic attitudes toward "expanding social service," this is it.

The president of the commission in 1943 was Msgr. Patrick J. McCormick, Rector of the Catholic University, now Auxiliary Bishop of Washington. The chairman of the Executive Committee of the commission was Bishop Francis J. Haas, of Grand Rapids, Michigan, the director of the commission was the late Msgr. George Johnson, of the Department of Education of the Catholic University of America and director of the Department of Education of the National Catholic Welfare Conference.

Anyone interested in making a competent investigation of Catholic attitudes, teaching, and leadership in the field of social policy could hardly have escaped knowing about Bishop Haas of Grand Rapids. That name alone, as the chairman of the Executive Committee of the Commission on American Citizenship, should prompt any serious scholar who was studying the social policy attitudes of Catholic Americans to read the booklet *Better Men for Better Times.*

A few items taken from *Who's Who in America* indicates something of the experience and standing of Bishop Haas in the field of social service:

> Professor of Sociology, Marquette University, 1922–1931; impartial chairman Milwaukee newspaper industry, 1929; general secretary Milwaukee County Association for Promotion of Old Age Pensions, 1925–1931; member National Labor Board, 1933–1934; member Labor Advisory Board, NRA,

[4] Washington: The Catholic University of America Press, 1943.

1933–1934; honorary LL.D. University of Wisconsin, 1935; member Labor Policies Board, Works Progress Administration, 1935–1939; Chairman President's Commission on Fair Employment Practice, 1934; co-chairman Council Against Intolerance in America; vice-president American Association for the United Nations; director Carnegie Church Peace Union; Bishop of Grand Rapids, since 1943.

I quote below (with permission) from *Better Men for Better Times.* While this book is not an infallible statement of social doctrine binding on all Catholics, it has back of it more impressive Catholic opinion and endorsement than almost any other comparable publication on the subject.

Political freedom becomes a hollow sham when it attempts to function in the midst of economic bondage.

. . . our zeal for the preservation of individual liberty must be matched by our devotion to the cause of social security. . . Of late years, there has been an acceleration in the framing of social legislation on all levels of government. Those who would prefer to let nature take its course have been fearful of this development and have seen in it the ultimate doom of free institutions. Their forebodings have not frightened us. We are convinced that it is possible to bring our economic system into conformity with the principles of sound reason and justice without doing violence to the essentials of democratic government [pp. 5-6].

It is increasingly apparent that we have need for more effective means of social control. Individualism and free enterprise need to be restrained and disciplined if we are to spare ourselves confusion, insecurity, and misery. Society must find better instrumentalities for implementing its common will [p. 85].

Society has the obligation of intervening when children are abused in the home or deprived of those things which are their due. The child is commanded by the Law of God to disobey his parents when they order him to do what is wrong. Obedience does not mean that we sacrifice ourselves to the arbitrary and *irrational* [p. 4].

He would be presumptuous indeed who would attempt to define in any specific manner the proper limits of State activity. In times like these when human values are at stake, doctrinaire quibbling is out of order. No one has summed it all up better than Pius XII in the following words taken from the Encyclical on the *Function of the State in the Modern World:* "No one of good-will and vision will think of refusing the State, in the exceptional conditions of the world of today, correspondingly wider and exceptional rights to meet the popular needs" [p. 91].

Other Catholic writers express the same basic attitude toward social thinking and policy. One more quotation will have to suffice.

> Communists justly castigate a political system which stands by indifferent while the more talented (or less scrupulous, as the case may be) give free vent to their greed at the expense of the masses. Benevolent industrialists, by incessant propaganda, have succeeded fairly well in getting over the idea that "free enterprise" is somehow a corollary of democratic government. Actually, endorsement of free enterprise, in the sense of allowing the economically powerful to absorb the weak has no connection with good government of any type, democratic or otherwise.[5]

When one writes "liberal Catholic" or "Catholic liberal" it should not be interpreted as indicating that either the Catholicism or the liberalism of the person so characterized is different from the Catholicism of other Catholics or the liberalism of other liberals. These expressions are much like Canadian Catholic, Catholic Republican, Southern Catholic, Catholic layman, Catholic Negro, or German Catholic. When some Catholic writers cease to give the impression that good Catholics cannot be liberals, and some liberals cease to give the impression that good liberals cannot be Catholics, America may accomplish the idea of unity without uniformity, of diversity in unity, of the right to be different, and at the same time to be frank, to be friendly, to cooperate in the things we agree about and to differ without bitterness and suspicion in regard to the things on which we differ. This will be a happy day for all Americans who actually believe in personal and religious freedom and in genuine liberalism. And it will be a bad day for those who seek power, office, or cash by dealing in racial and religious antagonism.

In spite of all of the above, and of the consistent record of individual Catholic American liberals, there are too many Americans who believe that there is something inconsistent in being a Catholic and a liberal. There is even a section of genuine American liberals, (i.e., supporters of economic, political, and international measures commonly called "liberal" by most Americans) who seem not to want to treat Catholics as even *possible* liberals.

[5] Sheppard, *Religion and the Concept of Democracy, op. cit.*, p. 40.

I regret to say, also, that there is a type of Catholic who seems to think the word "liberal" is a word of reproach. The use of the words "liberal" and "liberalism" by some Catholics in discussing racial, economic, or political questions in contemporary America, as though the words had the antireligious, *anti-Catholic, doctrinal meanings* of other times in other countries, is unwarranted and harmful to American Catholics in general.

We have too many monolithic liberals in this country. They are less than enthusiastic about having Catholics take prominent parts in liberal movements. They seem to believe that the *only* liberals are those who agree with them *in everything*. Liberalism is to them only their own hard and fast, monolithic creed. You take it all, or else you are not a liberal.

To be a liberal, *according to the monolithic liberal,* one must believe in something more than civil liberties, social security, racial equality, decent labor laws, better public education, "expanding social legislation," universal suffrage, religious freedom, no public favoritism for any one religion (i.e., equality *before the law of all* religions), the New Deal, and the Fair Deal. This program, which I think most informed people will agree is substantially the American program of political, economic, and social liberalism, simply does not satisfy many Americans who think of themselves as among the leading liberal propagandists of the country. I have met and worked with liberals of this type in educational movements, and in the American Civil Liberties Union, and have had illuminating questions from some of them in forum meetings at which I have spoken.

Any American Catholic can heartily subscribe (if he wants to) to every one of the liberal objectives and theories mentioned above. Catholics, as others, will of course differ on the merits of particular measures put forward to promote these ends. I am convinced, however, that the majority of Catholic Americans believe in most of the listed items. I cannot prove this statistically, but all the evidence I know (as that in this chapter) indicates this. The monolithic liberals never offer comparable evidence of the nonliberalism of American Catholics. They rest almost wholly on assumptions which they refuse to examine.

I know of just one partial excuse or explanation for this attitude. It is not adequate, but it is something, and it should cease to be available to those who wish to persuade the uninformed that the Catholic influence in America necessarily *has to be reactionary.* I refer to the previously mentioned, improper use of the word "liberal" in too many Catholic books and periodicals.

Sometimes careless writers in the Catholic press (it has them as does the secular and non-Catholic religious press), in commenting on some proposal which they do not like, ascribe it, gratuitously and inaccurately, to "the liberals," with the implication that it is the position of all liberals. This kind of writing on the part of a few Catholics gives to those who are anxious to make a case against all American Catholics the sort of help that Father John Courtney Murray[6] called "some bones" out of which to construct their monsters of anti-Catholicism. Such lapses on the part of some Catholics increase the opposition of the monolithic liberals, which in turn increases the disdain of the Catholic conservatives. This childish game of guidance by labels and slogan thinking should be dropped by both sides. Men who are mature citizens should work together cordially for the things they believe in and differ with respect, and still cordially, in regard to things on which they cannot agree.

Part of this whole problem arises from a lack of understanding on the part of both the monolithic liberal and the Catholic conservative in regard to certain Catholic denunciations, in papal encyclicals and elsewhere, of practices and doctrine labeled "liberalism" which do not apply to modern American problems. (See pp. 33–34, 62–63, 88.) A little competent study is indicated for the protagonists in both camps. More light for home consumption and less heat for export to one's opponents would be a good program for both sides—and especially this would be good for the United States of America.

The monolithic liberals demand, at least implicitly, that anyone to be labeled a liberal must subscribe to their programs in such matters as birth control, euthanasia, therapeutic abortion, total secularism in education, the omniscience of science in matters of religion and ethics,

---

[6] *The American Mercury,* September, 1949.

the infallibility of political majorities in the realm of morals, and their unhistorical and legally absurd interpretation of the religious clause of the First Amendment. These matters have little or nothing to do with improving the condition of those of our fellow men who are "ill clothed, ill housed, and ill fed." Any attempt to use legislative compulsion in regard to them means the introduction of the omnipotent state and the destruction of personal and religious freedom. Such a program cannot be brought about by compulsive legislation so long as we remain a free society. Therefore, the monolithic liberal who makes this program a part of the "liberal program for America" is doing something which no real liberal should do.

He is checking the use by the liberal forces of America of one of the largest and most potent reservoirs of liberal voting power in the United States for the genuine and relevant objectives of realistic liberalism—the twenty-odd million American Catholics. By so doing he is postponing the realization of the proper objective for which all liberals should be working in the area of political, economic, and international liberalism.

American Catholics are "natural" liberals for various reasons. Most of them are not in the higher income brackets and have an inevitable interest in equality of economic opportunity. They are conditioned to international-mindedness by reason of belonging to the world-wide Catholic Church. Except for a few who seem to be ignorant of the Church's doctrine of the equality of all men of all races, there are no "racists" among them. Finally the specific teachings of the Church on the Ten Commandments and the brotherhood of man under the Fatherhood of God inculcates (not always perfectly) an attitude toward one's neighbor that necessarily underlies the truly liberal attitude.

The lack of thoughtful, "thought-out," and *consistent* liberalism on the part of the monolithic liberals, is the subject of one of Dr. D. W. Brogan's sharp paragraphs in "The Catholic Church in America." [7]

> If religious intolerance is absolutely wrong (which is what the *liberals* say), then it is wrong as an accompaniment of revolution in Mexico and Russia; and when that persecution was going on in Mexico, or when it is

[7] *Harper's Magazine*, May, 1950, p. 43.

going on now in Lithuania, one might expect (if one were naive enough) impassioned protests from the run-of-the-mill liberal. If they have been made, they have been *sotto voce;* at any rate, few American Catholics seem to have heard them. The liberal, lay or cleric, does not seem to this American minority to come into court with clean hands. There may be doubts and ambiguities as to the Catholic position, but there are or should be none as to the liberal or modern Protestant position. Their duty was and is to affirm their faith in religious liberty in Lithuania and Vera Cruz, as well as in Spain or Italy. That no doubt means quarreling with allies and defending enemies, but what of it? Nor has the consistency of the liberals been surpassed by their foresight or understanding of the modern world. Indeed, looked at from the outside, the readiness with which the American liberals have followed their hearts, not their heads, with tragic or comic results, would suggest that modesty or even timidity would become them better than the naive assumption in 1950 of the old justifiable compacency of the youth of John Dewey or H. G. Wells.

This same tendency on the part of some liberals was discussed recently by Father George G. Higgins, Assistant Director, Social Action Department, National Catholic Welfare Conference, in his weekly column "The Yardstick." [8]

The American Civil Liberties Union refers to itself, and not without justification, as the "watchdog of freedom." And so it is—up to a point. Probably no other voluntary American organization has done as much to protect the liberties of unpopular minorities.

But it's one thing to protect a man's constitutional liberties and quite another to determine authoritatively what his liberties are and what they are not. ACLU, sad to say, sometimes overreaches itself and tries to carry out the latter function, for which it has no particular authorization, as well as the former, for which it is admirably suited. . . . It hands down decisions based on "liberal" slogans and clichés which are nowhere to be found in the Constitution or the Bill of Rights—the two documents, and the only two, which ACLU claims to be defending.

Some American Catholics are fervently opposed to much, or most, of the program of genuine economic and political liberalism which I listed earlier. They can properly be called Catholic conservatives or conservative Catholics. They have the same legal, intellectual, and

---

[8] *Catholic Transcript,* Hartford, Conn., June 29, 1950.

moral right to be conservative as non-Catholics have—or as other Catholics have to be liberals. I believe, however, that they are a dwindling minority of American Catholics. I believe that they are as numerous as they are at the present time partly because of the attitude of suspicion and opposition on the part of the monolithic liberals toward many things Catholic which have nothing whatever to do with the essence of economic, political, and international liberalism.

Mr. Blanshard misrepresents Catholic teaching and practice in the field of social policies throughout his book. The chief theme of his book is that the Catholic Church is an enemy of American freedom because the hierarchy through the priests controls the thoughts and actions of American Catholic laymen (p. 34, 44, 1 to 6); directs them how to vote (p. 29); controls the decisions of Catholics in public life (pp. 4–40 ff.), and enforces in detail decisions made in Rome concerning the *social policies* which Catholics *must support or must oppose* (p. 39). These positions are assumed and asserted always without proof. The evidence that they are false is abundant and unanswerable. I have given some of it above. Three more instances of Mr. Blanshard's unreliability should be sufficient.

First, One of Mr. Blanshard's most absurdly unfounded charges is his claim that the Catholic hierarchy is opposed to *expanding social service at the hands of the government.*

Mr. Blanshard writes (p. 265):

> The most questionable feature of Catholic labor policy in the United States is the hierarchy's doctrinaire opposition to the expansion of government social services. The National Council of Catholic Nurses opposed the Murray-Wagner-Dingell public health bill ostensibly on the ground of excessive government control. Catholic hospitals might be compelled to drop their sectarian medical code if they came under federal supervision.

Note the innuendo of the word "ostensibly" and the inaccurate "medical code" for "moral code." Mr. Blanshard must know, if he has followed even casually the extended public discussion of the Murray-Wagner-Dingell bill, that opposition to this bill on the grounds of the danger of "excessive government control" was widespread. The leading Republicans who opposed it on these identical grounds were (at least most of them) non-Catholics. However, if Mr. Blanshard granted Catholic *nurses* an interest in, and some knowledge of, the proper conduct of hospitals, as a basis for opposition to a federal health bill, he could not use their position as an attack on the hierarchy. Further, if he had competent scholarship plus a desire to communicate accurately with his readers, he would have written "moral code," not "medical code." The Catholic Church teaches morals, not medicine.

Mr. Blanshard has been a journalist for many years, and occupied an important public position in the LaGuardia administration in New York City. He must have been a fairly regular reader of newspapers and follower of election returns. But either he did not know or did not wish his readers to know, since he did not mention the fact that the three authors of the health bill, Senator Murray, Senator Wagner, and Congressman Dingell, *were all Catholics.* It follows inevitably that either (1) Mr. Blanshard's position that Catholic public officials must, and do, follow the direction of the Catholic hierarchy or (2) his position that the Catholic hierarchy is opposed to expanding government social service has to be false. In fact both of these positions are false. *Mr. Blanshard nowhere offers any evidence whatever* to show that either one of them is true.

Further, the expanding social policy programs of the Roosevelt and Truman administrations are well known, and Roosevelt and Truman have regularly rolled up big majorities in heavily Catholic sections of the country. He could have discovered this, as well as the official public record of Catholic members of Congress, as shown above.

Second, Mr. Blanshard tries to persuade his readers that there is fundamental, even doctrinal, opposition between the Catholic Church in the United States and the National Conference of Christians and Jews. These are some of his misleading phrases (pp. 300–301): "The Catholic Church has given relatively little active support to this movement. . . . The Conference . . . acts as if devout Roman Catholics could be full fledged, *bona fide* members of the triple alliance. The public impression created by the publicity [of the Conference] is that the Catholic Church believes in the same kind of inter-denominational cooperation that is endorsed by liberal Protestants and Jews . . . the basic anti-Semitism of priestly doctrine . . .

Catholic anti-Semitism is only one feature of a large discriminatory program."

Probably one of the best witnesses to the relation of Catholics to the National Conference of Christians and Jews is the Rev. Everett R. Clinchy, President of the National Conference. Dr. Clinchy is a Presbyterian minister who has been the chief executive officer of the Conference from the beginning, and president since this office was created about a decade ago. In a full-page letter to *America,* a national Catholic weekly, Dr. Clinchy discussed Mr. Blanshard's charges in part as follows: [9]

His clinching argument in support of this allegation of anti-Semitism is that "The Church did not remove the phrase 'perfidious Jews' from its Good Friday prayers until 1938." It was the International Council of Christians and Jews, among others, which urged the authorities in Rome to give consideration to the Good Friday prayers. Hence I feel warranted in saying that our study of the case convinced us that the Catholic Church has never taught that the Latin *pro perfidis Judaeis* means "perfidious Jews." The phrase meant "unbelieving Jews," the word "unbelieving" having reference to belief in the Divinity of Christ. In response to several petitions, and in order to make this unmistakably clear, a declaration of the Holy Office *was* issued in 1948. The Church did not "remove" the phrase. . . .

He implies that non-Catholic Americans cannot get along with their Catholic fellow citizens except under the condition that the Catholics surrender their Catholicism—that they disavow their spiritual allegiance to the Pope; that their moral preceptors abdicate their right to pass judgment on the morality of such things as contraception and euthanasia; that they yield their powers and privileges to maintain hospitals and medical schools consistent with their moral principles; and that they give up the right to provide a religious education for their children even in their own schools.

Dr. Clinchy also wrote an answer to some of Mr. Blanshard's misstatements and insinuations [10] concerning the Church and the Conference in *The Christian Century.*[11] He said in part:

Mr. Blanshard indicates that Catholics are not very cooperative with Protestants and Jews in this Protestant-Catholic-Jewish organization. Some

[9] May 7, 1949.
[10] "The Catholic Price for Cooperation," *The Christian Century,* May 5, 1949.
[11] June 1, 1949.

Catholics are not. The same may be said of some Jews, particularly many of the Orthodox, and of some Protestants, particularly Southern Baptists, Lutherans, et al. There is no way of calibrating the situation, of course; but it is our impression, not wholly without foundation, that the number of cooperative Catholics is greater *in proportion* than the number of cooperative Protestants.

Mr. Blanshard criticizes the National Conference because it does not condemn the Catholic Church for its "policy of non-cooperation on both the religious and civil levels." It does not condemn the Catholic policy of non-cooperation on the civic level because there is no such policy. It does not condemn the policy of non-cooperation on the religious, that is, the theological, level, for two reasons:

1) The National Conference does not exact, as a condition for participation in its work, that Jews acknowledge Christ as the Messiah, or that Protestants deny the Trinity; neither does it demand that Catholics admit that Christ did not found a Church or that this Church is not the Catholic Church. Universal cooperation on the theological level is impossible to anyone subscribing to a definite, super-natural religion, whether it be traditional Protestantism, Judaism, or Catholicism.

2) The title, National Conference of Christians and Jews, is shorthand for National Conference of Protestants, Catholics, and Jews. Such a conference obviously *cannot* condemn Protestantism, Catholicism, or Judaism. Mr. Blanshard is not proposing that the National Conference alter its policies but that it go out of business.

Mr. Blanshard argues that it is intolerant of the Catholic Church to believe that Catholicism is truer than Protestantism and Judaism, and to take steps to protect the faith of Catholics through marriage legislation, the maintenance of Catholic schools, etc. If this be so, it is equally intolerant of Protestants to believe in Christ and of Jews to reject such belief, and of both to believe in a Supreme Being who is the author of an immutable moral law which Mr. Blanshard—judging from his book, of which this article is a paraphrased excerpt—does not seem to accept.

Mr. Blanshard did not permit his pretense of allowing the members of the hierarchy to "speak for themselves" (p. 6) to interfere with his campaign on this topic. He could have filled ten times the space he devoted to attacking the Catholic bishops and the National Conference, to quoting bishops to exactly the opposite effect from the one he tries to create. So of course he quoted no bishops.

In June, 1944, the seven bishops of Texas and Oklahoma published a statement from which I quote:

Our collaboration with men of good will must be organized and fortunately there are among us numerous societies and groups deserving of our support. Many intelligent citizens are studying and laboring to establish enduring peace; others are planning helpful social legislation greatly needed in our time. Problems of health and recreation are being analyzed, and the needs of industrial and agricultural workers are being studied. Discussion clubs and open forums are available everywhere. The National Conference of Christians and Jews—a civic organization—seeks to overcome bigotry, to draw citizens together in the bonds of fraternal charity, to protect the rights of all men sincerely, to believe and practice what God has taught without punishment or persecution and to create a spirit of good will and fair play in the sense that a man's dignity and personality must be respected even if his religion cannot be accepted. Every thoughtful man, every good citizen should support such objectives.

On October 30, 1946, Archbishop Murray, of St. Paul, issued a statement containing the following:

> To counteract divisions, schism, prejudices and conflict while seeking to develop good will in the common cause of happiness in the entire family of the human race all our people should not hesitate to unite with groups such as the Conference of Christians and Jews in their individual capacity as citizens for the good of all.

Bishop Carroll, of Wichita, wrote a similar appeal to the clergy and laity of his diocese on February 16, 1948.

Third, Mr. Blanshard's one comment (p. 78) on the Commission on American Citizenship is sneering and inaccurate:

> The work of cleaning out all undesirable books and substituting Catholic syllabi and textbooks in parochial schools has been undertaken by a priestly group from the Catholic University of America that uses the euphonious title, "The Committee on American Citizenship."

The book *Better Men for Better Times,*[12] which Mr. Blanshard does not mention, is a detailed statement of the position of the Commission on American Citizenship, and it is about as authoritative as a publication could be in the matter of American Catholic attitude on social policies. It is a complete refutation of Mr. Blanshard's position on this

---

[12] *Op. cit.*

subject. Here are some specific samples of his misrepresentation (with no proof or documentation of course):

The lay members are carefully guided by the hierarchy into ways of separatism and monopoly. They are segregated from the rest of American cultural and social life as much as possible in order to preserve their faith unsullied [p. 31].

. . . American Catholicism is still *compelled* to follow the pattern of separatism [p. 101].

The following are from *Better Men for Better Times:*

We, as Catholics, should be much more fully conscious than we sometimes seem to be of our obligation to participate wholeheartedly in community action [pp. 12-13].

. . . we should not get ourselves into a position of being active in community life solely in defense of our own interests. We must guard and protect what is the very essence of our religious freedom, but we also have the obligation of working with men and women of good will toward the making of a better world [p. 13].

The Catholic citizen has a very special obligation to enter actively into community activities. . . . We have something to give, and we are derelict to our duty in the degree that we separate ourselves from other people and hoard up the grace that is in us [p. 15].

Membership in the Church does not require that the Catholic isolate himself from those of his neighbors whose persuasions in matters religious differ from his. It does not confine him within the walls of a ghetto. On the contrary, it imposes upon him the obligation of taking an active part as a good citizen in activities that promote the general welfare of the community, the nation, and the world at large. Outside the Church there are multitudes of men and women who are people of good will whose lives give evidence of the noble ideals they cherish and who are intensely devoted to everything that promises a fuller measure of human happiness [p. 80].

10

CATHOLICS AND "MEDICINE"

IN opening his chapter on "The Church and Medicine," Mr. Blanshard writes of (p. 107) "the actual titles of priestly articles on medicine in Catholic magazines" and "denominational excursions into the field of practical medicine." He mentions no such articles or excursions and gives no references to sources in which they can be found. He does give the titles of eight articles in Catholic magazines none of which indicates articles on medicine. Some are titles of articles on morals and some are titles that could apply to discussions of legal, moral, or medical aspects of certain subjects. To sharpen the unreal distinction he is trying to establish between Catholics and others concerning "medicine," he writes: "Most Americans would be somewhat startled if they picked up a medical journal [*sic*] and read . . . BAPTIST TECHNIQUE FOR STERILIZATION OF THE FEEBLE MINDED." He continues (p. 108):

> Catholic priests tell Catholic physicians when the life of a soul begins in the womb, what the surgeon can and cannot do concerning the ending of the life of the fetus, and what must be done to the new-born child immediately after birth. In the field of sexual conduct the priests not only lay down very definite and detailed instructions concerning courtship, marriage and divorce, but they also proclaim rules concerning contraception, abortion, masturbation, artificial insemination, sterilization, sodomy and the manners of the marriage bed. They believe that celibacy does not disqualify them from giving advice on such matters.

Questions concerning the existence of the soul or "when the life of a soul begins in the womb" are *theological* questions. If Mr. Blanshard does not believe in the existence of the soul or, believing in it, has no interest in the answers to any questions concerning it, he is under no compulsion to seek such answers. However, if any sincere scholar wants to find answers to theological questions, he necessarily looks for the answers in the field of theology. He follows this procedure, whether he wishes to make the answers the subject of a reasoned discussion, the butt of ridicule, or the source of personal enlightenment. No rational person should expect to find answers to theological questions in books on zoology, physiology, or anatomy, or in the sex experience of men or animals.

Nothing in Mr. Blanshard's chapters on medicine, sex, and marriage proves his charge that the Church tells physicians and surgeons what they "can and cannot do." His use of "can and cannot" for "ought and ought not" leaves his statement wholly indefensible to any informed and literate person. The Catholic Church, as all other religions, teaches the moral code it believes in, and instructs its members as to what they *should do* to live up to that code. *All* teachers of morals necessarily do the same.

In his sweeping attack on the Catholic hierarchy in his "Personal Prologue: The Duty to Speak" he indulges in this same misuse of language (p. 4) to include Catholics in professional and public life in general: "The Catholic hierarchy tells Catholic doctors, nurses, judges, teachers and legislators what they can and cannot do in many of the controversial phases of their professional conduct."

This is Mr. Blanshard's *distortion* of the fact that the Catholic Church has a moral code which it teaches, preaches, and exhorts all men to follow. Not only all religions, but a variety of nonreligious organizations, teach moral codes. As in the case of doctors and nurses, the Church does not tell teachers, judges, and legislators what they *can and cannot do,* only what according to its doctrine they *should and should not do in moral problems.* A scholar ought to know the difference between these two statements, and use the one which is true.[1]

[1] For a demonstration that the hierarchy does not dictate to legislators, see pp. 129–134 in Chap. 9.

Any professional man who follows the moral teaching of the Catholic religion, or of any other religion, or of Mr. Blanshard, must, in our country, first *choose of his own free will* to do just that. None of the churches, nor Mr. Blanshard, has any way of compelling obedience or of punishing disobedience. There are two reasons why, in my opinion, one should not list as "punishments for disobedience" the denial of the sacraments of the Catholic Church, or the exclusion from membership in any Protestant church, or the denial of privileges in any Catholic, Jewish, Christian Scientist, Adventist, or other institution administered by a religious organization. *First,* the person who does not wish to meet the requirements for the sacraments, the membership, or the privileges has (in a free society) no real grievance when he is denied them. *Second,* we in America could not, as a result of Mr. Blanshard's "resistance movement" (pp. 303 ff), refuse to religious organizations the opportunity to conduct institutions, according to their own religious and moral principles, for the service *of those who wish the services,* without destroying the personal and religious liberty which all loyal Americans support.

Baptists as well as Catholics teach morals and theology, and neither teaches the *technique* of sterilization, abortion, or artificial insemination. Mr. Blanshard's whole discussion of purely moral and theological questions, under the headings of medical and sexual *practice* or *technique,* is nonsense. It should impress only the thoughtless or the illiterate. His assumption that a person's standing as a teacher of *morality* in matters of sex depends upon the teacher's sexual experience, if accepted as valid, would (I hope) disqualify most ministers, priests, and rabbis from preaching against drunkenness, robbery, murder, drug addiction, and sex crimes and perversions. And after all, why not? If parents want their children to learn the "practice" or "techniques" in these arts and crafts they should seek the teachers of their offspring not among the graduates of religious seminaries but among the inmates of our better prisons and asylums. Then the little ones will have teachers who really know what they are talking about. If Mr. Blanshard sticks to his doctrinal position (pp. 44–55), in which he attacks the Church for its teaching that the moral laws of God and the individual conscience have priority over the enactments of a state legislature, he would have no *moral* grounds on which to oppose any of the above in the event the "people's government" or a popular referendum "repealed" the Ten Commandments.

The question of how best to perform an abortion (for instance) is a medical question. Whether an abortion *ought* to be performed is *always* a moral question, regardless of how it is answered. Obviously, it may *at the same time* be a medical question, and a legal question, and perhaps even a financial question. The Church does not teach the surgeon how to operate, nor the district attorney what the law of his state is, nor the surgeon's secretary how much money the patient has.

Only after it has been decided to perform abortion, sterilization, or to commit euthanasia (or other type of murder)[2] does the medical, surgical, ballistic, chemical, or other question of method or technique arise. The question of whether these acts are sinful or immoral according to the commandments of God is *always* a theological or philosophical question. The Catholic Church teaches, takes a position on, the moral and theological questions only. If Mr. Blanshard had railed against the Catholic Church for having moral and theological doctrines, even many of his most gullible readers would probably have said, "Well, why not? Don't all religions do the same thing? What are they supposed to do?" So Mr. Blanshard attacks not the theological or philosophical basis of the moral doctrines of the Church but denounces the "straw man" of "denominational excursions into the field of practical medicine."

Father George H. Dunne, S.J., discusses the Church's position on abortion in a passage which I quote with permission:[3]

> It is necessary to say one more word about abortion. Any objective discussion of the Church's position is impossible unless there is clear understanding of precisely what that position is. The fact that Norman Thomas, in reviewing Blanshard's book, obviously misunderstands the Catholic position suggests at least that Blanshard has not stated it clearly. The Church's position

---

[2] What is advocated today under the title of euthanasia is, and always has been, murder in every state in the United States.

[3] *Religion and American Democracy* (New York: America Press, 1949), pp. 30–31.

is not, as Mr. Thomas says it is, "that, if a choice must be made, the life of the unborn child, even the smallest embryo, should be preferred to that of the mother" (cf. Norman Thomas, *Nation,* May 14, 1949, p. 561). On the contrary, the position of Catholic moralists is that, wherever a choice must be made, everything possible should be done to save the mother even though the measures taken indirectly result in the loss of the child. The measures which may be taken, however, do not include the right directly to kill the child in order to save the mother.

The Catholic position is based upon respect for the individual human life, any human life; upon the principle that the direct and voluntary killing of any innocent human being, by the state or an individual, is murder; and upon the principle that the end, however good and desirable in itself, does not justify the means. Once these values are repudiated there is no *moral* limit to the crimes that can be committed against the human person. A rigorously logical path leads from abortion to euthanasia and the gas chambers. A logically satisfying case can be made out for the extermination of all Jews. Without Jews there would be no Jewish problem (though other scapegoats would be found to take their places). The extermination of all Catholics would be a logically satisfying solution to the problem that haunts Paul Blanshard—the Catholic problem. Once we claim the right directly to kill one innocent person in the name of a greater good there is left no *moral* ground upon which to protest the killing of tens of thousands of innocent persons in the name of a greater good—unless morals is a mere matter of numbers.

If the fetus is not a human being, then, of course, the Catholic position is based upon an erroneous premise. It would seem, however, that the burden of proving that the fetus is not a human being rests upon those who deny it and that they should assume this burden before proceeding to disembowel the fetus or to crush its skull.

Mr. Blanshard berates the Church for opposing artificial birth control and for not taking a similar position on the "rhythm method." This method means "continence during the same fertile period of the female cycle" each month (about ten days)[4] and he speaks of "the wholly specious distinction between 'natural' and 'unnatural' birth control" (pp. 143–144). Also, "The theologians call this rhythm

[4] The Contraceptive Safe Period—A Clinical Study," by Stephen Fleck, M.D., Elizabeth F. Snedeker, B.A., and John Rock, M.D. (of the Institute of Gynecology, Harvard Medical School), *New England Journal of Medicine,* December, 1940, p. 1005. In answer to an inquiry concerning later data, Dr. Rock wrote me on Jan. 27, 1951: "A recent survey of our cases almost up to date leads to the same conclusion that we expressed in that paper."

method 'natural' because it involves no medicine or contraceptive device" (p. 142). That the distinction between "natural" and "unnatural" as used in relation to any subject is "wholly specious" will be news to most readers. The theologians, not surprisingly, use the word "natural" as it is defined in standard dictionaries. According to Webster, natural means (in the definition applicable in this situation) "not artificial," and artificial means "made or contrived by art"—as medicine or contraceptive devices.

Concerning the reliability of the rhythm method, Fleck, Snedeker, and Rock write: [5]

> The 16th to the 12th days inclusive before the next expected menstruation constitute for us [6] the period during which ovulation may occur. An admittedly generous allowance of three days before and after this period is added for viability of spermatozoa and susceptibility of ova respectively. . . . We find a corrected failure rate of 2.9 per cent . . . [of] true failures in the sense that the occurrence of their pregnancies could not be reconciled with the concept of rigid periods of sterility and fertility. . . . The corrected rate for the true failures was only four pregnancies per 100 person-exposure years. These rates compare favorably with those compiled for other contraceptive methods [pp. 1007–1008].

Confirmatory testimony is offered by Katz and Reiner: [7]

> "We have yet to find a controlled report on several hundred women with written records . . . which serve to prove the validity of claims" that the rhythm method is not dependable [p. 74]. This factual evidence confirms our belief that the biological law of sterility and fertility as originally propounded by Knaus is correct, essentially practical, and workable [p. 79].

Not only linguistic absurdities, but other varieties of nonsense characterize Mr. Blanshard's discussion of birth control and the rhythm method. He repeats his position that knowledge of sexual morality is dependent on sexual experience (p. 138), since birth

[5] *Ibid.*

[6] The Free Hospital for Women in Brookline, which, at present writing, is the only free clinic in Massachusetts available of patients desiring contraceptive advice.

[7] "Further Studies on the Sterile and Fertile Periods in Women," by Leo J. Katz, M.D., LL.D., and Emil Reiner, *American Journal of Obstetrics and Gynecology,* Vol. XLIII (1942), p. 79.

control is in "a field of practical medicine unfamiliar to celibate priests." He uses the results of opinion polls, showing that various majorities of Catholic women believed in "the right to disseminate birth control information" as "the only real index of Catholic sentiment on birth control." Undoubtedly millions of Catholics believe in the right (of those who desire to exercise it) to disseminate information about birth control, and some of them live in Massachusetts and Connecticut, the only two states that place any restrictions on this activity. Believing in no restriction on information, as such, is, or should be, easily distinguishable from believing in the *practice* of artificial birth control or anything else. A knowledge of how various techniques in forgery, mayhem, or murder are carried out might well be sought or given by people not addicted to any of these crimes.

It is inaccurate to refer to the contest in Massachusetts over the amendment of the law concerning the spread of information on artificial birth control as one between Catholics and non-Catholics. Many non-Catholics have been active against the change, as a reference to the press of the state will make clear to any investigator. Dr. Walter A. Maier, a Lutheran, Professor of Old Testament Interpretation and History in Concordia Theological Seminary, St. Louis, a native and former resident of Massachusetts, in 1948 directed a long and detailed argument against the change to the voters of Massachusetts in a radio address on the International Lutheran Hour. I quote:[8]

> . . . a serious error to which Birth Control advocates repeatedly and unfairly resort, when they claim that the Catholic Church stands alone in opposing the spread of Birth Control information and practice. . . . My book, "For Better, Not for Worse," a Christian manual on matrimony, has the official sanction of my Church, when it denounces Birth Control. Moreover, other Protestant Churches take the same position.

Dr. Maier in his argument mentions birth control as "a definite departure from scripture," "unnecessary" for various reasons, the "crafty commercialism" and "the powerful money making propaganda supporting this proposal," "definite evidence of fraud and misrepre-

---

[8] *The Pilot,* Boston, Mass. Nov. 6, 1948.

sentation connected with this widespread sale," "the immorality produced by the ever-increasing Birth Control information and practice," "which have contributed to the sexual delinquencies of our day," "one of the most potent impulses pushing the sag of American morals to increasingly lower depths," and "a concession to impurity." He quotes Dr. Barton C. Hearst, Professor of Obstetrics in the Graduate School of Medicine of the University of Pennsylvania, as "decidedly opposed."

The Massachusetts statute involved is not a "Catholic law." It was passed in 1879, as an addition to a law first passed in 1845. Certainly in 1879 the Catholics of Massachusetts were in no position to dictate or pressure the legislature into passing a law that was not widely approved by Protestants. (Even today they are a minority, estimated at 35 to 40 per cent.) The so-called birth control laws of Massachusetts and Connecticut are (if they are to have any religious label) Protestant laws which so far Protestant and Catholic citizens in the exercise of their constitutional freedom and responsibility have united (wisely or unwisely in anyone's free opinion) to keep on the books. But to Mr. Blanshard the exercise of American freedom by Catholics is a threat to American freedom.

Mr. Blanshard reports, with no evidence or documentation of any kind in support, or even a suggestion of how *he* found out what he offers as fact, "The growing defiance by Catholic women, as well as men, has driven the priesthood into a corner" (p. 141); ". . . the priests have turned to a Catholic birth control formula of their own [*sic*]" (p. 142); "The priests accept this method as permissible only because they are fighting against such persistent and critical pressure for birth control among their own young married people that they must offer some compromise with reality" (p. 143); "The Church officially opposes the right [moral right or legal right not specified] of any American . . . to use contraceptives or to receive information concerning them" (p. 147). "Catholic sociologists [none named or referred to in documentation] refuse to concede that there is any such thing as over population" (p. 148); "American Catholic scholars . . . are under Papal orders to stress quantity rather than quality in population" (p. 149).

He not only writes nonsense, he quotes nonsense: From Professor Earnest A. Hooton of Harvard (p. 149), "The hypocrisy of certain organized religions and governments in endorsing deliberate killing in warfare, for what-ever reasons, and at the same time opposing the restrictions of that fatal overproduction of low-grade human life which leads to warfare, should not be tolerated by the leaders of human biological science." Professor Hooton omits to mention whether it was the "low-grade human life" in the United States, or in England, among the southern Secessionists, or Germany, which led to the Revolutionary War, the War of 1812, the Civil War, or the two World Wars, or which in Russia threatens World War III. None of these, incidentally, happen to be countries dominated by Catholic doctrines about birth control or anything else. He also omits to say how or why "the leaders of human biological science" *could or should* be in a position to say what should be tolerated in the family life of a free society.

This is the same Professor Hooton who was quoted in the New York *World-Telegram and Sun*[9] as saying that:

> If human life is "ever to be held sacred, it should be only when that life is of value to its possessor and to society."
>
> He admitted the Manchester doctor may have violated a law in a technical sense.
>
> "But in a moral and social sense," he continued, "he has risen above the law and has achieved a grandeur of self-sacrifice for the public good that will evoke the profound admiration of all enlightened men."

Bishop G. Bromley Oxnam is quoted (p. 150) in a long passage in which he mentions such nonsense as Roman Catholic "ignorance," "a vicious conception," "recommending continence for approximately twenty of the twenty-five years," "inevitable frustration," "sinful . . . destruction of the home," or else "women called upon to bear twenty children."

A question which seems not to have occurred to Mr. Blanshard and his supporters, Professor Hooton and Bishop Oxnam, but which should be constantly in the thinking of anyone dealing with social policies or

---

[9] Jan. 6, 1950.

personal and religious freedom in America, is: Should not Catholics as well as Protestants, Jews, Christian Scientists, secularists, and atheists have full freedom to believe and teach what they believe to be religious and moral truth, and even to seek in the democratic process to influence legislation on measures they hold to be good for our society? Or may only others than Catholic citizens properly debate such public questions as laws concerning: prohibition, religion in education, euthanasia, sterilization, betting on horse racing, federal aid to education, public health measures, birth control, and international relations? Is Freedom Everybody's Business—or only the business of everybody except Catholics?

Mr. Blanshard's discussion of miracles (pp. 211–220) contains a generous sprinkling of remarks about "superstition," "traditional magic," "primitive deception," the "exploitation" of the poor and ignorant, "a full-blown system of fetishism and sorcery," "the relics industry," and "necromancy or astrology." An intelligent discussion of any theological question on this level is obviously impossible. It would probably take a hundred or more pages to educate anyone who could be impressed by Mr. Blanshard's treatment. I shall use two quotations only.

Father George H. Dunne wrote: [10]

> It is not my purpose to defend here the Church's doctrine with regard to miracles and relics. The *rationale* of her position is exhaustively explained in countless volumes dealing with theology and apologetics. Or, if Blanshard regards any Catholic authority as suspect, I recommend for his reading C. S. Lewis' study, *Miracles* (The Macmillan Company, New York, 1947). The Catholic position is a reasonable position if one believes in God, the Divinity of Christ, the supernatural order. Catholics do. Blanshard evidently does not. That is the difference. If Blanshard were willing to state the difference in these terms, he might establish more plausibly his claim to be an honest critic. Nowhere does he even discuss the premises of the Catholic position—and this is characteristic of his whole book. Instead he *assumes* that those premises are ridiculous. And, of course, if the premises are ridiculous, the conclusions derived from them are ridiculous.

One of the high points of Mr. Blanshard's attack in this section is

---

[10] *Op. cit.*, pp. 37–38.

his report of his purchase for $2 of a reproduction of "the True Face of Christ from the Holy Shroud of Turin." I quote from a personal letter to me dated March 31, 1951, from the Most Rev. John J. Wright, Bishop of Worcester, formerly Auxiliary Bishop of Boston: "On page 218 Blanshard describes a 'racket' which had its headquarters at 287 Commonwealth Ave., Boston. What Blanshard does not tell is that this particular fraud was perpetrated by non-Catholics, was investigated by the Catholic Chancery and denounced by them to the police, who promptly terminated the racket. . . . It was not a Catholic affair and was exposed by the Catholic diocesan authorities."

11

PAPAL INFALLIBILITY

THE doctrine of the infallibility of the Catholic Church was not discovered or invented in 1870. It has been held and taught from the earliest days of Christianity. An interesting and simple American explanation of it in 1825 can be found in the work of Bishop John England.[1] It was first specifically *defined* by the bishops of the Church in a world council in 1870, as residing in the Pope, the successor of Peter.

The doctrine of papal infallibility is that *the Pope when he speaks ex-cathedra,* that is (1) *as pastor and teacher,* (2) *in defining a doctrine* (3) *regarding faith and morals,* (4) *to be held by the whole Church, is guaranteed against error by the teachings of Christ.*

Note that this infallibility refers only to teaching concerning faith and morals, and then only when the Pope speaks officially as teacher addressing the whole Church . . . that *neither impeccability nor inspiration is claimed;* that infallibility is personal to the Pope and independent of the consent of the Church. This doctrine the Vatican Fathers declared to be a "tradition handed down from the beginning of the Christian Faith," that it was implicit in the teaching of the Church up to that time. Infallibility does not by any means do away with the necessity of study and learning, but simply under certain conditions guarantees that the conclusions drawn from study and learning are free from error; the Pope's knowledge is not infused into him by God; he gains it much as does any other man, but he is assisted, watched over, by the Holy Spirit so that he does not use his authority and

[1] I. A. Reynolds, *The Works of the Rt. Rev. John England, op. cit.,* Vol. I, pp. 57–58.

his knowledge to mislead the Church at the times and under the conditions stated above.[2]

In discussing this doctrine scholars usually stress particularly St. Matthew 16:15–19 (Douay version): "Jesus saith to them: But whom do you say that I am? Simon Peter answered and said: Thou art Christ, the Son of the living God. And Jesus answering, said to him: Blessed art thou, Simon Bar-Jona: because flesh and blood hath not revealed it to thee, but my Father who is in heaven. And I say to thee: That thou art Peter; and upon this rock I will build my church, and the gates of hell shall not prevail against it." Also important are: St. Luke 22:32; St. John 21:15–17.

"Infallibility does not involve inspiration or a fresh revelation; the Church can teach no new dogma but only 'religiously guard and faithfully expound' the original deposit of faith with all its truths explicit and implicit."[3] Infallibility does not mean *impeccability,* omnipotence, or omniscience, or *ad hoc* inspiration.

Many people erroneously assume that anything the Pope does or says is believed by Catholics to be infallibly "true," to be accepted without question and applied as a rule of life *universally*. This theory is so wholly contrary to the teaching and practice of the Church, so wholly lacking in any credible basis, that little need be said in answer to it. However, see below (p. 163) in this book.

There seems to be on the whole more warrant for non-Catholics believing that the doctrine of Papal Infallibility applies to all papal encyclicals. But this also is incorrect. An encyclical is simply a circular letter addressed to a number of people. The word "encyclical" is usually applied to any document in which the Pope addresses the bishops of the world, or the members of the universal Church, or other large and widely scattered groups. Sometimes an encyclical is addressed to a special, small group, as the "Bishops and Faithful of France." Of course, an *ex-cathedra* definition of a matter of faith or morals addressed to the whole Church would usually be included in an encyclical. However, the fact that a statement is found in a papal

---

[2] Attwater, Donald (ed.), *A Catholic Dictionary* (New York: The Macmillan Co., 1943), p. 268.

[3] *Ibid.,* p. 267.

encyclical does not make the statement an *ex-cathedra* pronouncement to which the doctrine of papal infallibility applies. When an encyclical is concerned not with universal doctrine, but with some policy, event, or theory, related to an individual group, section, or country, it should be so treated, particularly by scholars (whether they approve of the contents of the encyclical or not).[4]

This theological doctrine of Papal Infallibility may be, and has been, discussed by theologians and other scholars for centuries. As a rational or intelligent discussion, it is necessarily a discussion in the field of theology.

I am not here arguing that non-Catholic scholars are expected to *believe* in the doctrine of infallibility. My position is only that the doctrine should be *understood,* and discussed accurately, honestly, without distortion or ridicule if the discussion is to be rated as "scholarly" by those who have any sound standards of scholarship. After all, the doctrine has been believed for centuries, and is believed today, by many competent scholars. All orthodox Christians would doubtless believe that Christ *could* do what this doctrine says He did do, and all Orthodox Jews would doubtless believe the same with "God" substituted for "Christ." Such theists would necessarily debate not the possibility but only the actuality of the divine granting of such power to any agent of God.

Anyone offering his contribution to the public in such a debate is, therefore, necessarily presenting himself as a debater in the field of theology. If he wishes to argue the position that this whole doctrine is fallacious *because there is no God,* he should first establish that premise as a valid theological conclusion. If he, in effect, asks his readers to accept this on his say-so, on the basis of *his own infallible revelation,* he is offering himself not as a debater but as one who is above evidence and argument. In these circumstances a cautious reader might properly ask how *he* got that way. The atheists and the unlearned could probably better achieve whatever ends they seek by trying to debate only matters more relevant to their interests and commensurate to their abilities.

The doctrine of infallibility does not seem to be simple nonsense to

[4] See *Catholic Encyclopedia,* Vol. 5, pp. 413–414.

all non-Catholic scholars, as probably most people know who have discussed it with such of them as are interested in Christian theology. I was once told by a distinguished Episcopalian minister that his only doctrinal disagreement with the Catholic Church was the doctrine of Papal Infallibility. He would accept the infallibility of the bishops of the Church. One might think that this difficulty would be answered by the action of the Vatican Council, since the bishops of the Church after months of debate decided by a great majority that the authority resided in the Pope.

Interesting in this connection is a statement by William Hurrell Mallock (1849–1923). He was the son of an Anglican clergyman. He won distinction as a young man at Oxford, particularly as a writer. Throughout his mature life he was active in writing and talking on the topics of the day. He was deeply interested in religion, a Protestant who was not satisfied with certain aspects of English Protestantism as he interpreted it in the latter half of the nineteenth century. The chapter from which I have taken this quotation is not defending the infallibility of the Pope, per se, but arguing that any "revealed" religion (as his own Protestantism) should claim infallibility *for itself*. This was written in 1879, when Mallock was thirty years old. It may have foreshadowed his conversion to Catholicism, but he was in no hurry to take the step. At the age of seventy-four, "on his death bed," [5] he became a Catholic.

> Any supernatural religion that renounces its claim to this [infallibility], it is clear can profess to be a semi-revelation only. It is a hybrid thing, partly natural and partly supernatural, and it thus practically has all the qualities of a religion that is wholly natural. In so far as it professes to be revealed, it of course professes to be infallible; but if the revealed part be in the first place hard to distinguish, and in the second place hard to understand—if it may mean many things, and many of those things contradictory—it might just as well have been never made at all. To make it in any sense an infallible revelation, or in other words a revelation at all, *to us,* we need a power to interpret the testament that shall have equal authority with that testament itself.[6]

[5] *Dictionary of National Biography,* 1922–1930 (London: Oxford University Press), pp. 556–557.

[6] Mallock, William Hurrell, *Is Life Worth Living?* (New York: G. P. Putnam's Sons, 1879), p. 267.

Cardinal Newman, who had been opposed to the *definition* of infallibility in 1870 (not to the ancient doctrine), discussed Papal Infallibility thoroughly and in plain English in his famous argument with Gladstone, which was published in 1874 under the title *A Letter to the Duke of Norfolk.*[7]

. . . a Pope is not infallible in his laws, nor in his commands, nor in his acts of state, nor in his administration, nor in his public policy . . . was Gregory XIII, when he had a medal struck in honour of the Bartholomew massacre? or Paul IV in his conduct towards Elizabeth? or Sextus V when he blessed the Armada? or Urban VIII when he persecuted Galileo? No Catholic ever pretends that these Popes were infallible in these acts [pp. 256–257].

Suppose, for instance, an Act was passed in Parliament, bidding Catholics to attend Protestant service every week, and the Pope distinctly told us not to do so, for it was to violate our duty to our faith:—I should obey the Pope and not the Law. It will be said . . . that such a case is impossible. I know it is; but why ask me for what I should do in extreme and utterly improbable cases such as this, if my answer cannot help bearing the character of an axiom? It is not my fault that I must deal in truisms . . . [p. 240].

But now, on the other hand, could the case ever occur, in which I should act with the Civil Power, and not with the Pope? Now, here again, when I begin to imagine instances, Catholics will cry out . . . that the instances never can occur. I know they cannot; I know the Pope can never do what I am going to suppose; but then, since it cannot possibly happen in fact, there is no harm in just saying what I should (hypothetically) do, if it did happen. I say then in certain (impossible) cases I should side, not with the Pope, but with the Civil Power . . . [p. 241].

Were I actually a soldier or sailor in her Majesty's service, and sent to take part in a war which I could not in my conscience see to be unjust, and should the Pope suddenly bid all Catholic soldiers and sailors to retire from the service, here again, taking the advice of others, as best I could, I should not obey him . . . [pp. 241–242].

Cardinal Turrecremata says, "Although it clearly follows from the circumstance that the Pope can err at times, and command things which must not be done, that we are not to be simply obedient to him in all things, that does not show that he must not be obeyed by all when his commands are good. To know in what cases he is to be obeyed and in what not . . . it is said in the Acts of the Apostles, 'one ought to obey God rather than man:' therefore, were the Pope to command anything against Holy Scripture, or the articles of faith, or the truth of the Sacraments, or the commands of the

[7] Pp. 240–257.

natural or divine law, *he ought not to be obeyed,* but in such commands is to be passed over (despiciendus).—*Summ. de Eccl.,* pp. 47, 48.

Bellarmine, speaking of resisting the Pope, says, "In order to resist and defend oneself no authority is required. . . . Therefore, as it is lawful to resist the Pope, if he assaulted a man's person, so it is lawful to resist him, if he assaulted souls, or troubled the state (turbanti rempublicam), and much more if he strove to destroy the Church. It is lawful, I say, to resist him, by not doing what he commands, and hindering the execution of his will."—*De Rom. Pont.,* ii. 29 [p. 242].

When, then, Mr. Gladstone asks Catholics how they can obey the Queen and yet obey the Pope, since it may happen that the commands of the two authorities may clash, I answer, that it is my *rule,* both to obey the one and to obey the other, but that there is no rule in this world without exceptions, and if either the Pope or the Queen demanded of me an "Absolute Obedience," he or she would be transgressing the laws of human society. I give an absolute obedience to neither [p. 243].

I cannot call to mind a passage in any other book comparable to Mr. Blanshard's which exhibits such weak "scholarship" as his pages 22–26. In these he discusses the Vatican Council of 1869–1870, and its definition of Papal infallibility.

When I say comparable to Mr. Blanshard's book, I have in mind, *first,* that Mr. Blanshard's book pretends to be accurate, scholarly, and unbiased; *second,* that it has some of the external *appearances* of scholarship—quotations, references, footnotes; *third,* that it is written by a literate man, of considerable education, a minister and a lawyer, and, *fourth,* that it has been praised as a book of "exemplary scholarship," "scrupulous documentation," "unbiased," "fair," and containing "proof" of the positions he takes. All this by men occupying positions of distinction and influence in American cultural life.

In these pages, Mr. Blanshard discusses an historical World Council, one that was attended by 774 bishops of an eligible 1,050. The Council lasted from December, 1869, to July, 1870. Various scholars have written discussions of this Council running from two to seven volumes each.[8] Mr. Blanshard mentions none of them. He makes no attempt

[8] Granderath-Kirch, *Histoire du Concile du Vatican,* 7 Vols. (Brussels, 1907); E. Cecconi, *Histoire du Concile du Vatican,* 4 Vols. (Paris, 1887); C. Butler, *The Vatican Council,* 2 Vols., (London, 1930); *Acta et Decreta Concilii Vaticani,* 4 Vols. (Friburg: Herder, 1892); E. Ollivier, *L'Eglise et l'Etat au*

whatever to discuss the theological problem or the Scriptural basis for it, but rather presents an attack on Pius IX and the Vatican Council which specifically *defined* (not invented or discovered) this doctrine.

Nowhere does Mr. Blanshard make the slightest attempt to give his readers a careful, accurate, authoritative explanation of what a Catholic theologian, or any other scholar, means when he uses the phrase "papal infallibility." He does quote the bare definition—and then apparently forgets about it. He does not explain the field covered by the doctrine, the limitations of the doctrine, the sort of utterances to which it applies, and those to which it does not apply. In his attack he has no *specific documentation of any kind that even refers to a single charge he brings against the Pope and the Vatican Council of 1870.* These five pages have a total of five footnotes attached to them.

Number 30 (p. 23) is a reference to the *New York Times,* from which he quotes a statement of Professor James Luther Adams, of the University of Chicago, on which some comment will be made later. This is not a quotation that *proves anything at all about anyone other than Professor Adams.*

Number 32 (p. 24) documents a widely known quotation from Lord Acton, inaccurately introduced by Mr. Blanshard, as I shall show shortly. This quotation from Lord Acton does *not prove anything at all concerning which there is the slightest controversy,* there being none about Lord Acton's opposition to the definition.

Number 33 (p. 25) is a reference to the papal document giving the definition of papal infallibility. No controversy here.

Number 34 (p. 26) is an accurate reference to a quotation from O'Brien's *The Faith of Millions,* which, of course, proves none of Mr. Blanshard's charges.

Note number 31 (p. 23) is the only documentation of any possible value in these five pages of misrepresentation and innuendo. This is a

Concile du Vatican, 2 Vols. (Paris, 1879). These are all referred to by the Rev. Edward F. Sheridan, S. J., Dean of Studies of the Theologate of the upper province of the Society of Jesus, Toronto, Canada, in "A Note on Mr. Blanshard," *Thought, Fordham University Quarterly,* December, 1950, pp. 692–697. I was privileged to read this manuscript some months before it was published, and was given permission to quote from it at will by both the author and the publisher. I gratefully acknowledge this kind and extremely helpful action on the part of both Father Sheridan and the editors of *Thought.*

general footnote introduced by the statement "among the many accounts of the struggle over infallibility may be mentioned . . ." Then he mentions nine. Any reader whose faith in Blanshard or whose contempt for all things Catholic is less than complete might like some support for these pages of accusation, explicit or implied. If he does, Mr. Blanshard says to him in effect, "Here are nine sources. If you care to look them up you may find something that may offer some proof of some of my charges."

Four of the above-mentioned references can be counted as the writings of Catholics: Döllinger, Acton, Scott, and Corrigan. Of the four, Döllinger's *The Pope and the Council* is probably the most important, even though this pamphlet was written *nearly* a year before the Council met,[9] a fact which Mr. Blanshard's "scholarship" omitted to mention. Further, Mr. Blanshard does not list Döllinger's *The Pope and the Council* in his bibliography and leaves out both publisher and *date* in his "documentation." It is still an important document on account of Döllinger's participation in the long pre-council discussion of the doctrine of infallibility and the desirability of specific definition in 1870. Further, Döllinger was, and is recognized as, a serious scholar. He attended the Council, was one of the most active leaders of the minority against the definition of the doctrine. He was excommunicated in 1871.

This general documentation *omits any reference* to the distinguished scholars who have written volumes on the specific subject of the Council, but is based almost entirely on non-Catholic, not to say anti-Catholic, sources. None of Blanshard's authors were present at the meetings of the Council (with the exception of Döllinger) and none of them was close to the Council in time or interest (in addition to Döllinger) except Acton.

The nature of Mr. Blanshard's nine general sources can be shown by a brief note on each one of them.

1. *Schaff.*[10] *This is a 680-page reply to Cardinal Gibbons' The Faith of Our Fathers.* The author gives considerable space to the need for the Reformation, Luther, the Protestant Movement, apology for

---

[9] Sheridan, *op. cit.*, p. 692.

[10] Schaff, David S., *Our Fathers' Faith and Ours* (New York: G. P. Putnam's Sons, 1928).

Luther's personal defects, and makes no mention of the movement commonly referred to by scholars as the Catholic Counter-Reformation. *He devotes a total of two pages to the Vatican Council.*

2. Bury.[11] The temper of this 175-page monograph on the Syllabus and the Vatican Council is indicated by the author's remark, quoted by the editor in the introduction, to the effect that he considered the Papacy "the other side of the history of the Freedom of Thought," and by such unscholarly statements in the text that he (the Pope) arrogated the right of making a new dogma (p. 49), and "the vague language of the Bull was a cloak" (p. 56).

3. *Cadoux.*[12]

This book of 690 pages of text devotes only a few lines to the Vatican Council of 1870. At "pp. 580 ff." (Mr. Blanshard's reference) there are a few harsh sentences scattered over a number of pages—in a 20-page chapter on "Catholicism and Truthfulness." There is no approach to a scholarly discussion of the Council, or any attempt to give the reader information, rather than epithets, about a seven months' long world council of nearly 800 Catholic bishops. The tone and scholarly level of Cadoux is indicated by his reference (p. 508) to the infallibility decree of 1870 as "the most spactacular instance of the historical untruthfulness of Catholic dogma." On p. 507 he mentions the "spectacle of a number of learned Christian men solemnly accepting and proclaiming, at the bidding of their ruler, a historical proposition which they had hitherto known and declared to be untrue to fact . . ."

4. *Lord Acton's*[13] essay on *The Vatican Council* (56 pages), with the introduction by Gertrude Himmelfarb, furnishes a good part of the substance and even the phrasing of Mr. Blanshard's account.

5. *Döllinger*[14] and Lord Acton are the only primary sources listed

---

[11] Bury, J. B., *History of the Papacy in the Nineteenth Century* (London: Macmillan and Co., 1930).

[12] Cadoux, C. J. *Catholicism and Christianity* (London: George Allen and Unwin, 1928).

[13] Acton, Lord, *Essays on Freedom and Power* (Boston: Beacon Press, 1948).

[14] *The Pope and the Council.* Published anonymously in the Augsburg *Allgemeine Zeitung,* March, 1869, revised and reissued as a pamphlet, *Der Papst und das Konzil von Janus,* Leipzig, August 19, 1869. See Granderath-Kirch, Vol. I, Chapter 3, pp. 204, 219.

by Blanshard. Acton was a pupil of Döllinger, and Döllinger was thoroughly against the definition before the Council met, and was a leader of the minority in the Council.

6. *Garrison,*[15] whose scholarship is not always objective when he touches Catholic matters (see pp. 226–227), gives *seven pages* of his 267 to the Vatican Council. In this book the reader can find, in a somewhat more temperate tone, at least a mention or insinuation of about all of Mr. Blanshard's charges.

7. *Encyclopedia Britannica:* The unbiased scholarship which should characterize articles in an encyclopedia is conspicuously absent. This is clearly indicated by such phrases as the following taken from the article in the fourteenth edition (Mr. Blanshard does not refer to any particular edition): "closest secrecy . . . Pius IX made no mention of his design. . . . The object of the Council was long a mystery . . . repudiation was energetic and unmistakable . . . by no means inclined to yield a perfunctory assent to the papal propositions . . . complacent majority . . . to end these unwelcome discussions. . . ." Such phrases do not fit the facts as reported below by scholars who made careful studies and detailed reports.

8. *Corrigan.*[16] Mr. Blanshard refers to this one as "a Catholic account of the Vatican Council," which is true. This book, which Mr. Blanshard also omits from his bibliography, has a 21-page chapter on the Council, and in addition eleven more page references to it in the index. There is nothing in it which offers any substantiation for Mr. Blanshard's specific charges and insinuations. Further, he does not use the factual data from it or from the *Catholic Encyclopedia,* which offers material taken from authentic sources and which refutes his pronouncements.

9. *Scott.*[17] This little 24-page pamphlet is a simple explanation of the doctrine, packed with quotations from the Bible which give the

---

[15] Garrison, W. E., *Catholicism and the American Mind* (Chicago: Willett, Clark and Co., 1928).

[16] Corrigan, Raymond, S.J., *The Church and the Nineteenth Century* (Milwaukee: Bruce Publishing Co., 1938).

[17] Scott, Martin J., S.J., *No Pope Can Be Wrong in Teaching Doctrine* (New York: America Press, 1941).

Scriptural basis for the doctrine. This is material which Mr. Blanshard omits to mention.

The worthlessness of Mr. Blanshard's 4-page attack on the Vatican Council is demonstrated by the fact that *the specific items of his indictment have no footnotes or proof of any kind attached to them.* The hostile criticism in this section carries no guide to any evidence or opinion which in any way substantiates Mr. Blanshard's charges and insinuations. The attack consists only of scores of *wholly unsupported* assertions. If Mr. Blanshard knows that any of them are true on any more specific and substantial basis than his private clairvoyance, he keeps this information strictly to himself. For instance, he says (p. 23) "that the American bishops opposed the doctrine of infallibility as either unfounded or untimely." When one uses the term "the American bishops" without qualification one should mean, and should be held to mean, *all* the American bishops. The truth is that some of the American bishops opposed the definition and that some favored the definition.

Maynard [18] writes concerning Cardinal Gibbons' attitude:

> Though, like most of the English-speaking bishops, he believed the definition inopportune, he voted *placet* [affirmative]. He was deeply impressed by the "fearless and serene conduct of the great majority, who, spurning a temporizing policy and the dictates of human prudence, were deterred neither by specious arguments nor imperial threats nor by the fear of schism from promulgating what they conceived to be a truth contained in the deposit of divine revelation." [19]

It would be interesting to have documentation for the particular statement that some American bishops "threatened to walk out of the Council if they were not given more time to consider it." Mr. Blanshard offers none.

Mr. Blanshard's undocumented accusation of the Pope for surprise and lack of time for discussion is proved to be unfounded by various facts. The question of the advisability of defining the doctrine of the

[18] Maynard, Theodore, *The Story of American Catholicism* (New York: The Macmillan Co., 1948), p. 545.

[19] Will, Allen Sinclair, *Life of Cardinal Gibbons,* 2 Vols. (New York: E. P. Dutton Co., 1922), Vol. I, p. 124.

infallibility of the Church had been hotly debated among theologians, and other scholars, Catholic and non-Catholic, for some time before the meeting of this Council. It is highly improbable that there was a single member of the Council who had not been considering the doctrine, and the desirability of specific definition at that time, not only for months, but for years.

Infallibility became a burning issue in the years intervening between the announcement of the Council in 1867 and its convention in 1869. It was the heyday of anti-Catholic liberalism, and discussion of the prerogatives of the Pope (primacy, temporal sovereignty, infallibility) by non-Catholics and by Catholics (gallican and ultramontane) was universal. Among Catholics discussion concerned only the scope and conditions of infallibility for there was moral unanimity on the fact. With the announcement of a council, controversy on infallibility and on the advisability of its definition became heated, especially in France and Germany where the greatest ecclesiastical names became involved.[20]

Mr. Blanshard implies that the Council was convened solely for the purpose of defining infallibility (pp. 22f.), a view which is thoroughly unhistorical. Infallibility did become the most violently agitated question in the Council, but the latter accomplished a great deal of other important work and projected more which was interrupted by the outbreak of war. The Constitution on Faith was no less important than the Constitution on the Church of which only a part dealt with infallibility. The Council convened in December, 1869, and the matter of infallibility was not opened in the Council until May of the following year. Since the Council closed in mid-July, only about one-third of its time was spent on infallibility.[21]

Consider the clear historical record, open to any scholar. On December 6, 1864, Pius IX directed the Cardinals of the Curiae to consider the advisability of an ecumenical council. Twenty reports were received in answer. Eighteen were for the holding of a council and two of the eighteen mentioned infallibility as one of the appropriate subjects for the council to consider.

In April, 1865, a similar inquiry was sent to thirty-six European

---

[20] Sheridan, *op. cit.*, p. 693. He cites, for accounts of these preconciliar disturbances, Granderath-Kirch, Vol. I, livre 2; cf. also Cecconi, *Histoire du Concile du Vatican,* Vol. II, livre III, cc. 4–6.

[21] Sheridan, *op. cit.*, p. 692.

bishops, and early in 1866 a similar inquiry was sent to the prelates of the Oriental Rite. These groups replied with practical unanimity advising that a council be held, and some of them again mentioned the subject of infallibility as a proper subject for discussion and definition.

In June, 1867, the Pope announced his intention to convoke such a council at the meeting of bishops in Rome to celebrate the anniversary of St. Peter's martyrdom. Five hundred bishops attended this meeting.[22] The Council met in December, 1869.

> . . . on January 28, 1870, more than four hundred bishops (better than four-sevenths of the Council) petitioned the Holy Father for permission to proceed to a definition of infallibility, less than two months after their arrival in Rome and almost four months before the debates on infallibility had even begun.[8] Lord Acton, no friend of infallibility, regarded the definition as inevitable from the beginning in the ordinary course of events.[9] The famous "Letters from Rome" of Quirinus, very hostile to the definition, express the same opinion.[10] The fact is that a sweeping majority for infallibility and its definition could have been obtained any time the Pope wished to present the matter to the Council through his representatives.
>
> Mr. Blanshard implies that the Pope badgered and hectored the Council into submission, "determined the general scope of discussion . . . controlled in one way or another not only the committee chairmen but the working majority of the bishops." These are facile assertions, and very general, but the stubborn historical fact remains that the debate on infallibility lasted two months and on July 4, 1870, all with a right yet to be heard renounced that right freely and the debate was closed.[11] [23]

When a writer refers to a vote of 451 to 150 as "a majority of only 451 to 150" he must have in mind careless readers, or those unac-

---

[22] *Ibid.*, p. 692.

[8] (In Sheridan)
Acta et Decreta, col. 923b; Granderath-Kirch, *op. cit.*, vol. IV, p. 139.

[9] (In Sheridan)
Action's *Correspondence*, Selections, section "Vatican Council," to Gladstone.

[10] (In Sheridan)
English translation (London: Rivington's, 1870).

[11] (In Sheridan)
Granderath-Kirch, *op. cit.*, vol. V, p. 86.

[23] *Ibid.*, pp. 694–695.

quainted with the working of democracy. A vote of 3 to 1 usually is considered a big majority, if not an almost unprecedented one where there is any real difference of opinion. But even in this item Mr. Blanshard is misleading.

The actual vote was 451 for definition of infallibility, 62 for definition with further precision of expression, and 88 against definition. Mr. Blanshard has no right to lump the conditioned votes with the negatives, since they were in principle affirmative, making the real majority 513 to 88.[24]

Since all these meetings and votes are items of historical record, they refute Mr. Blanshard's position that the doctrine of Papal Infallibility (which he mentions four times on page 23 as being proclaimed or promulgated, instead of *defined*) was sprung on the Council by a scheme of Pius IX, and quickly railroaded through without any observance of fair discussion and democratic procedure.

Mr. Blanshard states flatly (p. 23) that "an elaborate technique for smothering the opposition was worked out by the Vatican before the council began." What was this technique? Some tentative agenda for so important a meeting had to be prepared and several commissions charged with this work were appointed. The commission on dogmatic theology (infallibility falling under that heading) comprised twenty-four theologians under Cardinal Bilio. With the Latins there were five Germans, two Frenchmen, one Englishman, and one American, James Corcoran, vicar-general of Charlestown. These discussed the question of papal infallibility in February, 1869. All were of the opinion that the doctrine could be defined, but were equally unanimous that it should not be proposed for definition by the commission, but only on the request of the conciliar Fathers themselves.[7] The reason for this decision was to avoid as completely as possible any coercion of the Fathers on the part of Rome. However, since such a decree could hardly be left to improvisation on a moment's notice, a draft was prepared which could be brought forward for discussion and revision at the Council's request. Without hesitation Mr. Blanshard disregards this independent action of the commission and states that "Pius IX had arranged to have the question of infallibility brought up in the form of a humble petition to himself." [25]

---

[24] *Ibid.*, p. 697.

[7] (Sheridan)
Cecconi, *op. cit.*, vol. II, livre II, p. 281.

[25] *Ibid.*, p. 694.

Mr. Blanshard remarks that "the bishops who opposed Pius IX were risking their whole careers. They were living and working inside a tightly controlled, absolute monarchy [*sic*], and it took unusual courage to oppose the monarch." He offers, as usual, *nothing* to substantiate this point. The fact is that leaders of the minority did not suffer for their opposition to the definition. For instance:

. . . of the leading French opponents of the definition, Bishop Meignen of Chalons later became archbishop of Tours and cardinal; Bishop Ginoulhiac of Grenoble was elevated to the primatial see of Lyons late in the Council (June, 1870) after his opposition to the definition was well known. (He had signed the antidefinition petition, January 12, 1870.) John Henry Newman was not a member of the Council but had written influentially against the advisability of definition. He later became cardinal.[26]

The undocumented charges of railroading and improper procedure in general should be dismissed as unfounded accusations by anyone acquainted with democratic and parliamentary techniques in large assemblies.

Evidently, some machinery was needed to organize the proposals of seven hundred bishops from all over the world. It was Hefele, one of the leading antidefinitionists, who stressed the need,[12] and it was substantially his method of control which was adopted. The election of a unanimously prodefinition deputation was the work of the Council, not of Pius IX. In fact Friedrich, strongly partisan in favor of the minority, admits that Pius IX wished to see minority members and especially Dupanloup, leader of the antidefinitionists, elected to the more important commissions.[15] The whole complaint may be reduced to blame of a majority because it is a majority and elects whom it wills.[27]

An authoritative opinion on the freedom of the Council may be culled from Emile Ollivier, a non-Catholic, Prime Minister of France during the Council, intimate of the opposition bishops, and a historian of the first rank:

---

[26] *Ibid.*, pp. 693–694.

[12] (Sheridan)
Acta et Decreta, c. 1089 d.

[15] (Sheridan)
Ibid., vol. III, pp. 175 ff. Confer Butler, vol. I, p. 173.

[27] *Ibid.*, p. 695.

"Examined according to human standards the arguments for want of liberty do not bear discussion; and what if they are examined from the Catholic standpoint, that the Pope is vicar of Christ and Supreme Pastor? . . . For all spirits whom partisanship does not blind, it is certain that the discussion was as free as ever it was in any human assembly."[18] [28]

Mr. Blanshard introduced the widely known quotation from Lord Acton by the statement that *"many* leading Catholic theologians *denounced the doctrine"* (italics mine). He mentions *none.* If he meant that *some* Catholic theologians (according to the record of the Council a distinct minority) opposed the *definition* at that time—he would have been accurate. If Mr. Blanshard meant that "many leading Catholic theologians" denounced the *doctrine* of infallibility (and not simply opposed the definition at that time), either before or after the definition by the World Council, he certainly should have given his readers some proof. This he would have had difficulty in finding.

When he says that Lord Acton, "the foremost British Catholic, expressed the hostility of his people," he seems to be giving the untrue impression that English Catholics generally not only opposed the advisability of the *definition* of infallibility in 1870 (the only question seriously in controversy) but were hostile to the very idea of the doctrine.

However, Lord Acton's statement quoted by Blanshard (p. 24), despite Lord Acton's standing as a scholar, makes no sense. He wrote:

> It makes civil legislation on all points of contract, marriage, education, clerical immunities, mortmain, even on many questions of taxation and Common Law, subject to the legislation of the Church, which would be simply the arbitrary will of the Pope. Most assuredly no man accepting such a code could be a loyal subject, or fit for the enjoyment of political privileges.

Lord Acton must have been angry when he wrote this. The idea that the doctrine of Papal Infallibility in an *ex-cathedra* definition of

---

[18] (Sheridan)

E. Ollivier, *L'Eglise et l'Etat au Concile du Vatican* (2 vols.; Paris), vol. II, p. 43; quoted in Butler, *op. cit.,* vol. II, p. 195.

[28] *Ibid.,* p. 696.

some topic in the realm of faith and morals subjects to "the arbitrary will of the Pope" *civil* legislation on *all points* of *contract, marriage, education, mortmain,* and on many questions of *taxation* and *common law,* contains clear absurdities. The idea that no man accepting such a code could be a loyal subject, or fit for the enjoyment of political privileges, has been shown to be irresponsible nonsense by the lives and records of the millions of loyal subjects of the British crown, citizens of the American Republic, and of many other countries.

Mr. Blanshard writes (p. 21):

> If Catholic theologians were compelled to base their claims of Papal infallibility on the *character* of their Popes, they would be gravely embarrassed. . . . To reconcile their villainies with the exalted concept of Papal character held by most Catholics, the Church's theologians have developed the doctrine that an imperfect man may yet be a perfect conduit for divine grace. . . .

Mr. Blanshard, as a lawyer, must be familiar with the concept of *agency.* If so, he knows that in many areas the doctrine that the *character* of the individual making a certain decision, or taking other definitive action, has no effect whatever upon the legality, or the binding force, of the decision, or action. When an authorized agent signs the name of a principal according to proper legal forms, the agent's action is the action of the principal even if the agent is a thoroughgoing crook. When a corrupt judge on the bench renders a decision in the court, the decision is just as binding on the litigants as the decision of a judge of exemplary character. If, after a judge has served many years and delivered many opinions, it is proved that he has been a dishonest and corrupt judge throughout his career, such proof does not invalidate the decisions he made as a judge. The orders of a dishonest or incompetent military commander are still orders. They are effective, and must be obeyed by subordinate officers and soldiers who are living up to their duty of obedience to commanding officers. If Mr. Blanshard has investigated the meaning of "papal infallibility," he knows the ground on which it rests, which is not the character of an individual pope.

It seems unfortunate for Mr. Blanshard, and I should think embarrassing for Professor James Luther Adams and the University of

Chicago, to have Mr. Blanshard (p. 23) quote Professor Adams as having said that no individual except a mentally abnormal one would claim infallibility for himself, but that "the individual Catholic, whether lay or clerical, supports a church and a hierarchy that make precisely this blasphemous claim." Every intelligent person will doubtless agree with the statement about a person claiming infallibility for *himself,* and all well-informed persons know that neither the Pope nor any other Catholic "makes precisely this claim." The doctrine of infallibility applies to the *office*—to the Pope as Pope (in certain circumstances) not to the Pope as a person.

Mr. Blanshard (p. 25) falls back again on anonymous Catholics in saying that "some Catholic writers" claim that "there have been hundreds of infallible utterances, and others contend that the infallible pronouncements of the Popes can be counted on the fingers of one hand." He does not identify any of his sources.

Mr. Blanshard (p. 23) says that "the difference between an infallible and a fallible statement by the Pope is not important for the public at large. . . . It is a Catholic's duty to follow his teaching and directives [*sic*] in all things that affect religious life." Again no definition, no proof, no evidence, no documentation. When one considers the wide range of the variety of things that may "affect religious life," the statement that the Pope issues infallible *directives* on them that all Catholics are bound to obey is simply absurd, as is the idea that the difference between fallible and infallible statements is of no importance. The difference between what is "A" and what is "not A" is always of importance to people who are interested in accurate thought and expression.

Mr. Blanshard concludes his discussion of infallibility with the following sentence, again with no evidence, proof, or documentation (p. 26): "To answer some of the embarrassing questions with some show of consistency, the Jesuits have created several grades in Papal utterance. The most embarrassing Papal blunders are classified in one of the minor grades for which infallibility is not claimed."

It is unfortunate that Mr. Blanshard did not cite some of the embarrassing questions, and report when and where and by which Jesuits the several grades of papal utterances were classified. Particularly interesting would be some examples of Mr. Blanshard's selection of embarrassing papal blunders in *ex-cathedra* definitions of doctrine in the field of faith or morals.

The basic offense of this whole discussion is that its total effect is to misinform and confuse the uninformed reader about this doctrine, to make him believe that the Pope acts as a totalitarian dictator settling questions *ad hoc* in the total control of Catholics the world over. He gives the impression that all Catholics are bound to follow the Pope's minute directions and are even subject to the sort of punishment that a military commander, a dictator, or an absolute monarch might mete out to a disobedient subject. That this impression is totally false is obvious to anyone who has elementary information concerning the doctrine dealt with, regardless of whether the person is a Catholic, a Protestant, or an atheist. That Mr. Blanshard nowhere *proves* his charges and insinuations must be clear to anyone who understands the elementary principles of argument, evidence, and proof.

III

Blanshard's Attack on American Catholics

12

THE BLANSHARD DOCUMENTATION

MR. BLANSHARD'S documentation receives attention in much of this book. It seems well, however, to center one chapter specifically on his failure in documentation or proof for his alleged facts and sweeping charges.

The Blanshard volume is an attack on the American Catholic hierarchy. He makes this explicit at the beginning (p. 4):

> There is no doubt that the American Catholic hierarchy has entered the political arena and that it is becoming more and more aggressive in extending the frontiers of Catholic authority into the fields of medicine, education and foreign policy. . . . It uses the political power of some twenty-six million official American Catholics to bring American foreign policy into line with Vatican temporal interests.

Mr. Blanshard does not tell us how "entering the political arena" differs from the activity of leaders in other religious groups, as, for instance, Bishop G. Bromley Oxnam, of the Methodist Church, and the late Rabbi Stephen A. Wise.

In common speech "the American hierarchy" is shorthand for "all the diocesan bishops, including the archbishops and Cardinals, of the United States." Unfortunately for *American* Catholics, the word is a "foreign" word. It was brought to America. It is from the Greek and not an indigenous American Indian term. This makes it easier for Mr. Blanshard to use it to scare his untutored readers. So whenever a Catholic individual or organization does or says something which Mr. Blanshard does not like, it is "the hierarchy" that is doing or saying it.

"The American Catholic people have done their best to join the rest of America, but the American Catholic hierarchy, as we shall see in the course of this survey, has never been assimilated" (p. 10). There is no documentation for this language, nor any cross reference to a place in which a reader can see just what is meant by "joining the rest of America" and by "assimilation." Mr. Blanshard also omits to point out where he has shown in his book that the American hierarchy *have not been* whatever he means by "assimilated." American Catholics have no more occasion to "join" the rest of America than have American Protestants, American Jews, or American atheists. Members of the American Catholic hierarchy hardly need to be "assimilated" in their own country.

There are 181 Catholic Bishops in the continental U.S., including Cardinals and Archbishops. Of this number, only six were born outside the United States. And of those six, four of them received their college and seminary training in the U.S. Two of them were born in Ireland, two in Germany, one was born in Galicia, and the other one in Hungary. Three of the foreign-born Bishops are not of the Latin Rite. Bishop Senyshyn is of the Greek Rite, Bishop Ivancho is of the Byzantine, and Bishop Bohachevsky is of the Ruthenian Rite.[1]

Mr. Blanshard's idea that American boys who go into the Catholic priesthood, rather than into the Protestant ministry or the Jewish rabbinate, need to be "assimilated" in America, indicates fundamental religious discrimination which is quite contrary to the "American way." His basic philosophy of the omnipotent state (see Chapters 7, 8, 18) seems obviously inconsistent with the fundamentals of American democracy, religious equality, and religious freedom.

Mr. Blanshard speaks (p. 7) of the "great debt which I owe to hundreds of friends and advisers, Catholic and non-Catholic, who have helped me with valuable suggestions for this book." He does not name any Catholic who has helped him, or tell us what the "suggestions" were. He says he "had the assistance of some of the most

---

[1] A letter from the Information Bureau, National Catholic Welfare Conference.

distinguished and scholarly critics who ever united in the attempt to make a book factually impregnable. When the first draft of the manuscript had been completed, it was submitted for scrutiny and criticism to a panel of experts which included . . . Giovanni Pioli of Milan, former vice-rector of the Propaganda Pontifical College for Roman Catholic Missions, Rome; . . . and a leading American Catholic author." These two are clearly offered *as Catholics* who helped to make his book "factually impregnable."

Mr. Blanshard makes no statement as to what either the Catholic author or Giovanni Pioli said about the manuscript, or even that they had actually read it. He says it was "submitted" to them. He also omits to inform his readers that Giovanni Pioli is an ex-priest, who was removed from the office which Mr. Blanshard mentions, on January 18, 1908.[2] Thus, an aged Italian ex-priest removed from office forty-three years ago, and an unnamed Catholic author (from neither of whom any opinions are reported or quoted) constitute Mr. Blanshard's principal documentation for his pretense that his manuscript was prepared with Catholic advice and approval.

The "leading American Catholic author," mentioned but not identified by Mr. Blanshard, is Mr. Thomas Sugrue. His name appeared in a preliminary stage of the book with the notation to check for the use of the name. When the book was published Mr. Sugrue's name was missing. When I wrote to Mr. Sugrue concerning this situation, he replied in a frank and detailed letter, dated November 1, 1950, which he gave me permission to publish. From Mr. Sugrue's statement it is clear that he was not engaged as, and did not work on the manuscript as, an expert authority on Catholic belief or practice. He did a pre-printer's job which involved no responsibility for the factual accuracy of the book.

> First and most important of all, I am *not* a Catholic writer. I am a Catholic who happens to be a writer. I have never written for Catholic publications. I have never written from a Catholic point of view. . . . Any reference to me as a Catholic writer is erroneous. . . .

[2] Letter to J. M. O'N. from Archbishop Celso Costantini of the Congregation for the Propagation of the Faith, dated Vatican City, March 7, 1950.

Then mentioning that he is a professional writer, editor, and critic, who in the practice of his profession frequently read manuscripts for publishers and advised them on editorial and publication problems, he wrote as follows:

> . . . in my reading of manuscripts for publishers I specialize in the religious and the mystical, having a special interest in both, and particularly in the latter, both in its Oriental and Occidental aspects. Thus a few years ago when I was asked to read a manuscript by Beacon Press, I did so. The manuscript turned out to be that of Mr. Blanshard's book. I reported on it as a professional; I was concerned with such things as style, form, arrangement and length of chapters, etc. . . . I spent a day with Mr. Blanshard after submitting a written report on his manuscript. During that day I went over with him the points I had made in my report, particularly with regard to style, form, and arrangement of chapters. Half a year later in Tel Aviv I received a cable asking if Mr. Blanshard might thank me in his preface. I replied, declining. It was strictly a matter of professional manners. I was paid for my work; thanks are usually given to those who render amateur assistance. That's all there is to the story; I did not know a Catholic author had been mentioned in the preface. Perhaps I am the person mentioned, yet since I am *not* a Catholic author, but rather an author who happens to be a Catholic, I cannot be he.

Mr. Sugrue added that "being inclined toward the mystical element in religion, I naturally favor a broad unity rather than any kind of sectarianism. Thus to me the Blanshard book is a good thing; it puts the Protestant case on the table, and I would like to see the Catholic case on the same table alongside it. I hope you do this. Then perhaps both sides can talk plainly and move toward understanding, which Christianity in general needs so desperately."

In addition to the unnamed Catholic author (discovered to be Mr. Sugrue) and Giovanni Pioli, there remain three identified "experts" on the belief and practice *of American Catholics.* Let us see what are their qualifications for the advertised task.

1. Dr. Edwin McNeill Poteat, "former president of Colgate-Rochester Divinity School" (p. 7). This is all the information Mr. Blanshard furnishes. But, like Giovanni Pioli, Dr. Poteat has a more relevant past (so far as American Catholicism is concerned) which is not divulged.[3] He was one of the founders of Protestants and Other

[3] See Ebersole, Luke, *Church Lobbying in the Nation's Capital* (New York:

Americans United for the Separation of Church and State, a signer of its first manifesto (January 12, 1949), its president in 1949, and its current president in 1951. At the annual meeting of POAU in January, 1951,[4] in Washington, President Poteat shared the platform at the evening mass meeting of his organization with Mr. Blanshard. Dr. Poteat warned Americans of the dangers of a "clerical dictatorship," of making America "Catholic in legislation," of a "merger of Church and State," "Vatican attempts to break down the barrier between church and state in America." He charged that "a fundamental conflict exists between the ideals of democracy and the political ambitions of the Roman Catholic Church."[5] In addition to these visionary perils (wholly unsupported by the record of Catholicism in America from colonial times to the present) Dr. Poteat protested "the perverse effort to make us [POAU] appear an anti-Catholic organization."

William Rufus Scott, member of the National Advisory Council POAU, was reported as telling one meeting of the convention that the "Myth [*sic*] of martyrdom" surrounding Cardinal Mindzenty "must be shattered" and called on the House Committee on Un-American Activities to investigate "Vatican espionage here so that the leaking of our top secrets shall be plugged." He said that "the Catholic clergy has learned of American secrets hardly anyone except the President knows."[6] He was not reported as telling what the secrets were or how *he* came to know about them. His own system must be almost as good as the Vatican's.

Dr. Poteat's organization has been active since its foundation in making attacks on American Catholics and their relation to our government and the Constitution. And somehow the impression has got abroad that POAU is anti-Catholic.

2. The late Dr. Robert Latou Dickinson (he died in 1950, at the

---

The Macmillan Co., 1951), pp. 67–73. (Dr. Ebersole, of the University of Maryland, is a graduate of Crozier Theological Seminary (B.D.) and has a Ph.D. degree from the University of Pennsylvania.)

[4] See the *New York Times* or any Washington paper of Feb. 1 and 2, 1951.

[5] Robert Tate Allan, *Washington Daily News,* Feb. 2, 1951.

[6] *Washington Post,* Feb. 2, 1951. The *Post,* on Feb. 3, reported that Mr. Scott's statements were taken from a press release, and that family illness prevented him from appearing on the program.

age of 89) was one of the panel of experts on the affairs of American Catholics. Mr. Blanshard mentions only that he was "former president of the American Gynecological Society"—a strange guarantee of expertness in American social history and Catholic doctrine. But Dr. Dickinson had other "qualifications" for the task for which Mr. Blanshard chose him, though for some reason Mr. Blanshard failed to mention them in certifying his panel. Dr. Dickinson was (according to *Who's Who in America*) Senior Vice-President of the Planned Parenthood Association since 1939, President of the Euthanasia Society since 1946, and (according to Blanshard, p. 142) author of the "authoritative work, *Techniques of Conception Control.*" How could anyone ask for a better background for expert advice on the beliefs and practices of American Catholics, particularly in the realm of government and civil liberties?

3. Dr. George La Piana, Professor Emeritus of Church History in Harvard University, is the only one of the panel of experts who has qualifications for any part of the job of making Blanshard's book factually impregnable. His position for years in Harvard entitles him to respect. His education, at least in part, in Catholic institutions in Italy indicates some acquaintance certainly with Catholic doctrine and with Italian practices. In my search for definite information on his specific qualifications, I asked two members of the American Catholic clergy who were in positions indicating the probable possession of information. I received friendly reports: almost certainly a former Catholic, not one apparently since coming to America in 1913 at the age of 34, on the whole scholarly, fair, unbiased at Harvard, only occasionally some bitterness toward the Church, a few bad breaks in the book *What to Do with Italy,* on which he worked with Salvemini. I could get nothing that indicated clearly either special competence or incompetence as an expert on Catholicism in America.

I then examined the lectures which Professor La Piana gave in 1949 at Butler University.[7] They proved to be a mixture of quite fair attitudes, much sound information, some instances of, at best, gross carelessness in regard to the Church in America (as in the handling

---

[7] "A Totalitarian Church in a Democratic State," *The Shane Quarterly,* Butler University, School of Religion, April, 1949.

of the "heresy of Americanism," which is substantially the same as Blanshard's [see pp. 70–73], startling statements in regard to the First Amendment and the McCollum case, and an interpretation of the Church's doctrine of the relation of religion to government that is clearly inconsistent with that of many of the most distinguished scholars and theologians of the Church and particularly of the American hierarchy throughout our history. There is little to choose between Blanshard and La Piana in the matter of poor workmanship on the subject of the Church and American democracy.

However, it was still not evident that he had anything to do with making Mr. Blanshard's book "factually impregnable." So I wrote him a letter on January 22, 1951. I told him of my task, that I must discuss Mr. Blanshard's panel of experts, and asked him if he cared to tell me of his relation to, or contribution to, Mr. Blanshard's manuscript, and what is, or was, his relation to the Catholic Church, particularly in America.

I received an answer only from Mr. Blanshard, dated February 19, 1951. I quote Mr. Blanshard's first paragraph:

> Prof. La Piana has turned over to me your letter of January 22nd. He feels that it is a piece of inquisitorial impudence deserving no answer from him, since you have neither right nor reason to summon anyone to appear before you to give an account of his actions or opinions.

I submit that this is an absurd panel of experts on the threat of American Catholics to their country after 175 years of devotion. Consider the list in summary: one unidentified foremost authority on education; one unidentified American Catholic who was not engaged as an expert on the content of the book and who did not work as one; one president of POAU; one strong supporter of planned parenthood, euthanasia, and conception control; one Italian ex-priest (ex for 43 years); and one professor emeritus of Harvard whose relation to the Blanshard book neither he nor Mr. Blanshard is willing to divulge.

It seems clear that Mr. Blanshard prepared this attack upon his Catholic fellow citizens without taking adequate steps to check his alleged facts or his interpretations with competent and honest American Catholics. Certainly had he had any actual Catholic backing of this sort he would have listed it. There is none to be found within the covers of his book.

In some places Mr. Blanshard mentions, without any references which would allow a reader to check in any way, some unnamed Catholics. Here are some samples: "some Catholic writers" (p. 25), "Catholic writers frequently say" (p. 42), "as one Catholic writer has said" (p. 16). Also see p. 23, p. 26, p. 35.

He does, in some places, quote, or refer to, criticism of some things Catholic by Catholic writers. Such self-criticism of Catholic matters is common and well known to all readers of the Catholic press and books by Catholic scholars. The same is true of self-criticism in pretty much every area of life in our country, as one should expect in any free society. But not once in his volume does Mr. Blanshard name one American Catholic who in any way implies that *Mr. Blanshard's treatment* of any Catholic subject is "factually impregnable," or even well informed or unbiased.

Mr. Blanshard's "scholarship" should have revealed to him that all the *policies of a Catholic*, layman, priest, bishop, or Pope, teacher, writer, politician, or statesman, in any country are not necessarily *Catholic policies* in the sense in which Mr. Blanshard constantly uses the term. They are not Catholic policies in the sense that all Catholics approve of them or are supposed to follow them.

Any careful scholar discussing any large and complicated organization or enterprise, such as the Catholic Church, the United States of America, or World War II, ought to be capable of distinguishing between (*a*) the *fundamental doctrines* that are an inherent part of the faith of the church or the constitution of the country, or an inherent aspect or purpose of the enterprise, or at least a part of the objective of those operating the enterprise, and (*b*) the *specific policies* that are adopted or advocated from time to time by individual persons in positions of responsibility in the church, the country, or the enterprise.

For instance, in World War II, after Japan attacked us and destroyed our fleet at Pearl Harbor and Germany declared war on us, we adopted with substantial unanimity the *doctrine* that Japan and Germany must be defeated. In carrying out this doctrine many *policies* were advocated, or followed—island hopping in the South Pacific, a second front in Northern Europe, allowing the Russians to take Berlin, dropping atomic bombs. "Good Americans" supported the *doctrine* and differed decidedly in regard to the *policies,* such as dropping atomic bombs. So "good Catholics" believe in the Catholic doctrine in regard to the relation of government to religion, but differ as to the *policies* in this area of Spanish Catholics and others. Good Catholics believe in Catholic doctrine concerning religious training for children, but differ widely in regard to federal aid to education in relation to Catholic schools as expressed in any particualr bill.

It would probably take a number of volumes to explain away all the confusion that can result from the casual reading by the uninformed of Mr. Blanshard's discussion of what he calls "Catholic policies." As Father Dunne remarked in his pamphlet *Religion and American Democracy,* "Blanshard constantly confuses policy with doctrine, doctrine with policy, and confuses matters of pious belief, of opinion, and of historical interpretation, with doctrine." No loyal American is supposed to approve of all the policies of all the presidents of the United States. No loyal soldier, not even all the top-ranking officers of the United States Army, are supposed to approve of all the policies for which other officers, even their superior officers, were responsible in the conduct of World War II. The policy of a bishop in one diocese may be the exact opposite of the policy of a bishop of another diocese in regard to a good many matters. Particularly, Mr. Blanshard seems not to realize, at least he does not express the idea, that the policies and the language of any Catholic scholar, bishop, or pope are necessarily conditioned, not only by the fundamental doctrines of the Church, but by the particular circumstances in time, in place, and in persons that give rise to the policy, and the language. As Father Max Pribilla, a contemporary German Jesuit theologian, writes: [8] "We must therefore distinguish sharply between what is the strict teaching of the Church and what is only the theoretical echo of an historical

[8] "Dogmatic Tolerance and Civil Toleration," *The Month* (An English Jesuit magazine) (London: Longmans, Green & Co., Ltd., October 1950), p. 253. This is a translation, in slightly adapted form, of an article which appeared in *Stimmen der Zeit,* in April, 1949.

situation, the influence of which even outstanding theologians could escape only with difficulty. For even theologians are children of their age."

Mr. Blanshard regularly assumes that all Catholic priests and bishops think alike, that they all have identical policies, which they impose on the laymen, and that these policies are dictated from Rome. He offers no proof for this false assumption. (See pp. 129–134, Chapter 9.) Mr. Blanshard's book has scores of misstatements, charges, and insinuations for which he offers no support or documentation (see Chapters 7–17). But he protests in his book and elsewhere his admiration for Catholics other than the members of the hierarchy. "There is no personal bias involved . . . there is no disposition to question the moral worth or patriotic loyalty [*sic*] of the American Catholic people or their rank-and-file priests and nuns." [9]

Mr. Blanshard wrote in *The Humanist*,[10] quoted by Father Dunne, "Naturally, my criticisms would be offensive to a member of the priesthood because a priest is bound by oath to accept and propagate the very policies which I hold to be reactionary." A small amount of elementary inquiry could have saved Mr. Blanshard from making such a false statement. According to Mr. Blanshard's interpretation of the *Imprimatur*, the following statement of Father Dunne's should be accepted by him, not only as a sincere statement by Father Dunne but as a universal, authoritative Catholic doctrine, because it appears in a pamphlet carrying the *Imprimatur* of Francis Cardinal Spellman, D.D., Archbishop of New York: "I have not at any time taken an oath to accept and propagate any policies, nor do I know of any priest who has. I am a Catholic because I believe in the truth of the Catholic doctrinal position. I do not agree with all the policies of every or of any Pope, much less of every or of any bishop; nor is there anything in my faith which obliges me to do so." [11]

It is hard to pick out Mr. Blanshard's weakest chapter from the standpoint of sound, competently documented argument, but there are certain objective things about his Chapter 2, "How the Hierarchy

---

[9] *The Atlantic Monthly*, February, 1950, p. 78.
[10] August, 1948, p. 53.
[11] *Religion and American Democracy*, p. 8.

Works," that seem to make it the best example. It is his longest chapter, thirty-two pages; it has more footnotes than any other chapter, fifty-one; and as its title indicates, it is Mr. Blanshard's barrage of heavy artillery, to soften up his readers and prepare them for the infantry of the succeeding chapters.

This key chapter, on How the Hierarchy Works, opens on page 8. On page 6 Mr. Blanshard writes: *"Wherever possible I have let the Catholic hierarchy speak for itself."* He does not keep this promise in this chapter.

America has had well over five hundred members of the Catholic hierarchy. The total of the names listed in all the dioceses is 552,[12] but a number of bishops have served in more than one diocese. The current number in the American Catholic hierarchy is 181. They are all busy administrators, writing, speaking, issuing circular letters to pastors and people. The Catholic press carries news of their activities weekly, and the secular press quotes or reports them frequently. Mr. Blanshard could have let them speak for themselves for hundreds of pages showing "how they work," what they do, why they do it, how they do it. In this chapter of thirty-two pages and fifty-one footnotes he allows only two members of the American hierarchy, the late Archbishop McNicholas and Bishop Wright, to speak *just once each.* These are the instances: Blanshard writes (p. 32):

> Nothing enrages Catholic theologians more than "common denominator" talk. "It is sheer nonsense to talk of a common religion for all American children or a common denominator for the hundreds of religious beliefs that we have in America," says the most Rev. John T. McNicholas. . . .

Clearly this throws little light on how the hierarchy works. But let us examine it. If Mr. Blanshard has any accurate knowledge of the *variety* as well as the great number of "religious beliefs" in America, he must know that the late Archbishop's statement was not the expression of an enraged theologian, but an ordinary, sensible, accurate statement about a well-known aspect of the American scene by an informed American. We have over 250 different Christian denomina-

---

[12] *The National Catholic Almanac,* 1950, pp. 150–156.

tions, plus groups representing most, if not all, of the other organized religions of the world, plus a number of varieties of agnosticism and atheism—which also are "religious beliefs," if not organized and integrated "denominations." Presumably there are children in all these groups. If talk about a "common religion" for all American children is not nonsense, what is it?

The quotation from Bishop Wright (p. 35) has nothing to do with how the hierarchy works. It reads: "Auxiliary Bishop John J. Wright of Boston declared in 1948 that not a single Roman Catholic prelate in the United States is the son of a college graduate."

Mr. Blanshard inserts this quotation into a discussion of Catholic education. He does not demonstrate how the lack of a college education of the fathers of Catholic bishops has anything to do with the merits of Catholic education. Bishop Wright's comment [13] shows that his remark was not related to education:

> . . . gives as his source an editorial in the *Christian Century* which, while it disagreed with the conclusion I drew from certain facts, nonetheless cited the facts as I had given them.
>
> I was pointing out that in any alleged "century of the common man" the Catholic bishops of America should be in an excellent position to interpret the spirit of the people and to serve them with intimate sympathy. I pointed out that, far from being members of a social caste, they were without exception the sons of working men and of working men's wives. By way of illustration of this point I listed the occupations of their fathers, noting that they came from hard-working people, none of their fathers being college graduates. . . . The conclusion I made concerning the democratic background and spirit of the hierarchy runs counter to his preconceived thesis—[so he weaves] . . . the sentence into a paragraph on the Catholic educational system as he conceives it.

An examination of Mr. Blanshard's fifty-one footnotes in his Chapter 2 reveals the following:

> 23 notes deal with colorless, noncontroversial facts, population figures, etc., containing no substantiation or proof of any of the charges against the hierarchy. (Numbers 1, 2, 3, 4, 5, 8, 10, 11, 13, 14, 15, 16, 17, 18, 19, 22, 23,

---

[13] Personal letter, March 31, 1951.

35, 36, 44, 46, 49.)

6 deal with ancient, universal, well-known doctrines, not with how the hierarchy works. Notes 27, 28, 29 deal with the doctrine of infallibity as related to the offenses of "bad popes." But even on this he does not allow the hierarchy to speak, but refers to *Life* and to two laymen. In a nine line comment on this matter, Mr. Blanshard manages to be *irrelevant,* "if infallibility rested on the character of popes," *inaccurate,* "theologians have developed a doctrine to reconcile," and *vulgar,* "evil confined to one portion of the Pope's anatomy." Notes 39, 43, and 48 concern Catholic doctrine on salvation outside the Church, hell, and gambling. These are simple biographical references to quotations from others than bishops. The quotation for note 43, regardless of its accuracy, does not support what Mr. Blanshard uses it to support. He is speaking of the "faithful Protestant and Jew" (p. 34). Since a faithful Protestant or Jew is one who has *faith* in Protestantism or Judaism, he cannot possibly be one who believes in the Catholic Church but who pretends to be a faithful Protestant or Jew for some ulterior reason such as economic or social advantage. Therefore the doctrine Mr. Blanshard is here discussing has no relation to such a person.

5 deal with the doctrine of infallibility and its definition by the Vatican Council of 1870 (pp. 22–26). I have given this section special consideration, (pp. 165–169). As shown there these five notes furnish nothing to substantiate Blanshard's charges. (Notes 30, 31, 32, 33, 34.)

2 continue the text discussion, do not, even in form or phraseology, support the statements to which they are attached. (Notes 12, 41.)

3 give the sources (probably accurately) of three quotations, none of which has any relation to how the hierarchy works. (Notes 24, 26, 40.)

2 documented statements from two English writers, one a priest and one a layman, neither a member of the hierarchy. (Notes 42, 45.)

1 note (No. 47) is hard to catalogue. It is attached to Blanshard's statement that "Catholic groups" in New Jersey spear-headed a law "permitting gambling." This is the law which allows the playing of the game called "Bingo," a simple card game in which prizes are won. Probably his statement is true and probably the bishops approved. This hardly shows *"how the hierarchy"* works. Why should not citizens vote as they please on laws permitting or prohibiting Bingo, betting on horse racing (legal in many states), card playing, Sunday baseball, or beer drinking? It is no answer to say that these activities are *immoral.* There is a difference of opinion on that. Probably all Catholics, and most non-Catholics, agree that none of these activities is immoral *in and of itself,* that is, always and everywhere immoral. They all *may be immoral* under certain circumstances, as is the case with eating good food, writing your best friend's name, and driving an automobile.

1 (Note 6 p. 11) is on "loyalty," not on the work of the hierarchy (see p. 198). This footnote does not support the paragraph to which it is the only documentation.

2 (Notes 7 and 9) carry the names of four periodicals, as documentation which does not prove his statements (pp. 11, 13).

This makes a total of

45 notes out of the 51, in this longest and most documented chapter which do not support any of the sweeping statements and insinuations against the American Catholic hierarchy and other Catholics which constitute the bulk of this key chapter.

There remain

6 notes which document *something* having a bearing on how the hierarchy works. Note 20 is concerned with the bishop's power to suspend a priest; No. 21 documents the startling revelation that the Congregation of the Holy Office in Rome is composed of Cardinals, etc. and transacts its affairs in what is called in this country "executive sessions," as do most similar bodies in America (trustees, directors, governors, regents, etc.); No. 25 has to do with the method of selecting new bishops. Note 37 gives a book reference for statements about the organization of the National Catholic Welfare Conference. Note 50 is the support for a long passage on the "prices" for Masses, and says that the "data" were supplied by a priest "recently resigned" —name not given nor any source that can be investigated to check for accuracy, dependability, or identity. Note 51 contains the name of a Catholic paper. But it is difficult to see just what is being documented (presumably something about Masses or prayers for the dead). I know that Mr. Blanshard does not believe in these aspects of the Catholic religion, but I do not see how such prayers and Masses can be a threat to *American freedom.*

That's the lot. Six notes out of fifty-one, or most of the six anyway, have something to do with how the hierarchy works, but none of them has any support of any kind to offer for Mr. Blanshard's many sweeping and bitter attacks in this key chapter on the American Catholic hierarchy as a danger to America.

Dr. Guy Emory Shipler, editor of *The Churchman,* writes: [14]

In his chapter on "How the Hierarchy Works," Mr. Blanshard not only records the history of the hierarchy during the 200 years in which it has operated in the United States; he cites in detail its methods of procedure and its accomplishments, documenting all of his major statements. The same procedures are followed throughout. . . .

[14] *Lawyers Guild Review,* Vol. X, No. 1, Winter, 1950, p. 215.

Mr. Blanshard makes no pretense even of recording the history of the hierarchy; neither the American hierarchy nor the United States is two hundred years old; there clearly is no citation "in detail" or otherwise of either *methods* or *accomplishments;* and no one of his "major statements" in this chapter is documented at all.

One of the most serious faults in Mr. Blanshard's book is his constant misuse of the *Imprimatur.* He has scores of references to publications which have weight and value as he seeks to use them *only* on the assumption that he makes and expects the reader to make, that because these quotations carry the *Imprimatur* of a Catholic bishop the matters he quotes from them are *"official, authentic Catholic doctrine."* He uses this expression (or its equivalent) regularly in places where it could have no possible application except as the *Imprimatur* gave it validity.

Anyone who has even a passing interest in the meaning of the *Imprimatur* can find out easily that the *Imprimatur* is simply a statement of permission to publish, given to a subordinate by his superior. The only essential meaning of the *Imprimatur* is that, in the opinion of the official granting the *Imprimatur,* the document concerned contains nothing contrary to Catholic doctrine in faith and morals.

The truth about the *Imprimatur* is that "No implication is contained therein that those who have granted the *Nihil Obstat* and *Imprimatur* agree with the contents, opinions, or statements expressed." This is the official formula of the Catholic Archdiocese of New York. Note that not an *implication* is given—to say nothing of a guarantee—that the official granting the *Imprimatur* agrees with anything in the book or pamphlet. It says nothing about the contents of a book except that something is *not* included. The *Imprimatur* no more guarantees the accuracy, authenticity, credibility, or infallibility of the contents of the document to which it is attached than a government certificate on a bottle that it contains no *artificial coloring* is a guarantee that the contents will cure baldness, cancer, or arthritis.

The use of the *Imprimatur* in the Church substantially parallels the permission that subordinates in the army and navy are required to have from their superior officers for publications and important public speeches. The fact that a general gives a captain in the army permission to publish an article, or a book, or to make an important public speech does not mean that the general guarantees the accuracy or authenticity of everything the captain may say. It certainly does not mean that all men in the army, or all citizens whom the army serves, are supposed to believe everything such a captain may present to his audience or his readers. However, in the Church, as in the army and navy, it is held to be wise to have this check on the publication of erroneous *doctrines* that might do damage to the work of the Church—i.e., the salvation of souls. A subordinate is prohibited from publishing on faith and morals without a check by a representative of his superior—his bishop. Just so, precautions are taken to prevent subordinates in the armed forces from giving (unintentional) aid and comfort to the enemy.

Mr. Blanshard found many passages written by some Catholic which he could use to prejudice the uninformed against American Catholics. If any of these were published with an *Imprimatur,* he used that fact inaccurately to convey the idea that the passage was "authentic Catholic doctrine." Some of them were inaccuracies, some fragments which Mr. Blanshard misinterpreted, some just remarks in bad taste, some mere opinion that represented no one but the author.

One has to follow Mr. Blanshard through his arguments with some care to uncover his shifts of ground, his avoidance of a main point to contend with some minor aspect of the matter at hand, his repetition of earlier unsupported assertions and pretense. These techniques of bad argument are all well illustrated in his answer to Father Francis J. Connell's devastating review of his book.[15]

Mr. Blanshard writes in his book (p. 12): ". . . the parish priest often imposes a levy [*sic*] upon the Catholic community which burdens every one of its members for many years."

Father Connell quotes from Blanshard (p. 12): [16]

---

[15] *Father Connell and the Scholarship of Paul Blanshard,* a reply by Paul Blanshard, author of *American Freedom and Catholic Power,* reprinted from the *Cornell Law Quarterly,* Winter, 1951, distributed by the Beacon Press, Boston.

[16] Connell, Rev. Francis J., Book Review of *American Freedom and Catholic Power* by Paul Blanshard, *Cornell Law Quarterly,* Vol. 35, Spring, 1950, p. 678.

In 1948 the [Catholic] Church announced that it would spend ten billion dollars on construction in the United States in the next ten years. . . . If this program is paid for by contributions, it will mean an average levy of $385 on every Catholic man, woman and child in the United States.

Mr. Blanshard uses this factual assertion to confirm his serious charge that Catholic priests "frequently go to great extremes in their campaigns for building-funds, even in the parishes of the poor."

Then Father Connell pointed out that "the estimated figure of 10 billion dollars is for construction, remodeling, furnishing, equipment and maintenance," and was so reported in the article.

Mr. Blanshard uses this news story, or rather its headline, as "documentation" for his attack on the priests *for imposing levies on the Catholic community,* and *an average levy* on every Catholic man, woman, and child in the United States. If Mr. Blanshard knew the meaning of the words "impose" and "levy," plus Catholic policies and practices in this matter, he was misleading his readers.

Mr. Blanshard's answer to Father Connell on this point is a perfect example of how he argues: [17]

It is a perfectly sound inference that all the items cited in the Catholic survey, such as remodeling, equipment, etc., which I legitimately lumped under the journalistic term "construction," must come out of the contributions of the Catholic people. Where else could they come from? Regardless of the answer to this question, my reference is factually sound because it was conditional. I said: "*If* this program is paid for by contributions . . ." My inference was sound, but even if it was not, my statement was correct in every syllable.

The three little dots in Mr. Blanshard's statement are in place of the words "it will mean an average levy." His alibi is the suppression of this phrase plus the word "if." To make his answer look plausible he *has to omit* the word "levy." His question "Where else could they come from?" backs up nothing. It is an attempt to shift his burden of proof to his opponent. He asks a man who has challenged a Blanshard statement to prove that the statement is *not* sound. Clearly, *if* any money is raised by contributions, it is *not* raised by an imposed levy. Obvi-

[17] *Op. cit.,* pp. 7–8.

ously, *if* the priests raised ten billion dollars by *contributions* in ten years from 26,000,000 Catholics, it would mean an average contribution (not a levy) of $385 for ten years, or an average of $38.50 per year. What does this prove about *imposing levies* on "the Catholic community which burdens every one of its members for many years"?

He gives neither example nor authority for the idea that the parish priest can *impose levies* on a Catholic community; nor does he cite anywhere a single example of a Catholic parish in which any new buildings or other extensive improvements have ever been undertaken without the cordial support of the people of the parish. It is probable that there have been occasional cases of some opposition on the part of individual parishioners to such expenditures, but that when it happens, individual Catholics are *compelled* to pay what they do not want to pay, Mr. Blanshard does not show, and cannot show. There is no possibility of its being true. It is also *improbable* that there has often (if ever) been an instance in which a parish priest has undertaken an expensive enterprise without the backing of the parish. The difficulties would be too great. If Mr. Blanshard knows of any such instances, he refrained from mentioning them.

Just before making the above charge about levies, Mr. Blanshard writes (p. 11):

> Almost any "good" Catholic can give a dollar or two if he is loyal to the institution. By that test probably about half of our twenty-six million "Catholics" are real Catholics. Catholic writers who ought to know the field thoroughly have estimated that about half of the Catholic people in the United States give some kind of support to the Church.

Which one is right—the page 12 Blanshard who tells us about priests *imposing burdensome levies,* to show the greedy and grasping dictation of the priests? Or the page 11 Blanshard who tells us that probably about half of the twenty-six million "Catholics" are not real Catholics who *give any support* to the Church? Here Blanshard is trying to show the pretense and boasting of the Church. The reader can take his choice. Blanshard offers no evidence for either position. If the reader feels that he *must* get an unfavorable opinion of the Church on *each* page (and is untroubled by considerations of truth or logic) he can accept both.

It is interesting to put together Mr. Blanshard's charge (p. 4) that the hierarchy "uses the political power of some twenty-six million official American Catholics" to dictate American foreign policy and his statement above that only about one half of the twenty-six million are "real" Catholics. He nowhere explains how thirteen million "unreal" Catholics, who are not sufficiently "good" Catholics to give a dollar or two to the Church (which imposes levies on them and controls all their thoughts and actions), can still be *used* by the hierarchy to control American foreign policy. And I should think that the necessarily low opinion of the intelligence of the American State Department and the Presidency which this belief would require would destroy his frequently expressed faith in the infallibility of democratic government.

Another typical Blanshard answer when caught by Father Connell is the following. Mr. Blanshard wrote (pp. 82–83):

> For Catholic teachers in the public school system the hierarchy lays down the rules in the moral manuals almost as definite as the rules for parochial school teachers. . . . They must remember their moral responsibility to the Church and not become mere creatures of the state. "A teacher never is and never can be a civil servant, and should never regard himself or allow himself to be so regarded," said the Catholic archbishops and bishops of England and Wales in a declaration on this point in 1929. (A footnote refers to "Davis, II, 88.")

Father Connell comments: [18]

> The truth is that the statement from which Mr. Blanshard quotes has not a single word to say about the obligations of the public-school teacher toward the Church. It refers to the obligation of the teacher toward the *parents of the pupils.*

Mr. Blanshard made the following reply to Father Connell's exposure: [19]

> Of course this is what the English bishops *said,* but Catholic bishops always disguise their school doctrines wherever possible in nonCatholic countries.

[18] *Op. cit.,* p. 680.
[19] *Op. cit.,* p. 12.

13

BLANSHARD ON THE KNIGHTS OF COLUMBUS ADVERTISEMENTS

ONE of Mr. Blanshard's most elaborate series of misrepresentations is his treatment (pp. 295–299) of fourteen points which the Knights of Columbus called in an advertisement "erroneous ideas" about Catholics. Each one is clearly "erroneous." On that there can be no informed difference of opinion. Mr. Blanshard accuses the Knights of Columbus of adopting "the transparent device of mis-stating slightly the major criticisms of non-Catholics about the hierarchy's reactionary dogmas; then it denies this mis-statement lustily, attempting to give the casual reader the impression that the underlying criticisms on which the mis-statements are based are also untrue" (p. 296).

I do not know how widespread are the erroneous beliefs expressed in these fourteen points. I have, however, encountered twelve of them myself, expressed in exactly the terms of the advertisement. Most Catholics who have had close and cordial relations with many non-Catholics (as I have had in over sixty years as student or teacher in non-Catholic schools and colleges) have probably had a like experience. I have run across all but numbers 3 and 11. Certainly the "casual reader" of many pages of Mr. Blanshard's book would get the impression that he believed most of them—or at least that Mr. Blanshard wanted *his* casual readers to believe most of them. His parallel treatment of the Knights of Columbus' fourteen points (p.

299) is clearly designed to convince his casual reader that all this nonsense is essentially true. Not one of his fourteen points is true.

He says (p. 246) that he puts "on the opposite page the exact statement of Catholic doctrine that the hierarchy did not state in frank terms." (Note again that claim that it is the "hierarchy" talking when the Knights of Columbus speak. That would doubtless surprise and alarm the hierarchy!)

Mr. Blanshard does not state "exact Catholic doctrine" in a single one of his fourteen answers. He writes (p. 296): "It will be seen that the exact statements of Catholic doctrine [his fourteen answers] are almost as objectionable as the straw men which the Knights of Columbus demolish." He is right. His fourteen statements are almost as bad as the original list of errors. The "documentation" furnished for them is spurious.

It seems worth the space to publish in full the list of fourteen "erroneous ideas" about Catholics as given in the Knights of Columbus advertisement, and the parallel list of Mr. Blanshard's false statements which he offers as "exact statements of Catholic doctrine." This will exhibit the Blanshard "scholarship" and argument in their almost total unreliability.

I take them as phrased and numbered on Blanshard's pages 298–299. Under each I shall try to show the nature of Mr. Blanshard's error.

1. K. of C.: You hear it said that Catholics believe all non-Catholics are headed for Hell.
Blanshard: Non-Catholics who deliberately reject Catholicism are headed for Hell.

This would express Catholic teaching only if the word "deliberately" were taken to mean deliberate rejection of what the individual non-Catholic *actually believed to be the truth.* The deliberate rejection of the truth is condemned by the Catholic Church as an immoral act, a sinful act. It is similarly condemned by both Protestantism and Judaism. Hypocrisy, pretending to believe the opposite of what is actually believed to be the truth, is condemned by substantially all persons who have a moral code of any kind. Mr. Blanshard's statement would clearly include a non-Catholic who *deliberately* rejected Catholicism because he honestly and conscientiously believed it was not the truth. However, according to the teaching of the Catholic Church the person who rejects Catholicism *deliberately, in the sense of carefully following his conscience* (which should involve deliberation), is *not* "headed for Hell," in the phraseology of these tables. Either Mr. Blanshard does not know the Catholic doctrines concerning salvation "outside the Church" and the "priority of conscience," (see pp. 84–85) or else he does not wish his readers to know them.

In 1784 Father John Carroll (later the first Catholic bishop of America) wrote what was probably the first formal American answer to the false charge that the Catholic Church believes or teaches that there is "no salvation except to those in communion with the Church." In answering this old and still repeated accusation, Father Carroll said that "the members of the Catholic Church are all those who, with sincere heart, seek true religion, and are in unfeigned disposition to embrace the truth wherever they find it." [1]

The following passage from the work of an English Protestant, midway between Father Carroll and Mr. Blanshard, which repeats a Jesuit theologian, as quoted by Cardinal Newman, indicates how widely the doctrine of the Church is understood and how inexcusable is Mr. Blanshard's misrepresentation.

> She [the Church] condemns no goodness, she condemns even no earnest worship, though it be outside her pale. On the contrary, she declares explicitly that a knowledge of *"the one true God, our Creator and Lord,"* may be attained to by the "natural light of human reason," meaning by "reason" faith unenlightened by revelation; and she declares those to be anathema who deny this. The holy and humble men of heart who do not know her, or who in good faith reject her, she commits with confidence to God's uncovenanted mercies; and these she knows are infinite; but, except as revealed to her, she can of necessity say nothing distinct about them. It is admitted by the world at large, that of her supposed bigotry she has no bitterer or more extreme exponents than the Jesuits; and this is what a Jesuit theologian says upon this matter: *"A heretic, so long as he believes his*

[1] Shea, *The History of the Catholic Church in the United States,* Vol. 2, p. 229.

sect to be more or equally deserving of belief, has no obligation to believe the Church . . . [and] when men who have been brought up in heresy, are persuaded from boyhood that we impugn and attack the word of God, that we are idolaters, pestilent deceivers, and are therefore to be shunned as pestilence, they cannot, while this persuasion lasts, with a safe conscience hear us." [2] Thus for those without her the Church has one condemnation only. Her anathemas are on none but those who reject her with their eyes open, by tampering with a conviction that she really is the truth. These are condemned, not for not seeing that the teacher is true, but because having really seen this, they continue to close their eyes to it. They will not obey when they know they ought to obey.[3]

See Mr. Herberg's comment on this matter [p. 236]. Falsifying the position of the Church on this doctrine is a perennial tactic of those who seek to make out a case against the Catholic Church. Mr. Blanshard makes another brief reference to this doctrine (p. 32), which he characterizes as "narrowness of outlook," and adds that "the doctrine is still official that: outside of the Church there is no salvation." For Mr. Blanshard to repeat this ancient nonsense is inexcusable.

2. K. of C.: That they believe non-Catholic marriages are invalid.
Blanshard: Non-Catholic marriages involving a Catholic are invalid.

Mr. Blanshard is here confused about the distinction between civil laws and Catholic sacraments. The Catholic Church does not teach that a marriage between a Catholic and a non-Catholic is *invalid* in the sense of being illegal according to the civil law (this would depend on what the civil law is at a particular time and place) but that it is *invalid as a Catholic sacrament,* or a contract which *the Church* will recognize (see pp. 255–256). As documentation for this inaccurate statement Mr. Blanshard refers the reader to *five canons, and a textbook,* and uses one quotation from the *Catholic Almanac.* In other words, Mr. Blanshard is suggesting that an interested reader, who happens to have available a complete set of the canon laws of the Catholic Church, the *Catholic Almanac,* and the textbook referred to, who also

[2] Busenbaum, quoted by Cardinal Newman, *Letter to the Duke of Norfolk,* p. 65.

[3] Mallock, William Hurrell, *Is Life Worth Living?* (New York: G. P. Putnam's Sons, 1879), pp. 284–285.

has a few hours or days for study, might read up on the Catholic doctrines concerning the sacrament of marriage.

However, all any careful person has to do is to look at Mr. Blanshard's No. 2 and compare it with the No. 2 he is trying to answer. Even if Mr. Blanshard's No. 2 were accurate and true, it still would not show that there is any "mis-statement" in the Knights of Columbus advertisement. There the statement "non-Catholic marriages," unmodified, means all marriage among non-Catholics, and it *is* a belief held even today by some well-educated, fair-minded, unprejudiced non-Catholics that Catholics do not believe that these are marriages. I have talked to exactly that sort of non-Catholics who, at least until I talked to them, believed that the Catholic Church did not acknowledge *any Protestant marriages* of any kind as being valid marriages. The Church holds that a marriage between two baptized Protestants who are free to marry is a valid marriage *and a sacrament.* This is explicitly stated in the book[4] Mr. Blanshard refers to (generally *without any page numbers*) in his documentation. Mr. Blanshard should say what he means by "non-Catholic marriages" and by *invalid.* As it stands, Mr. Blanshard's No. 2 is a false statement.

3. K. of C.: Some think Catholics believe the Pope is God.
Blanshard: Catholics owe "complete submission and obedience of will to the Church and to the Roman Pontiff, as to God Himself."

If Mr. Blanshard has himself read the encyclical of Leo XIII to which he refers (without giving his readers even the title of a book in which it can be found, to say nothing of an accurate page reference), he must know that his statement here is wholly misleading. What he has quoted in his No. 3 is *only a fragment of a sentence* taken from a two-page paragraph in a 28-page encyclical. If anyone will read through the twenty-eight pages of this encyclical, he will discover that there is nothing in the entire encyclical concerning the belief that "the Pope is God" or indicating that "Catholics owe complete submission and obedience" to the Pope. Complete submission and obedience, unqualified, means submission and obedience *in all matters.*

---

[4] *Canon Law* by Bauscaren and Ellis (Milwaukee: Bruce Publishing Co., 1947), p. 398.

In the passage from which Mr. Blanshard selected this fragment of a sentence, the Pope was writing about (1) the *Christian Revelation* as expressed in various Scriptural passages accurately referred to, and (2) the matter of determining the doctrines *of faith* divinley revealed, and (3) the position of the Church and the *Pontiff as the Supreme Teacher*. Then comes the sentence which Mr. Blanshard misused to spread the false idea that Catholics owe *complete submission and obedience* to the Pope, as to God Himself.

The passage [5] says that *unity and perfect accord in faith* require the acceptance of the one teacher. All moderately well-informed people, whether Catholic, Protestant, atheist, or other, know that the "infallible rule" referred to in this passage applies only to matters of faith and morals, not to economics, politics, international relations, educational administration, diet, dress, or social policies. What this passage really shows is not that Catholics believe that the Pope is God, or that Catholics owe the Pope *complete submission and obedience in all matters,* but simply that *Leo XIII believed and wrote* that the Catholic Church was established by Christ to teach all nations the *Christian faith*. This position of the Pope should hardly surprise any scholar.

4. K. of C.: That he can do no wrong.
Blanshard: The Pope can do no wrong when he *speaks* as head of the Church in matters of faith and morals.

Even if one could accept Mr. Blanshard's No. 4 as absolutely true and accurate, it still comes nowhere near establishing that No. 4 in the list of errors (which was an unqualified statement that Catholics believe "that the Pope can do no wrong") was *not an error*. In other words, the Knights of Columbus No. 4 expressed the common misconception that "Papal infallibility" means "Papal impeccability." It is a fact (which I know from personal experience) that many non-Catholics, and even some uninformed Catholics, believe that this is the doctrine of the Church, but it is not taught or held by any well-informed person. Likewise Mr. Blanshard's No. 4 is not an "exact statement of Catholic doctrine."

---

[5] *The Great Encyclical Letters of Leo XIII,* with the Preface by the Rev. John F. Wynne, S.J. (New York: Benziger Bros., 1903), pp. 192–193.

There is no teaching that the Pope could not "do wrong" or *make a mistake* in a document in which he was speaking as the head of the Church *about* faith and morals. In making an address about some matter of faith or morals a Pope might make mistakes in historical data or might "do wrong" (in the opinion of some Catholic theologians or others) in regard to some particular *policy* for a certain situation. The doctrine of Papal Infallibility would apply to none of this (see Ch. 11). Mr. Blanshard here is guilty of misstating the doctrine—the fault he erroneously accused the Knights of Columbus of committing in listing commonly held errors.

5. K. of C.: That they owe him civil allegiance.
Blanshard: They owe him civil allegiance in matters of morals, education and priestly rights.

The key words here are *civil allegiance.* Mr. Blanshard cites nothing which justifies him in the statement that this wording expresses "exact Catholic doctrine." No well-informed Catholic citizen of the United States (or of other countries outside of the Vatican State) believes he owes the Pope anything that any literate person should call "civil allegiance." Mr. Blanshard's documentation has nothing in it that is capable of this interpretation. His documentation consists of some encyclical references, and two quotations none of which has any reference at all to "civil allegiance." The first refers to the general doctrine of the relation of the spiritual to the temporal realm, and the second to "moral conduct." Mr. Blanshard is probably confusing his readers on this point by an inaccurate combination of the Catholic doctrine of the relation of the temporal to the spiritual and the doctrine of the Church as an infallible teacher *of morals.* Only those who know substantially nothing about the matters Blanshard mentions in his No. 5, and who will not investigate his "documentation," should be deceived by this one.

6. K. of C.: And that he should have the political power to rule America.
Blanshard: He should rule America in moral, educational and religious matters.

Again if Mr. Blanshard's No. 6 were taken as accurate, it shows no inaccuracy in the No. 6 in the advertisement. That says the Pope should have political power *to rule America*—with no limitations. In Mr. Blanshard's No. 6, he has the modifications "in moral, educational and religious matters," but this also is not a statement of Catholic doctrine. There is no Catholic doctrine that the Pope should *rule America* in any matters. This is more twisting of the two doctrines mentioned under No. 5, and for documentation Mr. Blanshard offers only a reference to the unsatisfactory sources mentioned for that number. Anyone who wishes to discuss the position of the Church in regard to the temporal and spiritual powers, and the teaching of faith and morals, ought to try to understand these matters and ought to quote the doctrines accurately, and not present them as involving *the ruling of America.* Both doctrines are centuries older than America, have no more reference to America than to all other "temporal powers," and do not cover the *ruling* of any country.

7. K. of C.: It is said that Catholics want religious freedom only for themselves.

Blanshard: They advocate complete religious freedom for non-Catholics only as a temporary concession in non-Catholic countries, and in Catholic countries they restrict other cults.

What Mr. Blanshard says is flatly false, and is wholly unsupported by his documentation. Even if all Catholics would grant the absolute accuracy of every word in Mr. Blanshard's only documentation (a quotation from Father Connell's book), that does not substantiate what Mr. Blanshard says. Father Connell says that a Catholic cannot advocate *complete religious toleration "on the basis that all religions have a genuine God-given right to exist."* Probably no one who has any conception of the doctrines that are covered by such a phrase as "all religions" actually believes that all religions do have a *genuine God-given right to exist.* Some religions do not have even a *legal* right to exist under the Constitution and laws of our country. "Complete" religious toleration is unknown among civilized people—and *no* religious toleration is allowed by the uncivilized. No atheist, obviously, could possibly believe that any *religion* had a *God-given* right to exist.

In our country freedom is denied to groups indulging in practices held inimical to morals, safety, public decency, etc. Polygamy, "snake handling," certain features of "faith healing," and human sacrifice, all run afoul of the law.

Father Connell's further statement that the civil rulers *can consider* themselves justified in preventing denominational activities hostile to the Catholic religion is something that anyone who knows anything about the history of society, or about the present situations in various governments, would have to concede. Not only civil rulers *can* consider themselves justified but they *do* consider themselves justified. Certainly the civil rulers of countries with an established religion (Protestant, Jewish, Catholic, or other), such as Norway, Sweden, Denmark, Finland, Israel, Italy, and Spain, at the present time, all consider themselves justified in restricting denominational activities hostile to the religion of the state (See Ch. 6). Mr. Blanshard's No. 7 is an absurdly false statement and contrary to the belief and practice of Catholic Americans during the entire history of the United States. It is one of the fundamental misrepresentations of his whole attack. He offers no valid proof of it anywhere.

8. K. of C.: That they oppose public schools (as an evil which should be destroyed).

Blanshard: They oppose public schools for Catholic children as an evil which should be destroyed.

Again, if Mr. Blanshard's No. 8 were accepted as accurate, it does not prove that the Knights of Columbus No. 8 is in any way at fault. The idea of American Catholics wanting to *destroy* public schools in which most Catholic children are getting the only schooling they will ever have is too silly to take seriously. Again there is a canon referred to, 1374, which probably few readers will look up. This canon does not prove Mr. Blanshard's No. 8, that the American Catholic hierarchy are trying to get American public schools destroyed. It simply gives the well-known statement about Catholic and non-Catholic schools. Of course Mr. Blanshard knows (see his p. 101) that as it is interpreted and applied by the Catholic hierarchy in America not only are most Catholic children in public schools, but there are thousands of Catholics in non-Catholic colleges and universities. And the bishops appoint chaplains and approve the building of chapels to serve them. Finally, Mr. Blanshard refers again to Father Blakely's much-quoted statement which apparently never expressed the opinion of anyone but Father Blakely.

9. K. of C.: And separation of church and state as evils which should be destroyed.

Blanshard: They condemn separation of church and state and advocate support of both Catholic schools and churches by public taxation.

This point deals with our old friend, the ambiguous "separation of church and state." The statement that the American hierarchy condemns the type of separation of church and state which is expressed in the First Amendment to the Constitution of the United States is false (see Chapters 3 and 4); that they advocate support, unqualified, total, general support, of Catholic schools and churches by public taxation is also false. If Mr. Blanshard does not mean total support by public funds (which I believe would be refused by Catholic authorities if offered to them) but only some kind of partial support, as tax exemption, which would be offered to all religions impartially, he should have made this clear. *Some* Catholics have probably advocated *a policy* of total support at *some time, in some countries,* under *some circumstances.* However, that this is *the doctrine* of the Church or that it has ever been advocated by the American hierarchy for the past, present, or future of this country is again false.

This complex inaccuracy is documented by a reference to the famous *Syllabus of Errors* of Pius IX and is based upon Mr. Blanshard's clear misunderstanding of the import of one item in the *Syllabus* (see pp. 86–87). The other reference is credited to Monsignor O'Toole of the Catholic University of America in a document in which Msgr. O'Toole's function was that of a *translator,* not an author. The sentence quoted is to the effect that no Catholic may "positively and unconditionally" approve the policy of separation of church and state. This is true, or not true, according to what is meant in any particular context by the always ambiguous phrase "separation of church and state." In every reference to this phrase, whether in a propaganda speech, a textbook, a Supreme Court opinion, or the translation of a papal encyclical, the person who wants real understanding should keep in mind that this phrase *can have no specific meaning in any document* except as that specific meaning is given to the phrase by its context.

10. K. of C.: The claim is made that Catholics pay the priest for the forgiveness of their sins.

Blanshard: They pay the priests for Masses and those Masses are recognized as factors in securing forgiveness of sins, granted by priests.

In order to convey any truth at all, this reference to paying for Masses should be qualified by the word "generally" or "sometimes" or "some of them," and "forgiveness of sins" is the wrong phrase to use in regard to Masses. The "remission of punishment due to sin" is what Mr. Blanshard is here confusing with the sacrament of penance. The Knights of Columbus advertisement was evidently trying to answer what used to be a common belief of non-Catholics, and still is in some places, that Catholics *pay in the confessional.* Mr. Blanshard is here simply boiling down to a single sentence his misunderstanding and bias, expressed more in detail in his discussion of the sacrament of penance (see pp. 247–251). Also, in this sentence he is clearly mixing up the sacrament of penance with the Sacrifice of the Mass. The documentation quotes an ordinary statement about the Church's teaching on the expiatory power of the Mass and gives a reference to the *Catholic Encyclopedia* to the effect that certain payments are *"allowed"* and *"permitted."* As it stands, Mr. Blanshard's No. 10 is *not* a statement of Catholic doctrine.

All informed Catholics know (and it would not have taken much research for Mr. Blanshard to have found out) that what is called a "fixed Mass tax in each diocese" is an administrative convenience to be used as a guide, not an absolute rule, by the pastors of the various parishes. Mr. Blanshard could have found out in a few minutes that in the Catholic Church any pastor can and does waive, or refuse, any fee of any kind whenever that is appropriate. If Mr. Blanshard knows of a single abuse of this practice by even one Catholic priest in America, he omits to mention it. There probably have been some abuses, but abuse of the practice does not make the practice itself an abuse.

11. K. of C.: That they must buy their departed relatives and friends out of Purgatory.
Blanshard: They pay established fees for priestly Masses for the dead, and the Church guarantees that these Masses will help departed souls in Purgatory.

This is about the Catholic doctrine of Purgatory. In order to show that the Knights of Columbus advertisement was mistaken in denying that "Catholics *must buy* their departed relatives and friends out of Purgatory," Mr. Blanshard gives no additional documentation to that for No. 10 except a statement that in certain places a single Mass may be obtained for one dollar, etc. If Mr. Blanshard really looked into this matter, he knows (1) that Masses may be obtained for nothing; (2) that Catholics are not taught that they *must* have Masses said for the dead, at any fee at all or at none; (3) that they are taught, in common with Jews, "It is therefore a holy and wholesome thought to pray for the dead, that they may be loosed from sins" (II Machabees 12:46); in other words, (4) that their prayers may help to release their friends from Purgatory. Finally, he also knows, if he has made an investigation, that the overcommercial tone of some Catholic advertisements represents the bad taste of the advertisers rather than any *doctrine* of the Church. He could have quoted at length Catholic criticism of such advertisements. If he knows how the Church, or any other organization, can prevent some people from exhibiting bad taste he should have reported it.

12. K. of C.: That they adore statues.
Blanshard: They *venerate* statues by Canonical order.

Anyone who has read much anti-Catholic literature or who has even had friendly conversations with inquiring non-Catholics knows that the absurd idea that "Catholics adore statues" is still fairly common among otherwise enlightened people. Mr. Blanshard, in answer to this nonsense, does not say "of course it is nonsense," as he would have said if he knew and wished to spread the truth. His answer is that the Catholics "venerate" statues *by canonical order!* Anyone who is linguistically unable to distinguish between "worship" and "veneration" should refrain from discussing Catholic doctrine or Canon law. Webster's Dictionary says that "venerate" means "to regard with reverential respect, or with admiration and deference; to revere." The antonym for veneration, according to Webster, is "contempt, loathing, disgust, scorn, aversion."

Mr. Blanshard helps his readers on this one by simply putting forth as documentation Canon No. 1279 ff. If his readers will turn to their handy volumes of canon law and look up 1279 ff., they may or may not be surprised to find that that canon does *not order* Catholics to venerate statues. This canon does not even *recommend* the veneration of statues, but is essentially a list of directions to the clergy concerning the placing and care of statues, pictures, and similar objects. Of course, the doctrine of the Church is that Catholics should venerate *the saints.* There is a widespread belief, based upon a great deal of human experience, that the presence of statues and pictures may well help people to know about, appreciate, and venerate the saint whose statue or picture they see. They do not venerate the marble, or plaster, or bronze in the statue. If the sight of a statue moves one to any attitude of veneration, it is for the saint whom the statue represents, *not* the statue itself. The function of a statue in a church is similar to the function of a picture of Washington or Lincoln in a schoolroom.

13. K. of C.: Are forbidden to read the Bible.
Blanshard: They are forbidden to read any non-Catholic version of the Bible.

Mr. Blanshard's No. 13 is not true, and even if it were, it obviously shows no inaccuracy in the Knights of Columbus advertisement. When one says without qualification that Catholics are forbidden to read the Bible, one should be understood to mean exactly that. The *truth* is that Catholics are taught and urged to read the Bible. The only documentation that Mr. Blanshard offers for his untrue statement is Canon 1399. If anyone will take the trouble to read Canon 1399, he will find that Mr. Blanshard's No. 13 will need a good many qualifications put on it in order to make it even partially true. Canon 1399 is a long and complicated treatment of books, of interest chiefly to the clergy (as is all canon law), and contains *nothing* to substantiate Mr. Blanshard's criticism of the Knights of Columbus advertisement.

14. K. of C.: Use medals, candles and holy water as sure-fire protection against the loss of a job, lightning, or being run down by an automobile.
Blanshard: They use scapulars, relics and similar articles with the written assurance of their priests that these articles will help to protect the faithful against disaster.

The error in No. 14 in the Knights of Columbus advertisement is clear error to any informed person. This is an absurd misrepresentation of Catholic teaching in regard to medals, candles, and holy water. The one sentence which Blanshard quoted in his documentation is from St. Thomas Aquinas concerning relics and miracles and tells us what *God does* under certain circumstances, and not what is done by medals, scapulars, relics, or holy water. Catholic teaching in regard to use of certain religious articles, that these may help the faithful in various circumstances, is certainly not expressed by such phrases as "sure fire protection against the loss of a job." The title of the sample circular published with an *Imprimatur* is an example of the sort of promotion and advertising which is held in thoroughly bad taste by many Catholics. It will not be held to be an accurate expression of *Catholic doctrine* by any well-informed person, Catholic or non-Catholic.

14

BLANSHARD'S "CATHOLIC PLAN FOR AMERICA"

ON the first page of his chapter "The Catholic Plan for America," Mr. Blanshard writes (p. 266): "Many American liberals . . . have allowed the Catholic hierarchy, unchallenged, to use American freedom as a cloak for the systematic cultivation of separatism and intolerance among the American Catholic people." He then asks: "What would happen to American democracy if our alleged twenty-six million Catholics grew to be a majority in the population and followed the direction of their priests?"

These expressions contain two of Mr. Blanshard's fundamental *assumptions:* (1) that the Catholic hierarchy is using American freedom *as a cloak* to work against the essence of American freedom and (2) that the American Catholic voters do, or are supposed to do, what the *priests tell them to do in political affairs.* Anyone who is willing to believe these two assertions, without any evidence, is doubtless beyond the reach of evidence and argument. But if anyone is interested in proof and looks for it in the Blanshard book he will find there is none there.

Mr. Blanshard gives a hypothetical Constitution of the United States which he offers as the Catholic Plan for America after a couple of centuries, if America at that time should become predominantly Catholic. His Plan is a summary of the principal charges against American Catholics which constitute his book.

My position concerning his Catholic Plan for America is this:

1. His assumption that the hierarchy, priests, or Catholic people do not, and cannot, believe in American Freedom, but pretend to as a temporary expedient until strong enough to destroy it, is viciously false. He does not prove it. He cannot prove it.

2. His assumption that the Catholic laymen do, or are supposed to, adopt political, social, and economic policies required by the priests, and vote as the clergy tell them to, is also false. The evidence that it is false could hardly be avoided by anyone who had even a tentative curiosity about it. Positive proof that it is false is found in my Chapters 5 and 9.

3. His specific documentation or proof for his Catholic Plan for America is worthless. It should deceive no one who has even a little knowledge of Catholicism or of argument.

He says (p. 269) that "there is not an original thought and scarcely an original word in my entire three Catholic amendments [to the United States Constitution]. They are mosaics of official Catholic doctrine. Every concept, almost every word and phrase, has been plagiarized line by line from Catholic documents. The most important phrases are derived from the highest documents of Catholicism, the encyclicals of the Popes." Note here his reference to *official Catholic doctrine* and *Catholic documents,* and *the highest documents of Catholicism.* It is clearly inaccurate to refer to every document written by any Catholic person, or by any *agency of a government* made up predominantly of Catholics, as a "Catholic document." It is a Catholic document only in the sense that Mr. Blanshard's book and mine are *American documents.* His assumption to the contrary has no foundation in fact; and he offers it as a simple assumption. He does not even try to substantiate this position in any way.

Mr. Blanshard's further assumption that any such document necessarily contains *official Catholic doctrine* is equally absurd. His position that all statements in the encyclicals of the Popes are to Catholics *ex-cathedra* statements of universal Catholic doctrine is unfounded. It could not possibly be believed by anyone who had taken the trouble to find out: (*a*) the meaning the doctrine of Papal Infallibility, as defined by the Vatican Council in 1870 (See Ch. 11) or (*b*) the way in which papal encyclicals have been interpreted, taught, and applied by Catholic scholars and administrators throughout history. In fact an understanding of what the phrase "a statement of doctrine" means, as distinct from "a statement of policy," "a statement of opinion," or "a report of fact," should keep any person from such erroneous writing.

Papal encyclicals are not *per se ex-cathedra* utterances.[1] This does not mean that no pope ever discusses an infallible, dogmatic position of the Church in any encyclical. Obviously, an encyclical may deal with universal Catholic doctrine. No informed person, however, can honestly take the position that any "important phrase" that can be found in a papal encyclical is necessarily a statement of doctrine which Catholics universally are supposed to accept and believe.

Many papal encyclicals and many parts of other encyclicals deal not with formal doctrine of universal application (to which only the doctrine of Papal Infallibility applies), but are concerned merely with *specific events or policies* in *particular countries* at *particular times.* A little elementary understanding of this situation should be an effective preventive of any apprehension induced by most of Mr. Blanshard's "Catholic Plan for America." It should totally dispose of his ridiculous pronouncement that almost every word and phrase used in his prophecy expresses official Catholic doctrine. A document may be written by a Catholic for Catholics about something of interest to Catholics without being *official.* And no document expresses Catholic doctrine unless it is, *first,* about doctrine, and *second,* about doctrine that is universally Catholic. Encyclicals of the Popes may or may not fit these conditions.

There are in Mr. Blanshard's Plan a few statements that are characteristic of *any established* religion in any country. They are given on *the assumption* that in a predominantly Catholic America the Catholic Church would be the established religion of the country. Anyone is free to guess as to what the situation would be if the country in two centuries should be predominantly Catholic, or predominantly Methodist, Lutheran, Jewish, or something else. Mr. Blanshard

---

[1] See Corrigan, *The Church and the Nineteenth Century,* pp. 176–177; *The Catholic Encyclopedia,* Vol. V, pp. 413–414; see also my quotations from Cardinal Newman, p. 163.

is entitled to take his fling at prophecy with whatever type of aid he wishes to use. But no rational person should accept it for anything other than just that.

Some of Mr. Blanshard's statements here express essentially what one should expect in any country which is overwhelmingly populated by people of any one faith, *unless the people had a thorough indoctrination and background in constitutional democracy and religious freedom.* The provisions are much like the restrictions on dissenters today in Sweden, Spain, Israel, and most of the other countries of the world which have an established religion (see Ch. 6). But he nowhere submits any valid evidence of any kind that there necessarily would be an establishment of the Catholic religion in such a future as he imagines.

Mr. Blanshard's documentation, the quoted sources for the phrases he has allegedly taken from "Catholic documents," has the form but not the function of documentation. His sources are drawn in part from the *Spanish Law of Succession* (p. 335). He nowhere explains what this "document" is. Further, neither in (*a*) this note (p. 335) nor in (*b*) his bibliography (p. 310) does he give his reader (*a*) any quotation from the Spanish law or (*b*) *any reference* which would enable the reader to look up the Spanish law to check (*a*) the accuracy of what Mr. Blanshard got out of it or (*b*) the sponsorship or status of the Spanish law itself. As documentation this amounts to little more than saying that he found *something* in print *somewhere.*

Next he relies on the *Vatican-Italian Concordat of 1929* which was a working agreement with a totalitarian dictator, and as such has obviously no necessary application to affairs in a constitutional democracy or any other type of government, or even to another concordat with another totalitarian dictator. The very nature of such an agreement makes it conditioned to time, place, and persons, which deprives it of the universality that is essential to a *Catholic doctrine.*

The word "concordat" may properly be used in somewhat different meanings in different contexts. As commonly used in Catholic affairs it is an agreement, contract, or treaty, between ecclesiastical and civil authorities, made for a certain country in regard to specific matters which in some way concern both the Church and the government making the agreement.[2]

Two of his sources are the *Italian Constitution of 1947* and the *Spanish Bill of Rights, Article IV*. Again, neither in his notes nor in his bibliography does he give the reader a reference to a publication in which either of these documents can be examined; nor does he report in the text (p. 267) or in his notes (p. 335) (by either quotation or paraphrase) what he found in these "sources" on which to build his Catholic Plan for America.

Notice here again how completely he has failed to live up to his claim that wherever possible he allows the *hierarchy to speak for itself* (p. 6). He could have quoted hundreds of pages from members of the American hierarchy concerning their hopes and plans for America. He did not quote one line. He preferred presenting his readers with fragments from some Spanish law, a Spanish bill of rights, an Italian concordat, and phrases from encyclicals. All these last were, necessarily, taken completely out of context, without furnishing his readers any information in regard to the purpose, or the limited application, of any particular encyclical. Finally, he relied on the false assumption that any word or phrase he could pick out of an encyclical expressed "official Catholic *doctrine*."

Mr. Blanshard writes: "In a Catholic world every national government would establish the Roman Catholic Church in a unique position of privilege, and support its teachers and priests out of public revenue. That is what the Holy See has always demanded in every country where it has had the power to support the demand with reasonable strength" (p. 270). The first sentence is just another unsupported prophecy and his second statement is false, as Mr. Blanshard knows if he made any adequate investigation. In fact, if he had spent a half hour with Professor M. Searle Bates' book on *Religious Liberty*,[3] he would have known better. There he would have found that a Protestant scholar (whom he could hardly charge with being a dupe of the Pope) had presented, in a few pages following a detailed

---

2 *Catholic Encyclopedia,* Vol. IV, p. 196.

3 Bates, *Religious Liberty* (New York: Harper & Brothers, 1945), pp. 546–548. Also see Chap. 6 of this book.

report, a summary of the world situation which demonstrates that the predominantly Catholic and predominantly non-Catholic countries have approximately equal records in the matter of granting religious freedom to minorities—and that his charge is plainly false.

Mr. Blanshard (p. 271) quotes from a *Catholic Action Manual:* "Catholic action itself is an army involved in a holy war for *religion*" (italics mine). Mr. Blanshard blows this up into the following statement (italics mine): ". . . the Catholic Church can conquer the earth if its followers *obey their priests with military precision.* Its members are urged not to marry *the enemy.* . . ." Notice how he drops out the point of the quotation that *religion* is the objective of Catholic action. The idea that people interested in promoting religion obey their priests with *military precision* is, of course, sheer nonsense, or better, it is using emotionally loaded words to falsify the plain meaning of a quotation that is being attacked. Mr. Blanshard follows this by another quotation concerning which he similarly avoids the point, which is the idea of the use of influence "*seriously to conquer other souls for Christ.*" Mr. Blanshard is here simply changing the Catholic Church's concept of its obligation to live up to Christ's injunction "Go ye therefore and teach all nations" into a military attempt to conquer the world in the interests of political power.

In following out this misinterpretation, he is also attempting to spread the falsehood that there is little to choose between Catholicism and communism. He writes (p. 272): Note the words I have italicized.

> The *priests choose* Catholic laymen from Catholic Action to infiltrate non-Catholic organizations in much the same manner that Communists are chosen to infiltrate labor unions and political parties for the Kremlin. . . .
>
> The chief role of Catholic Action is in *politics,* where it serves as a general denominational *pressure* group "not only outside all parties but above them." How far above all parties it functions is a matter of dispute. Its nonpartisanship is nearly always *fictional* because, in practice, it throws its support to Catholic *parties* when some issue arises that is vital to the priests. [Are there Catholic parties in America? He uses the word elsewhere throughout the paragraph to mean political parties.] In the United States, Catholic Action has not yet become very important because the hierarchy is not yet ready to *participate openly* and officially in partisan politics, as it participates in Europe. The American hierarchy is *shrewd* enough to know that American

voters would reject a political party *controlled from Rome* almost as decisively as they now reject, and properly, a political party controlled from Moscow. Accordingly, Catholic Action in the United States is still largely in the talking stage. It is a *manufacturer of wordy propaganda* which seems to the outsider so abstractly theological that it is bound to repel all except the devout.

This whole paragraph of false and insulting charges and insinuations is wholly without documentation, evidence, illustration, or support of any kind.

Mr. Blanshard writes (p. 280): "When an American Catholic bishop says fervently that he accepts the doctrine of the separation of church and state, the skeptical inquirer may turn his eyes southward and see what the bishop means by this profession of an American doctrine." This passage contains Mr. Blanshard's chronic false assumption that Catholics do not and cannot actually believe in "the separation of church and state" in its form as "an American doctrine." It contains the equally false insinuation that American bishops believe in and desire the conditions that obtain in Latin America. Following his common pattern when his charges are most sweeping and without foundation, he has no documentation of any kind attached to this passage, nor elsewhere, that offers any substantiation. He could with equal justification say that when an American Lutheran or an American Orthodox Jew says he accepts the doctrine of the separation of church and state "the skeptical inquirer" may "turn his eyes" to Sweden or to Israel (see pp. 74–81) to get the measure of hypocrisy in such Protestant or Jewish "profession of an American doctrine." His expression (p. 280) "Church dominated governments" would probably better fit the facts if changed to "government dominated churches" to express the situation in some parts of Latin-American countries that have strong governments.

In this chapter, as elsewhere, Mr. Blanshard assumes that whatever is distasteful to Americans in Spain, Mexico, or South America is to be attributed to the influence in those countries of the Catholic Church. He should know, if he has made a thorough investigation, that most of the matters of which he disapproves in those countries are also emphatically disapproved of by many (probably most) Catholics in the United States, and by some of the Catholics in Spain,

Mexico, and South America. He knows, further, that similar practices are *not* found in other predominantly Catholic countries, such as Ireland and Belgium. Further, he takes no account of the tremendous divergence in temperament, history, economics, geography, and many other factors which differentiate the Catholics of the United States from the Catholics in those countries. In other words, it is not far from literal accuracy to say that Mr. Blanshard and other commentators on the Spanish and South American situation are inclined to attribute everything they do not like to the influence of the Church and to assume that everything they do like has been brought about in spite of the Church.

One of Mr. Blanshard's prophecies of a constitutional provision in his Catholic Plan for America is the present constitutional situation in the United States. "Compulsory education in public schools exclusively shall be unlawful in any state in the Union." I should expect that anyone who believes in personal and religious freedom would hope this provision would still express the constitutional situation in the United States "two hundred years hence" whether or not Catholics are in the majority. Mr. Blanshard's statism is contrary to our whole tradition. Compulsory schooling in public schools has never been lawful in any state. Mr. Justice Black was clearly in error when in the majority opinion in the McCollum case[4] he spoke of the "state's compulsory public school machinery." Neither Illinois nor any any other state has such machinery. When Oregon tried in 1922 to set up compulsory public school machinery the Supreme Court of the United States (in 1925) unanimously declared the scheme unconstitutional.[5] The court referred to the state law of Oregon as "legislation which has no reasonable relation to [any] purpose within the competence of the state." One way in which "the competence of the state" is limited was expressed by the court when it said: "The fundamental theory of liberty upon which all governments in this Union repose excludes any general power of the state to standardize its children by forcing them to accept instruction from public teachers only."

Two years before the Oregon case the United States Supreme Court

[4] 333 U.S. 203.

[5] *Pierce v. The Society of Sisters,* 268 U.S. 510.

overruled the Supreme Court of Nebraska[6] in declaring unconstitutional a state law which prohibited teaching any language other than English to any child below the ninth grade. The case concerned the teaching of German to a child in the eighth grade in a Lutheran parochial school. "It should be noted," writes Professor Robert E. Cushman, of Cornell,[7] "that the basis of the Court's decision is that the liberty of teachers and parents with reference to instruction in private schools is infringed by the statute. It does not hold that the state could not restrict the teaching of foreign languages in the public tax-supported schools of the state."

If the *Blanshard plan for America* (see Chapter 17) ever becomes an actuality, it seems clear that in the words of the Supreme Court "the competence of the state" will in no way be limited and that our "fundamental theory of liberty" will not be allowed to interfere with the "general power of the state to standardize its children by forcing them to accept instruction" in public schools only. The omnipotent state has to take over the training of children in order to have grown men and women who will be content to live without freedom. The Nazis and Communists have thoroughly demonstrated that in recent years.

Mr. Blanshard leaves no doubt as to his stand on compulsory public schooling (see pp. 109–110). He writes (p. 52): "Leading Catholics have repeatedly declared that if the United States ever adopted a law compelling all children to attend public schools, they would defy the law." He does not document this statement with a reference to any named Catholics. But he comments on the Oregon case on the same page, saying oracularly that the Oregon law "was declared unconstitutional partly because of special circumstances existing at the time." I suppose that every case ever decided by a court was decided partly because of special existing circumstances, in fact or in law or in both. Either his explanation of the Oregon decision is general enough to cover most, if not all, decisions in lawsuits or else it is clearly inaccurate. The Oregon decision did not rest on any *principles* that were peculiar to that time or to the circumstances of that case, as shown by the language of the court quoted above. It rested on the broadest

---

[6] *Meyer v. Nebraska,* 262 U.S. 390.

[7] Cushman, Robert E., *Leading Constitutional Decisions* (New York: F. S. Crofts & Co., 1937), 6th ed., p. 109.

principles of any free society, principles of the sort that the Supreme Court frequently says are "inherent in the scheme of ordered liberty."

Mr. Blanshard continues (same page): "Presumably if the Constitution were amended to permit such a law . . . the Catholic Church would make good its threat of defiance." I doubt if the Catholic Church would, or could, defy the law. But I am confident that thousands of Catholic parents would defy the law and would be joined by practically all non-Catholics who still cared anything about American freedom. Probably most Americans who are aware of what is going on in the world today have seen enough of the taking over of the children, by "the people's governments" in Germany and Russia and the satellite states, to be quite ready to defy the first big drive to force totalitarianism on America. This (if usual patterns are followed) will be the attempted destruction of religion by destroying religious education. Totalitarianism has to be antireligious. It follows that a tentative atheist who still retains something of a liberal philosophy, a belief in a free society, ought to join all those who believe religion has any helpful contribution to make to man in defying any law that would take the basic control of children's education away from parents and give it to the state. If Mr. Blanshard's plan for America ever becomes a "clear and present danger," those who believe in personal and religious freedom will have to fight it at some stage. They would probably wisely decide to fight on this first frontier of freedom—the right of parents to direct the education of their children so long as the schools they choose meet reasonable standards of the state in regard to desired common skills and knowledge.

Men of no religion do not have to be totalitarians. However, it seems clear that the tendency is definitely that way. Secularism easily becomes atheism, and atheism (a universal element of full-blown totalitarianism) seems inevitably to permeate eventually the whole creed of the omnipotent state of which it is always a basic element. The need to put something into the philosophic void left by a denial of God leaves the atheist little choice. As he becomes mature enough to know himself, self-worship becomes untenable. There is nothing left but to worship the state. So he adopts the Mussolini creed—"nothing above the state, beyond the state, outside the state."

15

OPINIONS OF BLANSHARD'S BOOK

MR. BLANSHARD'S book has been hailed by men of position and influence as a work of exemplary scholarship, scrupulous documentation, fairness, sound reasoning, complete proof, freedom from bias, freedom from attack on religion, and sympathy and admiration for American Catholic laymen. These words of praise have been written by men who hold positions from which one should be able to infer that they are responsible and competent *judges* of scholarship. I believe I provide in this book conclusive evidence that these terms of praise are literally and specifically, in every instance, contrary to fact and truth.

Space considerations make it impossible to do more than sample the inaccurate passages of uncritical endorsement that have done so much to promote Mr. Blanshard's book. The results have been to spread suspicion and antagonism among Americans of different religious groups. It seems clear that these unpleasant fruits of Mr. Blanshard's work are due, in large part, to the enthusiastic, unrestrained, uninformed endorsements of Mr. Blanshard's attack on American Catholics and their religion.

It is disturbing to find in positions of distinction in education and in religious life men who know so little about Catholic doctrine and practice, and who are so careless about the requirements of competent controversy. The unhappy result has been to spread and underwrite false, insulting, and unproved attacks on every American Catholic, and on the oldest and largest body of Christians on earth. When such attitudes are found among clergymen, editors of religious journals, and professors of philosophy, it seems time for others than the Catholic victims to be concerned. Amity, friendship, American unity, cannot long survive such dereliction on the part of influential men in education and religion.

In all this Mr. Blanshard has become a relatively unimportant part of the cast. The stage is occupied by his uncritical admirers and their editors. Explanations of the emotional, intellectual, or ethical shortcomings that excuse or explain Mr. Blanshard's text are not available to excuse reviewers, whose job is *evaluation,* or to excuse the editors of supposedly responsible journals whose job it is to spread accurate information and intelligent opinion, rather than misinformation and religious prejudice.

For purposes of clarity and condensation, I have selected only seven points involving inaccurate statements and unsupported charges, and ten men who have given these unproved charges unscholarly approval. The seven points will be discussed in order, and the ten men will be referred to by letters,[1] with all sources listed in one note.

---

[1] A—George Boas, Professor of the History of Philosophy in Johns Hopkins University. *Philosophical Review* (edited by the faculty of the Sage School of Philosophy in Cornell University) January, 1950, Vol. LIX, No. 1.

B—W. E. Garrison, Literary Editor of *The Christian Century, The Christian Century,* June 8, 1949.

C—Henry Sloane Coffin, President Emeritus of Union Theological Seminary, *Christianity and Crisis,* May 2, 1949.

D—Herbert West, Professor of Comparative Literature in Dartmouth College, *Dartmouth Alumni Magazine,* October, 1949.

E—Clifford Kirkpatrick, Professor of Sociology, Indiana University, *Annals of American Academy of Political and Social Science,* January, 1950.

F—John Dewey, Professor Emeritus of Philosophy, Columbia University (quoted widely in advertisements of the Beacon Press).

G—Charles Clayton Morrison, Editor Emeritus of *The Christian Century* and editor of *The Pulpit.* An advertisement of the Beacon Press, New York *Herald Tribune,* Oct. 15, 1950.

H—Harold A. Larrabee, Professor of Philosophy in Union College, Associate Editor of *The Humanist, The Standard,* February, 1950.

I—Clarence W. Hall, Managing Editor of *The Christian Herald, The Christian Herald,* July, 1950.

J—John Haynes Holmes, Pastor Emeritus of the Community Church, New York City, and Chairman of the Board of the American Civil Liberties Union. Quoted in advertisements of the Beacon Press.

1. Mr. Blanshard's pretense of Catholic approval and assistance in making his book "factually impregnable" is wholly unsubstantiated (see my pp. 182–184).

"D" said that "this book is a monument of scrupulous documentation and has been checked and rechecked by a distinguished group of scholars both Catholic and Protestant."

"I" wrote: "We doubt whether any other book has been subjected to such thorough checking by so many persons equipped to catch the slightest error." Certainly persons equipped to catch the "slightest error" in regard to the belief and practices of the American Catholics would have to have intimate and extensive knowledge of Catholicism in America (see pp. 184–188). This writer's statement that the critics employed by the Beacon Press "combed every sentence, checked every reference, examined every charge" can mean *only* either (1) most careless reporting or (2) that the "critics" were incompetent or deliberately deceived the Beacon Press.

2. Mr. Blanshard *assumes* that the American system of democracy and religious freedom, traditional and constitutional, is accurately expressed in the so-called "Rutledge doctrine" of the meaning of the First Amendment. Then he *asserts* without proof that American Catholics do not, and cannot, support "American freedom." This double misrepresentation of our American system and the attitude of American Catholics toward it is given sweeping, unscholarly approval by "A." He wrote that the Catholic Church is a "most bitter opponent of the liberal tradition, a tradition which, in a review of this size, may be defined as the principles enunciated in the First Amendment to the Constitution" (see Chapter 4). "B" wrote "that the Catholic Church *must* lay down social laws which it *must* seek to have endorsed by the state, *must* be intolerant of any religious system but its own, and *must* demand that the state support its claims wherever there is a possibility that this demand will be met—and meanwhile *must* work toward gaining such predominance that the demand will be met." (Italics by "B.")

These things which this reviewer says the Roman Catholic Church *must* do are deduced by him from an unscholarly interpretation of Catholic doctrine, plus a refusal to pay any attention to the record of the Catholic Church in such countries as the United States, Ireland,

Holland, and Belgium. He must know also that Mr. Blanshard has not *proved* any of these things (see Chapters 4 and 6). Granted, of course, that there have been in history some situations which offer some evidence that some civil governments have seemed to act on these principles. Further, there are, in certain papal encyclicals and other important documents written by Catholic scholars some statements, that are *capable* of these interpretations as applicable to some political situations. These facts, however, in no way prove the contention that the Church must teach, or does teach, these as principles of doctrine.

First, the actions of civil government (even of governments dominated by Catholics) do not necessarily express fundamental Catholic doctrine, but rather *government policies.* Second, the documents containing such statements are not *ex-cathedra definitions of doctrine,* but are, almost without exception, discussions of *policies* having to do with specific crises in specific countries and quite unrelated to the affairs of the American democracy. Third, and finally (and, I submit, conclusively), if one will grant that the Catholic bishops of America know and teach fundamental Catholic doctrine, then one must conclude that these principles are not fundamental Catholic doctrine. The Catholic hierarchy in America have taught the opposite consistently throughout our entire history (see Chapter 3).

The review by "H" accepted and passed on Mr. Blanshard's double error concerning American freedom and the attitude of American Catholics: "That the Catholic power-system in this country persistently and deliberately refuses to stick to its religious last in accordance with American conceptions of freedom." Concerning sticking to the "religious last," there is one fact of American life that no observant American should question. That is the fact that Protestant ministers and bishops, and Jewish rabbis, are frequent preachers of sermons, signers of petitions, members of committees, speakers at rallies, and officers of organizations that appeal to the American public week after week in attempts to affect public opinion, legislation, elections, and governmental decisions. It is also a fact that Catholic priests rarely do anything of the sort, and members of the hierarchy almost never.

I suggest that anyone who doubts this verify my statement by watching for a month or two his daily paper and the propaganda mail he receives. I am not suggesting that there is anything wrong about this activity on the part of ministers and rabbis. They are as free to work for the kind of society they believe in as are businessmen, lawyers, labor leaders, or farmers. They are also free to refrain from such activity in cases in which they think it would interfere with their more important duties. I protest against attacking Catholic clergymen for doing occasionally exactly what the clergy of other religious groups do frequently, with no hostile criticism from Mr. Blanshard or his supporters.

Maybe the secularists would have a harder time making secularism the established religion of the United States if all religious leaders (especially those of the large groups, Protestant, Catholic, and Jewish) would emulate the leaders of other professions in America and come out in public more often, more vigorously, and with more information and better logic, on all sorts of public questions. The idea that it is all right for leaders of Protestantism and Judaism to advocate one side of any question of legislation, or a political or economic program, but an unpatriotic threat to "American freedom" when Catholic religious leaders advocate the other (or the same) side is itself a betrayal of the essence of American freedom.

3. Mr. Blanshard's assertion that Catholicism is like communism (later expanded into his second book, *Communism, Democracy, and Catholic Power*) is accepted by two reviewers. "A" wrote of the Catholic Church as "on exactly the same basis as the government of Soviet Russia, and its members on exactly the same basis as the members of the Communist Party, in that both groups are said [*sic*] to be under the orders of a foreign power while retaining the rights and privileges of American citizens." Note the words "are said." If those who say things are sufficiently irresponsible, anything can be "said" about any person or any institution. The impact of this sentence on the uninformed is to give the totally false impression that the Catholic Church controls its members in the same way in which the Soviet government controls the people who are within range of its guns and clubs, its secret police, its army, navy, and air force. The charge is false, and not only totally unsupported by anything in Mr. Blanshard's book but

totally incapable of being supported, as any mature American citizen ought to know.

Reviewer "C" repeats the offense against both language and truth by calling the Church equally *totalitarian* with the Soviet government. In these times particularly, writers and editors ought to find out what "totalitarian" means, and ought to consider what they are actually saying in today's atmosphere to the careless and the uninformed about their Catholic neighbors. To call the Catholic Church "totalitarian" is on the semantic level of calling the Soviet dictatorship a "democracy." [2]

4. Mr. Blanshard's erroneous assertions about no freedom of opinion, thought control, and dictation by a foreign power are accepted by three reviewers.

"E" referred to Mr. Blanshard's book as "This superbly articulate attack on a demonstrated threat to freedom of thought." How the threat was "demonstrated" is not divulged.

"D" writes that Mr. Blanshard's book "points out to the democratic United States the dangers of a strong and militant authoritarian force which allows no freedom of thought within its ranks." All that anyone needs to know in order to know that this statement is not true is an elementary knowledge of the doctrines of the Catholic Church and of the beliefs and practices of American Catholics. One does not need to approve, or believe in, any of these doctrines, beliefs, or practices, but only to have information which is easily obtained.

All that anyone needs to know in order to know that this charge is not proved by Mr. Blanshard is an understanding of the elementary principles of evidence and proof.

"A"'s statement "The Church maintains that all questions are religious" is too absurd to be taken seriously by anyone with elementary knowledge of Catholic doctrine. He writes that the "issue boils down to whether it is better for individuals to make up their own minds about what they want to do, or to accept the dictates of an organized power." Anyone who is sufficiently aware of the nature of the mind knows that any member of a society reasonably free as to speech, press,

[2] However, for this reviewer's dissent from Mr. Blanshard's limited concept of democracy, see below, p. 244.

and assembly, and with a mind capable of functioning, has to decide for himself what he wants to do whether it is good for him or not. No one else can decide for him. If he decides to accept, or not to accept, the *teaching* of the Catholic Church, or of Mr. Blanshard, there is nothing anyone (in our type of society) can do about it.

The idea that the Church can or does "dictate" what Catholics think or do is silly. And to know this one does not even have to know the doctrine of the Church (though that would suffice) but only how the human mind works. Thought cannot be controlled in the United States by the Catholic Church, the United States government, the Communist Party, or the Sage School of Philosophy of Cornell University. Any individual of sane mind who is capable of thinking can think what he pleases. Furthermore, only an organization, as a government, which possesses instruments of force (such as armies, police forces, squads of gunmen) can either restrain the individual from putting his thoughts into action or can fine, imprison, torture, enslave, or execute him for his actions. Obviously, any force that can *control* all media of communication, such as education, press, radio, and assembly, can control the spread of ideas and information which are the stuff of most significant thinking. In such a situation something approaching "thought control" *may be* achieved. Nowhere does the Church have or seek such control.

Clearly, neither the Church nor the American hierarchy have any instruments of force of any kind with which they can restrain any individual from thinking what he pleases, or from carrying out the results of his thought. Nor can they "punish" him for any actions which he may take.

The Catholic Church cannot dictate. It has available only the "force" of its teaching, persuasion, and the privileges of its sacraments. It follows necessarily that any Catholic who decides not to accept its teaching or yield to its persuasion, who is not interested in receiving its sacraments, may simply disregard all of them. Members of the Church may attempt further teaching or persuasion, if such a person wishes to listen to them, and doubtless some Catholics will pray for him. To say that such activity on the part of any organization or individual in the Catholic Church is on a par with what happens under

Communist governments to those who openly disagree with, and attack, such governments is an irresponsible statement for any scholar to write and for any scholarly journal to publish.

5. Mr. Blanshard's erroneous charge that the hierarchy were responsible for the refusal of the Board of Superintendents of the New York City public schools to continue to subscribe to *The Nation* is repeated by three reviewers.

"A" wrote that Mr. Blanshard's articles in *The Nation* "aroused the hierarchy to such indignation that *they succeeded* in having the magazine *suppressed* in certain cities." (Italics mine.) This charge is without foundation in fact. Neither Mr. Blanshard nor "A" cites a single item of evidence to back it up. The Catholic hierarchy did not attempt to do anything to *The Nation,* and *The Nation* was not suppressed (see Chapter 8).

"C" repeats the misstatement about the *banning* of *The Nation* under "Catholic pressure." The Nation was not banned. Only subscriptions were not renewed. There was *no* Catholic pressure—not even a request or suggestion according to Superintendent Jansen and the Associate Superintendents (see Ch. 8).

"I" repeats the false statement, officially disproved a number of times before his article appeared, that the action of the New York public school authorities in not resubscribing to *The Nation* was "hierarchy sponsored action." His allusion to that as a "freedom-of-the-press fracas" is inaccurate reporting, since the so-called "fracas" concerned only the freedom of subscribers to decline to resubscribe. There were no problems of freedom of the press in any way involved in that action (see my Chapter 8).

The further reference to the Church or the hierarchy as "a power that could so effectively cow a great city's board of education and gag the American press" has three inaccuracies in it: (1) The action was not due to the power of the hierarchy. (2) The action was not taken by the city board of education, but by the professional educators on the Board of Superintendents. (3) No press was in any way gagged.

6. Mr. Blanshard's scholarship, documentation, and use of "authoritative Catholic sources" have been praised in superlatives by many enthusiastic promoters. Any reader who has in mind the facts I have

given in the three chapters immediately preceding this one should have no difficulty in assessing the workmanship as scholars of the seven distinguished commentators quoted below:

"F" wrote: "Mr. Blanshard has done a difficult and necessary piece of work with exemplary scholarship, good judgment, and tact."

"J" called Mr. Blanshard's work "accurate, sound in argument, objective in spirit—an outstanding piece of work, if ever I saw one."

"G" called it "the most penetrating analysis of the enormous power exercised by the Roman Church that has appeared in our time. . . . The documentation, mostly from Catholic authorities, makes his case invulnerable."

"E" speaks of "careful documentation largely from Catholic sources, a calm but razor-keen analysis."

"D" credits Mr. Blanshard with "scrupulous documentation."

"C" tells his readers that the book was "written by a scholar with precise documentation of every statement, and written with patent aim to be fair."

As already shown the book contains numerous charges to which no supporting footnotes are attached. The worst attacks on Catholic Americans and their religion have no documentation of any kind (see Chapters 12, 13, and 14, particularly pp. 195–196).

"B" is also impressed by Mr. Blanshard's "most precise documentation from Catholic sources . . . his quotations from authoritative Catholic sources." If all that any Catholic has ever happened to write is to be accepted as fundamental Catholic doctrine, then anyone can prove any charge he wishes to make against the Catholic Church without the slightest difficulty. This is simply another application of the preposterous notion that whenever a Catholic writes or says anything, particularly if it carries an *Imprimatur,*[3] the result must be *authoritative Catholic doctrine.* This makes it necessary for every Catholic to believe everything in innumerable contradictory, but "authentic," documents representing every shade in the whole spectrum of political, economic, and social opinion.

7. Mr. Blanshard's assertion that he is not attacking the Catholic

---

[3] For Mr. Blanshard's misuse of the *Imprimatur,* unnoticed by any of these ten reviewers, see pp. 195–196.

religion or the Catholic people is followed by direct and detailed attack on both (see Chapter 16). A surprising number of his endorsers failed to notice this discrepancy, or at least failed to remark upon this particular lapse on the part of Mr. Blanshard. His reviewers praise his objectivity, fairness, lack of bias, and the "rigid tests for accuracy" that were applied to the manuscript.

"I" says that "the manuscript was wisely put to the most rigid tests for accuracy." That the book approaches accuracy, or exhibits any competent attempt to prove its most bitter attacks, cannot be honestly held by anyone who reads the book with an intention to "test for accuracy" (see my Chapter 12).

"H" writes "Any reader who got as far as page 6 would have learned [*sic*] that 'It is not a book about the Catholic faith but about the cultural, political and economic policies of the rulers of the Catholic Church.' "

"E" joins "H" in accepting in simple faith the pretense and the advertisement, even though these are in direct conflict with the contents of the volume. He says: "A prologue makes crystal clear to all fair-minded readers that Mr. Blanshard . . . is not attacking Catholic people, or Catholicism as private faith and ritual. To this pledge he adheres with remarkable consistency." If he read beyond the prologue, whom and what did he think Mr. Blanshard was attacking? Are not Catholic bishops, priests, nuns, and laymen *people?* And are not the sacrament of penance, the sacrament of marriage, the Catholic doctrines of transubstantiation, prayers for the dead, the intercession of the saints, aspects of the *Catholic religion?* The extent to which these commentators believe in, or approve of, these or other doctrines of the Catholic religion are their affair, not mine. However, Mr. Blanshard's pretense that he is not attacking his Catholic fellow citizens and their religion, followed by some three hundred pages containing inadequately documented, unproved attack should be recognized by reviewers as just that (see especially my Chapters 3, 6, 12, and 13).

"I" writes that Mr. Blanshard's book is "a scholarly and well-documented examination into Roman Catholic policy as it applies to the freedoms in which we all, Catholic and non-Catholic alike, have a precious stake." "It is not a slashing attack on the Catholic faith, nor on the Catholics as a people." Mr. Blanshard's pretense of admiration for Catholic *people* is echoed again in the next sentence. "If it were we would join its detractors, for we have too much admiration for the sincerity and devotion of too many fine Catholic friends to wish to see their religion ridiculed." This reviewer's "fine Catholic friends," if they read the book, read a great deal of ridicule of their religion and necessarily found that in it they themselves, and every other Catholic in America, is held up to ridicule.

In the same vein "I" writes: "the facts of Blanshard's life prove him neither an irresponsible scholar nor a 'Catholic-baiter.'" The facts of Blanshard's life are irrelevant. The facts of a man's life are nowhere accepted by reasonable people to prove that he did not commit any offense which ample and unquestionable evidence shows he did actually commit.

It is probably unnecessary to give any extended discussion of Catholic opinion of Mr. Blanshard's book. It is almost unanimously and completely adverse. A number of Catholic commentators have made the sound observation that a scholarly, factual, unbiased discussion of Catholic affairs by a non-Catholic might do a great deal of good. Regret has been expressed that Mr. Blanshard's book is not of this sort, and that his inaccuracy and bias have made ineffective those of his observations which have some basis in fact.

In the light of Mr. Blanshard's inaccuracies about Catholic doctrine in relation to Protestants and Jews, it seems worth while to show some of the important instances in which members of these two groups do not agree with him. This disagreement is much more general, of course, than the reviews mentioned below demonstrate. Most Protestant and Jewish leaders have not endorsed Mr. Blanshard's book or joined in any way in the current attempt to stir up religious animosity in America. After all, fortunate for America and for American Catholics, most such leaders know more about the ancient Church and their Catholic neighbors than Mr. Blanshard gives evidence of.

I do not wish to be interpreted as endorsing all the comments in the unfavorable reviews by non-Catholics. Obviously no reviewer of a current book should be expected to check the accuracy, the validity, and the sufficiency of all footnotes. Nor should one expect non-Catholic reviewers to catch *all* the misstatements and misinterpretations concerning Catholicism in Mr. Blanshard's text. However, some non-Catholic reviewers were well informed on Catholic doctrine and practice or else did some careful checking.

In discussing the *Times'* attitude toward the Blanshard book, Managing Editor Edwin L. James says: "it was regarded by our daily book review editor as being excessively contentious, quite unfair in its criticism of the Roman Catholic Church, and with no large literary merit. So he decided not to review it." As for the advertising problem, Mr. James says that "the advertising department took an analogous position, and on the grounds that the book constituted a biased attack on the rites, customs and teachings of a religion with millions of adherents in the United States, the advertisement of the book was rejected, as would have been a comparable attack on any religion." [4]

One of the most penetrating reviews of the Blanshard book is that of Mr. Will Herberg in *Commentary*.[5] Mr. Herberg wrote:

> For Mr. Blanshard's work . . . is permeated with anti-Catholic bias and is vitiated by a secularist-statist philosophy that, in this reviewer's opinion at least, is far more dangerous than anything in American Catholicism to which the book calls attention.
>
> The anti-Catholic bias, despite repeated and no doubt sincere disavowals, is pervasive and often quite offensive. What is it but vulgar anti-Catholicism to sneer "at the whole segregated system of nuns, wimples and convents" as "medieval posturing and useless mortifications (page 287)? What is it but vulgar anti-Catholicism to ridicule the very names of Catholic religious institutions—"The Sisters of Our Lady of Charity of the Good Shepherd" is Mr. Blanshard's prize exhibit—as reflecting "a medieval attitude of piety and feminine subordination" somehow incompatible with the robust spirit of American democracy? . . . But our confidence in his findings and, above all, in his conclusions is greatly shaken by a certain feeling that the author is not quite candid with us, or perhaps, for that matter, with himself. There

[4] The review in the *New York Times Book Reviews,* Sunday, May 9, 1949, was written by Mr. John W. Chase, a Catholic and a frequent reviewer for the *Times.* Any reader will find it a restrained and temperate review, containing no hint as to the writer's religion.

[5] *Commentary* (New York: American Jewish Committee, August 1949), pp. 198–200.

is an air of such calculated special pleading, of such arguing for effect rather than for the balanced truth, that it is really difficult to know how far one may safely follow Mr. Blanshard in his indictment of the Catholic Church.

. . . He repeats (page 299) the familiar charge that Catholics hold that "non-Catholics who deliberately reject Catholicism are headed for Hell," when he is aware or ought to be aware that the phrase "deliberately reject" is officially understood in such a way as not to mean this at all [see pp. 202–203]. He goes into great detail (Chapter 11) describing the Vatican's rapprochement with the fascist regimes of Italy and Spain but has not a word to say about the same Vatican's impressive efforts on behalf of the Jews during the Hitler terror.

Mr. Blanshard does not hesitate (page 301) to call the Catholic Church anti-Semitic on the ground that "The hierarchy teaches Catholic children (1) that they should not marry Jews; (2) that they should not go to school with Jews in a neutral atmosphere; and (3) that they must not read any Jewish literature that states the case for Jewish as against Catholic faith," [on this see pp. 251–252] without suggesting that these same tests, particularly the first, would expose most believing Jews and very many believing Protestants to condemnation as bigoted anti-Catholics. The last point, by the way, is a good example of Mr. Blanshard's method. He knows—indeed, he points out—that the Catholic ban on intermarriage, secular education, and reading anti-Catholic literature is not in any way directed against the Jews but is quite general in its application. He is not content, however, to criticize such a policy for what it is; he must pretend it is anti-Semitism . . .

Mr. Blanshard's prejudices make it impossible for him to appreciate the deep concern that many religious people feel about an allegedly "neutral" school system that in fact indoctrinates the child and young person with an outlook on life in which man is held to be sufficient unto himself and God is treated as an outmoded irrelevance. This secularism, linked to an exaltation of the "social-welfare state" as an omnicompetent agency for the total control of social life, prevents Mr. Blanshard from understanding how people may seriously insist that since social, family, and educational problems are at bottom moral, they cannot be separated from one's religious faith, and if that faith is institutionalized in that form, from one's church.

His perfervid nationalism and statism make it hard for him to grasp how any person genuinely devoted to democracy can nevertheless contend that there is a higher law in the name of which the dictates of the state may be disallowed if these dictates are felt to come into conflict with obedience to God. Mr. Blanshard excoriates (pages 52–53) the Catholics for affirming that they would disobey a law outlawing parochial schools and compelling parents to send their children to the public schools. He thinks such an attitude outrageously undemocratic and a menace to American freedom. To me, on the contrary, this attitude seems not only intelligible but thoroughly in line with the best of democratic tradition, which has always rejected the pretensions of the state to a monopoly of social and cultural life.

Mr. Herberg's review was criticized in a letter to *Commentary* which was later answered by Mr. Herberg in a letter [6] containing some passages which merit wide circulation.

Mr. Blanshard's book does display vulgar anti-Catholicism on almost every page.

To me bigotry is bigotry whether directed against Catholics or against Jews.

The Catholic doctrine of salvation may or may not be as liberal as Rabbi Baeck's, but it is emphatically not what Mr. Blanshard in his book suggests it is. Nor is it particularly "complicated." Even if it were "complicated," it would have been Mr. Blanshard's obvious duty to find his way through the complications before using it in his indictment of the Church. He need not have gone to recondite treatises of theology or canon law. He could, for example, have consulted such popular but fully authoritative handbooks as *The Faith of Millions,* by the Rev. John A. O'Brien, which has sold in the hundreds of thousands, and he would have found (pages 55–56) that only those are condemned "who are convinced of the truth of the Catholic Church but for some selfish reason fail to profess their faith in her."

However great may be the merits of the public school system, American democracy does not grant it a monopoly of education. On the contrary, American democracy recognizes the right of parents to send their children to private or parochial schools or even to educate them at home, provided the level of teaching meets certain standards. To deny this right would be totalitarian statism and would justify defiance in the name of the "higher law." When Catholics say this, they are right, and when Blanshard attacks them for saying it, he simply reveals the totalitarian and statist strain in his own thinking.

Mr. T. Robert Ingram, a former newspaperman and naval officer who served in the assaults on Palau and Okinawa and who is now studying at the Episcopal Theological School in Cambridge, published a discussion of Mr. Blanshard's book in *The Atlantic Monthly* (February, 1950) from which I quote:

[6] *Commentary, op. cit.,* March, 1950.

For all his impressive "documentation," Blanshard does not help to clarify the issue, but seems rather to confound confusion.

. . . Blanshard takes issue with the Roman Catholic Church on the crucial point for all of us: he judges that church to be a sinister threat to the public weal because it "refuses to admit that the Church in the social field is simply one agency within the state." . . . All Christian profession, whether Protestant or Catholic, explicitly declares that the church derives its existence and its authority directly from God in Christ, and that it never can bow to the supremacy of the state and still be a Christian.

The four Evangelists went to great pains to write in ways that would leave no doubt upon this point. The Gospel writers profoundly believed that the church is *not* simply one agency within the state, but that it has an authority above the state. The church has so believed ever since. What Blanshard seems to be unable to comprehend is that both Roman Catholics and Protestants accept the Christian view with all the assurance of truth evident in the secularist religion, and with equal if not greater, experience and reasoning power, and certainly with as much integrity and candor. . . . American dissenters who colonized and founded this country were in dissent at home, not against Rome, but against churches established, maintained, and supported by the force of law in their own countries. Exactly the same point is at issue today in Czechoslovakia where the Communist government is attempting to form a church that will acknowledge subservience to the state. It was the quarrel in Hungary, involving Lutheran Bishop Ordass as well as Cardinal Mindzenty, and was the story of German Christians under Adolf Hitler.

In the same number, Mr. Blanshard publishes a reply to Mr. Ingram which does not answer Mr. Ingram's argument, but defends his book largely by repeating positions which he took in the book. "With the help of some of the world's finest and most generous scholars, I loaded down every charge against Catholic policy with detailed documentation out of the mouths of Catholic authorities themselves . . . not about the Catholic faith" (see Ch. 12). He remarks that Mr. Ingram "does not try to deny that the Roman Catholic Church is a complete dictatorship." Any modern who knows what "a complete dictatorship" does to the lives of people within the horizons of its power knows already that the Catholic Church is not a complete dictatorship, and anyone who examined Mr. Blanshard's book with care knows that he in no way establishes anything of the sort. He testifies: "I favor a democratic state against an authoritarian church because I do not like *governments operated by terror* [italics mine] military or theological."

Mr. Blanshard repeats: ". . . there is no disposition to question the moral worth or patriotic loyalty of the American Catholic people or their rank-and-file priests and nuns." How completely his book belies this protest, I have shown by accurate quotations (see Chs. 3–12–13). He observes with accuracy that "the Roman Catholic Church . . . in the United States is not an American Church." True, but neither is Protestantism nor Judaism. In fact, the American people have many aspects of cultural and spiritual life which are somewhat older than the United States of America. Importation of ideas even in the realms of religion and philosophy from distant lands and times has never been frowned upon by most Americans who can read and write.

Mr. Blanshard here again ascribes to the "censorship" of the Catholic hierarchy his difficulty in getting his book published: "Politicians and publishers are usually so amenable to Catholic pressure that no overt threats are necessary. Several of the ten publishers who rejected *American Freedom and Catholic Power* admitted quite frankly that the real reason for the rejection was that they feared Catholic reprisals, but I do not believe that one of them was approached or threatened directly by any agent of the hierarchy." Notice the closing statement. If politicians and publishers improperly follow imagined threats which are not expressed, Mr. Blanshard should attack politicians and publishers, not members of the hierarchy. If he doesn't *assume* that the publishers declined his book through fear of reprisals, rather than its extreme bias and inaccuracy of factual statement and interpretation, he should present some evidence.

Mr. Blanshard reports here that only seven out of one hundred fifty daily newspapers published a review of his book. He assumes that they were afraid.[7] He says that only seven of them "ventured" to touch it.

---

[7] I was surprised and disappointed that a number of newspapers and magazines did not review my last book (*Religion and Education Under the Constitution*). I do not know why. They were free to do as they pleased. I should not feel free to *assume* a derogatory reason and publish it. There would be no free press if they were not free to review (or to refuse to review) any book for any reason, or for none. J.M.O'N.

How does he know that *fear* was responsible? If he knows, why not give his readers the evidence? Editors often omit things which writers would like to have published. To most Americans, I believe this is an indication of the freedom of the press rather than "censorship by suppression."

Under the heading "censorship by vilification" he writes: "Any person in public life who directly criticizes Catholic policy as stupid or reactionary is vilified by the hierarchy [*sic*] as 'anti-Catholic' or 'bigoted' . . ." In other words, Catholics may be properly called "stupid" and "reactionary," but if so, it is vilification for them to answer back by using such words as "anti-Catholic" and "bigoted." I wonder what kind of censorship Mr. Blanshard would like which would permit such epithets being directed against Catholics, but would prohibit such answers.

Professor D. W. Brogan, of Cambridge University (who described himself as "an agnostic, brought up as a Catholic in Scotland, where I attended both Catholic and Protestant schools"), has commented at some length on Mr. Blanshard's book.[8] Perhaps his best summarizing sentence is this: "Thus in Paul Blanshard's book, a great deal of his argument for changing American Catholicism is simply a plea for resuming the Reformation, for converting the benighted Catholics from their superstitions."

Professor Brogan gives an interesting explanation of the fear of "Catholic power"—when it is sincere even though not well founded. It is due, he says, to

> . . . a great over-estimation of the power of the American Catholic clergy . . . and to a grossly exaggerated fear of Catholic clerical power among politicians and among hostile and, sometimes, envious Protestant ministers. It is easy to see why this mistake is made. The politicians or the minister sees crowds pouring into the local Catholic Church, crowds going to a series of "services" on a Sunday morning when the ministers of the community are each fighting an often losing battle with the attractions of golf or the inertia bred by a hangover. If the Catholic Church were a Protestant Church, such crowds would be proof positive of the personal weight and power of attrac-

[8] "The Catholic Church in America," *Harper's Magazine,* May, 1950, pp. 40–50.

tion of the minister. Sometimes that attraction is much to the credit of the minister and the congregation: sometimes as in, say, Fort Worth, Los Angeles, and Minneapolis in fairly recent times, it was to nobody's credit—from a "liberal" point of view. The Protestant church may be full because the minister is Harry Emerson Fosdick; it may be full because he is Elmer Gantry. But the Catholic Church may be, and usually is, full because it is the only Catholic Church in a defined territory and its crowds prove no more about the abilities, the character, or the popularity of the parish priest than do crowds in a post office, . . .

Look, for example, at the controversy over banning the *Nation* because of Mr. Blanshard's articles. . . . The *Nation* has not been suppressed; . . . But the New York school authorities decided that the taxpayer's money should not be used in circulating a magazine which so deeply offended the parents of so many tens of thousands of school children and, of course, so many hundreds of thousands of voters.

In commenting on Mr. Blanshard's discussion of abortion, Professor Brogan reaches the basis of Mr. Blanshard's moral philosophy,—"statistical morality."

One could go on; one could recall the notorious fact that many abortions are performed to save trouble, not life, that one of the makers of the modern liberal mind defended infanticide, the killing of fully delivered children whose presence embarrassed their (unmarried) mothers. . . . They [Catholics] agree with Cardinal Newman that it is not "a slight benefit to know what is needed for the proof of a point, what is wanting in a theory, how a theory hangs together, and what will follow if it be admitted." There's the rub, what could follow might be Auschwitz, the extermination of Jews and Gypsies. And on the principle of what may be called statistical morality; if that is what the majority wants, it is all right. If it isn't, again, why not?

Professor Brogan makes a good point when he says: "Catholics in America have to take the rap for bigotry or folly in Spain or Latin America, while northern Protestants need accept no responsibility for southern serpent handlers, or American Protestants in general for the latest news of barbaric race pride plus vaunting Protestant orthodoxy in South Africa."

While I agree that Dr. Brogan's point here is well taken, I believe also that American Catholics have to take this particular "rap" to a large extent through their own fault; and that on two counts. First, many (both clergy and laymen) who disapprove of the conditions in Spain and in Latin America do not say so often enough or loud enough. Nor do they say often enough and loud enough how bad are the restrictions *imposed upon the Catholic Church* in some, if not all, of these countries. Second, enough of them do not proclaim and protest what I know they understand and believe, concerning why, when, how, and how much weak Catholic bishops were responsible for the development of the disapproved conditions. However, granting all of this, no one who has made a reasonable (not to say a "scholarly") investigation of the situation in Spain and Latin America is justified in saying that these conditions are the natural or necessary result of *Catholic doctrine* concerning the relations of government and religion, or that the reproduction of them in the United States is any part of the hopes or plans of the American hierarchy, or other American Catholics.

Dr. Brogan might have added that neither Mr. Blanshard nor his enthusiastic endorsers have so much as mentioned the fact that American Protestants take no responsibility for, or even protest against, the restrictions on Catholics in such countries as Sweden. They are the essential parallels of those which the government of Spain imposes on Protestants (see pp. 80–82).

Finally, Professor Brogan writes: "I have said that Mr. Blanshard makes some valid points. I think, for example, that it is scandalous (as far as it is true) that Catholic nurses should be encouraged to dodge their duty of getting patients the religious comfort they want. If a Catholic nurse is to behave in this way, she has no more place in a public tax-supported hospital system than a zealous Quaker has in West Point." It is not true that Catholic nurses should as a matter of doctrine act this way. But in so far as, and wherever, it is true, I agree that it is scandalous. And I agree with the addition that I would say such a nurse has no place in any hospital or at the bedside of any sick person in a hospital or elsewhere. And I have distinguished backing.[9]

A long and thoughtful discussion of the Blanshard book was written

---

[9] Rev. Francis J. Connell, C.S.S.R., Professor of Moral Theology in the Catholic University of America, in a letter dated Jan. 12, 1951, and in conversation Feb. 2, 1951.

by Mr. David Rome,[10] press officer of the Canadian Jewish Congress and editor of *The Congress Bulletin*. Mr. Rome puts his finger on Mr. Blanshard's worst offenses with admirable precision.

This [Mr. Blanshard's] emphasis upon the majority and its state is a frightening one to any democrat today. For one thing, it is not at all a libertarian concept and this is a period when liberty should be cherished more than ever. Indeed it is distinctly totalitarian and the only equality inherent in such a point of view is the equal flatness in the track of steamroller. Mr. Blanshard's concept of democracy in this phase is a "democracy" that finds some ninety percent support in every vote taken behind the Iron Curtain. It fits poorly into a defence of American democracy and sounds unpleasant in the ear of a Jew.

By the same token a Jew finds it queer to hear of the imputation of Catholic disloyalty because American Catholics contribute to the support of the Vatican and its works or because they find a spiritual leadership outside the boundaries of the U. S. . . .

Mr. Blanshard claims to be honestly engaged in an objective search for the truth. He denies any anti-Catholic motivation or a desire to arouse anti-Catholic sentiments. Whatever his intentions he has scored at least a stylistic failure in this regard for the book is written in an anti-Catholic tone. His facts are marshalled with an effect to arouse anti-Catholic feelings and even prejudice. . . .

Mr. Blanshard *confuses documentation with validity*[11] and exercises his scepticism all too seldom when he has a juicy paragraph to quote.

Concerning Mr. Blanshard's pretense, stated in various places, of his admiration for the Catholic laity, coupled with his extreme denunciation of the priests and bishops, Mr. Rome remarks with a good deal of insight:

In the case of the argument on Catholics this appeal to the rank and file is even more fallacious from the very definition of the terms. The Church is by its very constitution and philosophy an authoritarian institution. Its constitution is basic to the creed. It is not a body governed by its communicants or preaching a truth arrived at by a consensus of opinion. To appeal to Catholics to change their leaders or their mode of church government is, in effect, to ask them to leave the church and to abjure their religious principles.

---

10 *The Congress Bulletin:* Canadian Jewish Congress, Montreal, July, 1949.

11 Italics mine. This is the most complete, compact, and accurate evaluation of Mr. Blanshard's book that I have found.

What, then, is wanted of the individual Catholic and of the growing Catholic church in this country and on this continent? Are they being asked to renounce their rights and influences in the state or to confine them to certain areas of social action? If they are, the appeal must necessarily be in vain. But even more, it is an undemocratic appeal, for democracy must have all its citizens exercise their franchise on all questions.

To be concrete, Catholics are a majority in the province of Quebec and nearly a majority in Canada. The Church has a distinct interest in many political and social questions and has certain views on questions of democracy. Does anyone expect that these will be laid aside because Canadian democrats of Mr. Blanshard's denomination do not share the Catholic views? Why is anyone surprised that the church is powerful in a country where it has so many loyal communicants?

Further Mr. Rome notices that Mr. Blanshard has made his case

. . . by bringing together all the evidence which strengthens such a case and omitting all the facts which point in a contrary direction. He has cited all the zealous and fanatical statements and rulings and omitted all the milder, more restrained and better balanced statements and practices. The result is not a judgment but a case for the prosecution.

To question the Catholics' right of organization and propaganda when all other groups are encouraged to interest themselves in public affairs and to urge their views on legislator and president is to weaken democracy, for it is to suggest that democracy as a form of society is closed to persons of a certain creed, that there is no room for Catholics in a democracy. This is a serious limitation upon the democratic definition which Mr. Blanshard as a democrat should be slow to accept.

Dr. Henry Sloane Coffin [12] recognized Mr. Blanshard's limited grasp of genuine democracy and his preference for the omnipotent state—which is totalitarianism.

Dr. Blanshard gives the appearance of an undiluted secularist, with a naive faith in the moral impeccability of the "social welfare state." He seems ready and eager to hand over all education from the kindergarten through the university entirely to the State. He ignores, or by inference condemns, the many schools and colleges founded and maintained under Christian auspices, which continue with more or less devotion to educate in a Christian atmosphere and to furnish courses in Christian convictions and morals. His

[12] *Op. cit.*, footnote 1.

denunciation of the supra-national character of the Church of Rome would logically include the ecumenical church for which Protestants and Orthodox pray and labor.

He does not face the fact that Christian faith in man, in truth, and in the world as God's world lies at the root of our American freedoms, nor does he seem to see that without the maintenance in vigor of that faith and the saturation of our education with it, our freedoms will fade and die. He does not appear to recognize the spiritual limitations of a social welfare state, which in itself may readily become barrenly secular.

16

BLANSHARD'S ATTACK ON RELIGION

MR. BLANSHARD claims (pp. 3, 6) that his book does not attack the Catholic religion. The claim is false. The various passages that demonstrate the untruth of this statement also exemplify Mr. Blanshard's failure in scholarship. He not only attacks Catholicism *as religion;* he attacks it by *ridicule*—not in terms of scholarly discussion in what he says is his subject: "the arena of controversial social policy" (p. 3).

Here are some samples [1] of Mr. Blanshard's expressions concerning Catholicism as religion in America:

> In a sense the survivals of magic in the Catholic system give the priest an enormous advantage over his Protestant and Jewish confreres in controlling a congregation [p. 38].
>
> The Catholic priest is also armed with several special and effective devices of control over his people [p. 35].
>
> He blesses certain articles, and thereupon they take on some of the mysterious qualities of a primitive charm [p. 36].
>
> To a certain extent the priests are victims of the medievalism of their own Church, imprisoned by ancient beliefs and forced into the role of a "good" magician [p. 36].
>
> . . . there is no doubt that the ceremonial accompaniments of prayer and indulgences are paid for in cash at standard prices, and sometimes at competitive prices [p. 36].

[1] It is impossible to include in one chapter all of Mr. Blanshard's direct attacks and insinuations against Catholicism as religion. Some of them are more naturally treated in sections dealing with other specific subject matter. See particularly Chaps. 10, 11, and 13.

The Blanshard treatment of the Catholic confessional (pp. 38–39) perhaps throws the most doubt on both his claim of not attacking religion and his standing as a scholar. The following passage, it will be noticed, is composed almost exclusively of insulting assumptions and sweeping assertions, without one footnote to back them up. It has literally no documentation or evidence.

> Most important of the devices of priestly control is that of the confessional. Every good Catholic is supposed to kneel down at least once a year before the dark screen in the Church where, in a confession box, a priest is posted unseen to hear him confess his innermost thoughts. Particularly when the penitent is a woman, her mind in the process of unburdening her regrets and worries is delivered, so to speak, wide open to the priest. The joy of release for pent-up emotion and the comfort of communion are mingled with personal submission and the yearning of the grown-up child for a substitute father.
>
> The priest is trained to supply promptly a definite answer for every situation, a Catholic formula approved by the Holy See and given out as the law. The latest devotional manuals even tell the priest precisely how to take a confession in an airplane. As we shall see in our chapters on medical and sexual matters, the young celibate priest has only one Catholic answer for the mature married woman inquiring about birth control, or for the experienced surgeon on therapeutic abortion. In each case the priest delivers the answer confidently, declaring that he speaks the word of God in the field of religion and morals.
>
> Is it surprising that, with such a perfect instrument for the control of conduct, the priest does not hesitate to extend the directive power of the confessional into the regions of politics, sociology and economics? Who would resist the temptation to mold character at its most malleable moment, when a consciousness of imperfection makes the mind receptive to priestly guidance? At any rate, the record shows that in many parts of the world the confessional is used not only to keep Catholic girls pure and Catholic boys honest but also to defeat British control in Malta, birth control reform in Massachusetts and democratic government in Spain. The priests would be more than human if they did not use this remarkable instrument for the attainment of the *whole* Catholic program. And the whole Catholic program, as we shall see in our next chapter, is almost as much political as spiritual [p. 39].

There is only one sentence in these paragraphs that any informed person could accept as possibly true—the one about confession in an airplane. That *may* be true. However, what the "devotional manuals" are is not clear, and there is no reference to the source of this information.

All the following phrases are biased, untruthful, impossible to reconcile with scholarly discussion: "devices of priestly control," the penitent confessing his "innermost thoughts" (instead of his sins), "a woman, her mind . . . delivered wide-open to the priest," "pent-up emotion," "personal submission," "grown-up child," "substitute father," "a woman unburdening her regrets and worries." These are useful only to stir the unintelligent, antagonistic reactions of the previously uninformed, and now misinformed, reader toward a purely religious aspect of the life of some of his neighbors. What possible relation this has to "facts that every American should know" (p. 6), Mr. Blanshard makes no attempt to reveal.

Following out the idea of the "controlling" of Catholics by the priests through the confessional, Mr. Blanshard informs his readers that the priest has a definite answer *for every situation.* Even a moderately well-trained Catholic child would know that such a statement has no reference to the teaching of the Church, or the experience of the penitent in the Catholic confessional.

We also find in the references to "the celibate priest" and "the experienced surgeon" an idea that is repeated elsewhere in Mr. Blanshard's book (pp. 132 ff.) to the effect that the answer to *theological* or *moral* questions can properly be found in sexual experience, the biological laboratory, or the surgical clinic. He clearly indicates, here as elsewhere, that he believes that adequate answers to certain *theological* and *moral* questions are dependent in large part on the *sexual experience* of the answerer.

The question with which Mr. Blanshard opens the third paragraph on page 39, quoted above, is a good example of his rhetorical method, which avoids either direct statement or evidence. He gives his readers the impression that it is an unquestioned fact, beyond doubt, or is generally known, that the priest uses the confessional as an instrument to control the conduct of Catholics, in politics, sociology, and economics.

He gives no evidence. He has no evidence. There is no evidence *possible,* that this is normal, common, or even *permissible,* use of the confessional. Obviously, no one could surely say that there has never been an instance in which a priest has tried this sort of thing. It is impossible to prove a universal negative.

No informed person, Catholic or non-Catholic, questions the fact that there have been unworthy and incompetent priests in the Catholic Church, or unworthy and incompetent ministers, rabbis, college presidents, and plumbers. However, any even poorly trained Catholic, or moderately informed non-Catholic, could hardly help knowing that any *control* through the confessional of the citizen's voting or free decision in politics, sociology, or economics is wholly contrary to Catholic doctrine and authorized practice, and *impossible* in America or any other free society with a secret ballot.

Mr. Blanshard seems unable to understand how a priest in the confessional could be interested in a soul's salvation and not in politics, sociology, and economics. "Who could resist the temptation to do these things?" he asks.

Probably the peak of the outrage in this false discussion of the confessional is his statement that "*the record* [*sic*] shows that in many parts of the world the confessional is used . . . to defeat British control in Malta, birth control reform in Massachusetts and democratic government in Spain." Mr. Blanshard avoids saying what record he refers to. He knows of no record; there is no record; in the very nature of things there cannot *possibly* be any record. Even if the confessional had in some isolated instances been so misused, there could be no *possible* way of having any record of it.

No Catholic priest who had any respect for his training and his vows (or who wished to remain a Catholic priest for another week) could possibly divulge any *record* of what went on in his confessional.

Probably no Catholic penitent that Mr. Blanshard ever heard of has ever repeated to anyone, much less made a public record of, his conversation in the confessional. Further, the *political* questions concerning the government of Malta, legislation in Massachusetts, and the form of government in Spain are not questions that are covered by Catholic doctrine. If the priest and the penitent both knew how to act in a confessional, such matters would never be mentioned. Clearly such questions would normally be settled by votes in the ballot box. Even if settled by open voting in the legislature, there could be no *possible* way of anyone's knowing that any vote was the result of experience in the Catholic confessional. No Catholic who understood the teaching of the Church would mention in the confessional his vote on any such question. If he were asked about how he voted, or intended to vote, on such a question, he would know that something was wrong.

There is probably no other relationship known among men that is so absolutely confidential as that of the confessor and the penitent in the Catholic Church. The Church punishes *direct* violation of the "seal of confession" with her most severe penalty. "The confessor who *presumes directly* to violate the seal of sacramental confession incurs *excommunication ipso facto. . . .*"[2] "Direct violation" occurs when a confessor makes known "the sin and the sinner" to another person, even without divulging that his information was obtained in the confessional. "Indirect violation" probably more completely reveals than does "direct violation" the length to which the Church goes to protect the seal of the confessional. Indirect violation is that in which there is *danger* that the sin and the sinner *may be known* from the confessor's words or actions—his behavior in the presence of the penitent. This is a serious offense and may be severely punished, but the punishment is not automatic. Furthermore, confessors everywhere are instructed "to avoid imprudent references to matters learned in confession, even when there is no danger that any particular person will suffer."

In addition to all the above, the seal of the confessional is respected in the courts of civilized countries. If some unwise or poorly trained judge should instruct a Catholic priest to break his vow by violating the seal of the confessional in court, he would almost inevitably receive a flat refusal regardless of the consequences. And Mr. Blanshard is free to make what treason or disloyalty he can out of this.

In spite of all these guarantees that *no one* except the penitent and the priest will ever know what took place, Mr. Blanshard pretends that "the record [*sic*] shows that in many parts of the world the con-

[2] Lydon, P. J., *Ready Answers in Canon Law* (New York: Benziger Brothers, 1934), p. 473.

fessional is used" in political controversies. A better example of an attack on *religion* and of the antithesis of "unbiased scholarship" could scarcely be found.

In this passage Mr. Blanshard exhibits his almost total misconception of the purpose, teaching, spirit, and atmosphere of the Catholic Church. This misconception is unpardonable in any person living in the midst of millions of Catholic fellow citizens and pretending to write a scholarly, "factually impregnable" book (p. 7) about the beliefs and practices of American Catholics. He assumes that this outrageous and wholly improper use of the Catholic confessional (which he may conceivably have taken from some such source as *The Converted Catholics* or *The Menace*) is a natural and inevitable result of the doctrine of the sacrament of penance, and that it *must be used* for the attainment of the *whole Catholic program.*

The confessional has nothing whatever to do with any part of "the Catholic program" (either the true Catholic program or Mr. Blanshard's nightmare), except the sins and the reformation of the individual penitent.

One of the clear possibilities of some passages in his book is that it may contribute to bad feeling between Catholics and Jews. That this has not been the result is shown in some reviews in outstanding Jewish publications (see pp. 235–244). In his discussion of mixed marriages (pp. 162–163), Mr. Blanshard twists a rule concerning "nonbaptized persons" to direct it "against Jews." If he had said marriage with a person who is not "a validly baptized Christian," this would have taken some of the sting out of it. Altering it as he does conveys the impression that the Catholic Church is particularly hostile and intolerant toward Jews. He writes: "The impediment to marriage between a Catholic and a Jew is called an 'annulling impediment,' whereas the impediment to marriage with a Protestant is only a 'prohibitory impediment.' " What he should have said, if he were talking the language of the accurate scholar, is that the impediment to a marriage between a Catholic and *any non-Christian* is an annulling impediment, whereas the impediment to marriage with *a non-Catholic who is a Christian* is a prohibitory impediment. In other words the Catholic Church makes a distinction among non-Catholics between

Christians and non-Christians. This is a distinction which, I think, anyone should expect the Church to make.[3]

Mr. Blanshard (p. 301) proclaims "the basic anti-Semitism of priestly doctrine," "Catholic anti-Semitism," and "the fundamental fact of the clergy's anti-Semitism." He reports that "the hierarchy teaches Catholic children" not to marry Jews, not to go to school with Jews, and not to read certain "Jewish literature." By way of an appearance of the externals of scholarship he mentions the numbers of three canons. He does not tell his readers what the canons are about, leaving the simple impression that they express unadulterated anti-Semitism. He does not quote the canons. That would defeat his purpose. The three canons which he misuses on this page deal with marriage, education, and books, in the ordinary terms known to all those who are familiar with the Church's position on these matters, and the word *"Jew"* does not appear in any one of them. The Church's position in these areas is no more anti-Semitic than it is anti-Islamic or anti-Protestant, or than Protestantism and Islam are anti-Catholic. Naturally the Church's position is more antiatheistic in all three instances than anti-Jewish or anti-Protestant. However, Mr. Blanshard could hardly arouse anti-Catholicism by mentioning that the Church is antiatheistic, while anti-Semitism is today an easily inflammable subject.

A Catholic cannot be an anti-Semite without stultifying himself; for a Catholic accepts the Old Testaments as an integral part of divine revelation. He considers the Jewish race as the "chosen people" from which the Redeemer was to come. He recognizes that the Founder of Christianity, His Mother, the Apostles, the early converts, were all Jews.

In 1928 the Holy Office solemnly declared that the Catholic Church "just as it reproves all rancours and conflicts between peoples, particularly condemns hatred of the people once chosen by God, the hatred that commonly goes by the name of anti-Semitism" (Binchy, p. 610). In September 1938, Pius XI told a group of Belgian pilgrims that "The promise made to Abraham and his descendants was realized through Christ, of Whose mystical Body we are the members. Through Christ and in Christ we are Abraham's

[3] See Bouscaren and Ellis, *Canon Law* (Milwaukee: Bruce Publishing Co., 1947), pp. 459 ff.

descendants. No, it is not possible for Christians to take part in anti-Semitism. Spiritually we are Semites."[4]

Mr. Blanshard goes on to say that if the general rule against mixed marriages were strictly enforced "we would have an American community split clean down the middle by religious bigotry" (p. 163). In other words, the open, clear, ancient statements of the Catholic Church concerning the sacrament of marriage, based on what Catholic scholars sincerely believe to be the teaching of Christ, are to Mr. Blanshard a manifestation only of religious *bigotry.* This is hardly the language of an unbiased scholar.

If Mr. Blanshard wishes to discuss the validity of the conditions the Catholic Church lays down for the reception of Catholic sacraments, including the sacrament of marriage, he should study the subject, and probably discuss it with Catholic theologians, and moral philosophers. He should be prepared to react in rational good temper to the explanation that such study and discussion would present to him as the basis of Catholic teaching. Clearly, he should not attempt to discuss the matter in terms of religious bigotry. Had he followed such a program, he would not write such nonsense as that at the bottom of page 173: "they would not be married at all, and the bishop could dissolve their marriage." How or why a bishop would go about dissolving a marriage between people who are "not married at all" is a bit hard to understand. Also he would not talk (p. 164) of the marriage of a Catholic with a non-Catholic as a matter "of low ethical significance." He does not (and could not) give a single example of, or citation to, anything that would indicate that Catholic girls are taught to approach marriage with a non-Catholic as a matter of low ethical significance. Obviously, to receive the Catholic sacrament of marriage, anyone has to meet the conditions of the sacrament. Anyone who is not interested in receiving that sacrament is not pursued and punished by the agents of the Church.

Mr. Blanshard is wrong in saying (p. 164) that Catholics and non-

[4] *London Tablet,* Sept. 24, 1938, "The Catholic Church and Fascism," reprinted in *World Policy Conference Report,* Feb. 15, 1944, p. 8. Published monthly by World Policy Conference, St. Paul, Minn.

Catholics cannot have the wedding ceremony performed in the church. Reading the daily newspapers or making a telephone call would have easily given him information on that point. A great many marriages between Catholics and non-Catholics are performed in Catholic churches.

Throughout his chapter on marriage Blanshard makes sweeping, unsupported assertions for which he has, and can have, no valid evidence: "Non-Catholic men do not carry out the promises as faithfully as women" (p. 165). Perhaps a legitimate guess in regard to the differences in the behavior of men and women in various situations, but in the nature of things, this can be nothing more than a guess. And he doesn't say how faithful that is for either men or women, and of course he doesn't know. "There is a tendency for the mixed family to adopt the religion of the wife or no religion at all." On what evidence? "Catholics, as well as non-Catholics violate the privileges so frequently that the priests are thoroughly alarmed" (p. 165). On what evidence is this frequency and alarm reported? Mr. Blanshard furnishes none. These particular assertions do not have even one of Mr. Blanshard's footnotes attached.

He pays the American people the doubtful compliment of referring to the breaking of solemn pledges as arising from the "fundamental fair-mindedness of the American people," and opposition to the breaking of vows as "the narrowness of priestly practice" (p. 165).

Mr. Blanshard writes: "In practice 'heretic' means Protestant, and 'schismatic' means Greek Catholic. Jews, Moslems and, in general, non-baptized persons *exist on a special tertiary level*" (p. 162). This is neither accurate nor unbiased. One can almost imagine the Jews and Moslems (as Mr. Blanshard saw them) condemned by the Church to live on the lower levels of subterranean caves. This phrase helps him on with his attempt to show especial intolerance of the Catholic Church toward Jews. He does not indicate what "practice" he is writing about. If he is confused by such terms as "heretic," "schismatic," "Greek Catholic," etc., he should refer to a good dictionary or encyclopedia, such as Attwater's *A Catholic Dictionary* published with the *Imprimatur* of Cardinal Hayes, or the Catholic

Encyclopedia. As a matter of fact anyone can find the definitions of such terms in Webster's International.

The words "heathen," "pagan," "heretic," "infidel," "schismatic," as used by scholars in the Catholic Church are not instances of name-calling. They are objective labels for doctrinal positions or groups of people who have (or are supposed to have) a common philosophy—like Democrat, Republican, dissenter, Covenanter, or Communist.

Mr. Blanshard must know (if he read the passages in the books he refers to which cover the Church's position on the matters he was discussing) that his use of the words "valid," "invalid," "legal," and "illegal," as applied by Catholic scholars to various marriages, and actions that were *not* marriages, is quite indefensible. He uses these words throughout this chapter in expressions which tell the reader who is not well versed in Catholic doctrine, clear untruths about Catholic doctrine concerning the sacrament of marriage. He does not clear up and *keep clear* the distinction between the Catholic sacrament and the *civil requirements* and effects of marriages that meet, or fail to meet, the laws of the civil state. Any discussion of the Catholic doctrine on marriage that does not conform to this fundamental distinction cannot properly be called "scholarly" regardless of the footnotes attached. It can only be confused and confusing.

He does refer his readers to papal encyclicals, textbooks, canon law, etc., usually in general references but in some that are more specific. But none of them contains material which proves that his remarks in the text are true. If an occasional reader works hard enough to get the passage referred to and finds in it the words "valid," "invalid," "null," "illegal," etc., he may (and probably will) believe, as Mr. Blanshard implies, that these refer to the total conditions of the marriage concerned, both as a civil contract and a Catholic sacrament. And this will spread misinformation and antagonism among Americans.

Mr. Blanshard could easily have given his readers the Catholic doctrine from various distinguished Catholic scholars. Here is the way Dr. Heinrich Rommen, of St. Thomas College, St. Paul, puts it: [5]

[5] Rommen, Heinrich A., LL.D., *The State in Catholic Thought* (St. Louis: B. Herder Book Co., 1947), pp. 575–576.

This claim of the Church over the bond of matrimony does not mean that the Church claims an exclusive jurisdiction in matrimonial law. *It means only the precedence of the sacramental law over the civil law in matters that concern the sacramental character of matrimony for members of the Church.* Yet the Church does not deny that matrimony, as it serves for the preservation and propagation of human society, is closely connected with human relations that immediately follow from matrimony but belong to the sphere of secular life, such as the property relations between husband and wife, the legal liabilities of the husband for the wife and vice versa, the mutual duties of support and also all those matters that are connected with matrimony as a social and economic union. To regulate these relations between husband and wife and between the married couple and third parties is clearly in the competence of the secular authority, to which is entrusted the care for the common good and whose duty it is to direct the social community of matrimony and of the family to the common good. Yet the state, the civil law, has no authority *to void the sacramental union between members of the Church.* It is thus impossible for the Church to acknowledge a right of the state to void the matrimonial bond between validly baptized persons on account of racial discriminations, as the Nurnberg anti-Semitic laws provided. [Italics mine.]

Mr. Blanshard writes: "declaring that a valid American [*sic*] marriage does not exist" (p. 156); "declare a marriage annulled in Catholic law without any reference to American marriage law" (p. 157); "Marriage, according to this theory, is an ecclesiastical rite and not a civil ceremony [*sic*]" (p. 157); "American law recognizes civil and religious ceremonies as equally valid" (p. 158); "The Church regards Matrimony as a sacrament over which she alone has jurisdiction, and jurisdiction which she cannot transfer; she cannot permit any other agency to take over the administration of *those laws with which she has* surrounded the sacrament" (p. 159); "the Church alone has the right to authentically declare in what cases *the Divine law* [n.b. not the *state* law] forbids or annuls a marriage" (p. 159, italics mine).

The last two passages are quoted from the writings of two Catholics: Mr. John G. Brunini and Msgr. John A. Ryan.

Mr. Blanshard indulges in no theological argument to show that the Church has no warrant for her position. He does not explain what is wrong with the idea of the Church's having laws or rules about her sacraments or why the Church should not teach the marriage requirements of the Divine law, *as the Church understands it.* "There you have," he writes in the next sentence to the one about the divine law (p. 159), "the Catholic marriage gospel in its full presumption."

He does, however, indicate *his* remedy for the requirements of the Church for the Catholic sacrament of marriage. This will surprise no one who has grasped the full significance of Mr. Blanshard's basic philosophy of the omnipotent state (see Ch. 17). "The most the hierarchy will concede to any government is that the people have the right to adopt certain rules concerning the purely 'civil effects' of marriage." In other words, the Catholic Church will not "concede" control over the spiritual and moral teaching of the Church "to any government." Mr. Blanshard emphatically disapproves. There you have his gospel of the omnipotent (and omniscient) state "in its full presumption."

The sum of Mr. Blanshard's complaint seems to be that Catholicism is Catholicism, and not statism. If he competently expressed his position, nothing other than an omnipotent state (see pp. 46–55) will appease him. Any religion which denies the *complete* authority of the state over all its moral teaching and practice (which every positive religion will forever deny) seems to run counter to Mr. Blanshard's position. He wants the Church not to be the Church, but to surrender its function to the governments of Vermont, New York, and Russia. Quite evidently he will not be content until either the Catholic Church goes out of existence or the United States gives up its policies of personal and religious liberty and forces the Catholic Church to abandon its teaching about sacraments, fidelity to vows, adultery, artificial birth control, abortion, euthanasia, and the rest of *its interpretation* of the Gospels and the Ten Commandments.

It is true that the Church takes the position that she alone has jurisdiction over her sacraments—just as Harvard University has jurisdiction over her degrees. This is the essence of Mr. Blanshard's discontent. If anyone wants to receive a Catholic sacrament or a Harvard degree, he has to meet the requirements of the Church or of Harvard. If anyone does not want to receive such a sacrament or such a degree, neither the Church nor Harvard will dragoon him and force him to accept. Each will continue to say (until Mr. Blanshard's statism takes over to make decisions for the churches, if any, and the private universities, if any) if you want the advantages, whatever they are in the next world or in this, from the hope of Heaven to getting into a Harvard Club,[6] you will have to meet the requirements which the Church or the university imposes. I have faith that the overwhelming majority of the American people agree with me that the Blanshard position is an attack on religion and is the antithesis of "American freedom."

---

[6] My purpose here is not to disparage Harvard University or Harvard clubs, I speak as a former president of the Harvard Club of Madison, Wisc.!

17

THE BLANSHARD PLAN FOR AMERICA

MR. BLANSHARD, in opening his chapter on "The Catholic Plan for America," asks (p. 266): "What would happen to American democracy if our alleged twenty-six million Catholics grew to be a majority in the population and followed the direction of their priests?" In support of the nightmare with which he seeks to answer this question, he claims that the details are "mosaics of official Catholic doctrine. Every concept, almost every word and phrase, has been plagiarized line by line from Catholic documents" (p. 269). In my Chapter 12 I have shown the inaccuracy of his use of the terms "Catholic doctrine" and "Catholic documents."

In discussing the "Blanshard Plan for America," I start with a similar question: *What would happen to American democracy if Mr. Blanshard, and those who agree with him, became strong enough to take over America?* In answering this question I shall not rely on "mosaics" taken from the writings of other men in far-off countries, and applicable not to the United States but to nondemocratic areas and problems. And I shall "plagiarize" no one. I shall quote accurately with full documentation and shall also cite references to magazine articles discussing Americans in American publications.

To what extent Mr. Blanshard would change any of his articles if he were to rewrite them now, I have no way of knowing. Also no one has any way of knowing to what extent there would be changes in a rewriting today of the Spanish Law of Succession, the Concordat with Mussolini, the Spanish Bill of Rights, the Italian Constitution of 1947, and even the particular papal encyclicals—from which he plucked "important phrases." These are the sources of his imaginary amendments to the Constitution of the United States in his "Catholic Plan for America." However, any informed person knows that none of these has any bearing on the relation of American Catholics to American freedom and anyone who has examined Mr. Blanshard's book knows that he did not name a single American Catholic whom he asked to what extent, if any, this documentary "plan" expressed the belief and practice of American Catholics. He simply exercised his "exemplary scholarship" far away from American Catholics, in distance, atmosphere, democratic experience, and outlook, and then (through "mosaics," "plagiarism," and "important phrases") held up American Catholics to ridicule and accusations of docile stupidity, hypocrisy, and disloyalty.

Mr. Blanshard is greatly concerned (p. 46) over the *un-Americanism* of the Catholic Church in teaching that the spiritual order is superior to the temporal order, and, therefore, that men should refuse to observe unjust and immoral laws of *any government* which violates the conscience of the citizen by requiring the performance of actions which the citizen sincerely believes to be immoral. He seems disturbed (rather strangely, it seems, for a minister of the Congregational Church) [1] by the doctrine that a person who has a moral code will refuse to abandon it on the basis of its rejection *by other people*—even by a majority vote in a political democracy. He seems to deny the civil right of any American to believe that God is greater than government.

Mr. Blanshard writes (p. 51), "Unquestionably Catholics have a moral right to oppose any law in a democracy *so long as they believe in submission to law.*" (Italics mine.) This is the point of the whole matter. People with *moral codes* do not believe in "submission" to immoral laws—even the laws of a democracy. This sentence of Mr. Blanshard's reveals clearly his philosophy of the omnipotent state as it

[1] He was ordained in 1917 and was pastor for a short time of the First Congregational Church of Tampa, Fla. Dale Francis (*op. cit.*, p. 32) quotes him as writing: "The only church I had asked me unanimously to continue, and nominally I have never demitted, as the word goes, from the Congregational ministry because the polity of that church is so loose."

would operate in a democracy. Once the political majority has spoken and has passed a law, over the opposition of the Catholics, or the Protestants, or the Jews, or any other group, "submission to law" must be taught and observed. This is the essence of totalitarianism, the heart of the teaching of Communism, Nazism, and Fascism. This is not only the position of Mr. Blanshard, it is also necessarily that of those who unreservedly endorse him.

This ancient position of Judaism and Christianity concerning, for instance, the superior moral force of the Ten Commandments over the decisions of a state legislature is the essential target of most of Mr. Blanshard's attack on the Catholic Church in his chapter on "Church, State and Democracy."

These are some further expressions of Mr. Blanshard's position:

"In particular areas the authority of the Church is superior to that of the United States government and of all governments, and no government is conceded the moral right to deny this" (p. 45). This is correct. Note that it is concerned with *moral right.*

Mr. Blanshard then quotes from the Encyclical *Christian Constitution of States,* of Leo XIII [2] as follows:

> The Almighty, therefore, has appointed the charge of the human race between two powers, the ecclesiastical and the civil, the one being set over divine, and the other over human things. Each in its kind is supreme, each has fixed limits within which it is contained, limits which are defined by the nature and special object of the province of each, so that there is, we may say, an orbit traced out within which the action of each is brought into play by its own native right.

Mr. Blanshard comments on this statement: "The snare in this innocent-sounding proclamation is that if there is a dispute between the Catholic Church and the state over the right to rule any specific area, the Church and the Church alone has the right to decide who wins" (p. 45). Here Mr. Blanshard expands the position of the Church as *teacher in the field of faith and morals* to "the right to *rule any specific area*" and "*the right to decide who wins.*" Notice also the words "snare" and "innocent-sounding." It seems obvious that who wins in

---

[2] Reprinted in Wynne, *The Great Encyclical Letters of Leo XIII,* p. 114.

any particular contest should be discovered after the contest is over by noticing the outcome. Whether the Catholic citizens would win a contest with a specific government, in regard to obedience to a law which violated the consciences of individual Catholics, could not possibly be decided by the Church. What the Church claims is *the right to decide to enter the contest.* The Church claims its right and responsibility to teach what it sincerely believes to be the moral laws of God. Scholars in the area of philosophy and religion ought to know that this basic responsibility to teach, and the insistence on the moral right to teach, is common to substantially every type of religion known to man, and *scholars* should neither use nor endorse the use of the emotionally loaded words of this Blanshard comment.

"In Catholic theory the Church and the state are parts of a single temple with movable interior walls, and the Pope has the power to say where the separating partitions will stand," says Mr. Blanshard (p. 46). Again, note the word "power." The only *power* that the Pope has for doing whatever Mr. Blanshard is trying to express in this figurative language is the power to teach and persuade, and the right to exercise his responsibility under what he believes to be the injunctions of Christ. Of course, he has the potential influence that comes from his position, like every other teacher or teaching institution on earth. Mr. Blanshard objects to the Church's teaching what the Church believes to be right in faith and morals.

Again Mr. Blanshard: "In practice, as we shall see, 'immoral and irreligious laws' are sometimes laws that non-Catholics consider supremely moral" (p. 46). If Mr. Blanshard believes that Catholics are not entitled to their *own opinions* in morality and religion, unless these positions are *endorsed by non-Catholics,* would he say, therefore, that non-Catholics have no right to take moral or religious positions *unless they are endorsed by Catholics?* Seemingly the position that Mr. Blanshard takes indicates that neither Catholics nor non-Catholics have a right to take any positions which are not approved by a majority vote of the civil society in which they live. This means moral standards by popular vote.

"If the hierarchy once conceded that ultimate sovereignty lies wholly in the people, anything might follow" (p. 47). Certainly anyone who concedes that *ultimate sovereignty* lies *wholly* in the people must necessarily concede that *anything might follow* if "sovereignty" covers individual morals and religious faith.

Obviously, anything "might follow" according to Mr. Blanshard's philosophy of government and morals (if the omnipotent state should be set up by the vote of a political majority). Any popular atrocity from confiscation of all property to slave labor and gas ovens for disliked minorities could result. Any opposition based on the integrity of the individual and the priority of the individual conscience would, to Mr. Blanshard, be immoral. This is the essence of the philosophy of the omnipotent state—what Dr. Brogan called "statistical morality" (see p. 241). Under this philosophy the individual citizen would do as he was told by the government (in morals, religion, child training, and education) or take the consequences. If "the people" happened to vote complete dictatorial power to such chiefs of state as Mussolini, Hitler, Stalin, Franco, Tito, or Peron, Mr. Blanshard and the other advocates of this philosophy would seem to have no possible basis for claiming that any action of any such dictators is immoral or should be refused obedience by their subjects.

"American Catholic bishops who praise democracy always utter their praises with an important mental reservation, that the real source of the authority of the American government and of all governments is God and not the people. Under this theory the frontier of the people's authority is set not by the people themselves" (p. 47). To call the centuries-old doctrine of the Catholic Church, that the source of authority of all governments is God, a *mental reservation* is another example of Mr. Blanshard's misuse of language. The idea that the frontier of the people's authority has limitations that are not set by popular vote, but by the individual conscience of the citizen, is certainly a fundamental doctrine of Catholicism and also of substantially every other religion that teaches anything that can be called a moral code.

"American Catholics . . . have heard progressive American Bishops praise democracy so often that they honestly believe that their Church stands unequivocally for *complete* democracy in government" (p. 48). Anyone who has heard American Catholic bishops discuss democracy has necessarily heard them (substantially without any qualification whatever) praise political democracy and praise it as unequivocally as any others praise democracy in America. This statement is insulting in its implication that the bishops are insincere in praising political democracy. Mr. Blanshard offers no evidence whatever to bolster that pretense. Of course Catholic bishops, in common with substantially all other religious leaders in America, deny that democracy in government gives the government any status as *an infallible moral teacher*.

"But even in the United States, American Catholics are instructed by their hierarchy to defy the laws of the American people when these laws differ from the rulings of the Church" (p. 50). "American Catholics are instructed to accept the privileges of American democracy and work to force the lives of all the people, Catholic and non-Catholic, into the pattern laid down in Rome" (p. 50). A more accurate phrase than "instructed by the hierarchy to defy" would be to say that American Catholics are taught by all Catholic teachers, in conformity with the doctrines of the Church, just as substantially all other Americans are taught (who happen to be so placed that they are taught anything about religion and morality), that the laws of civil governments should not be held to excuse them from observing the superior laws of God.

There are other expressions of this same philosophy of the infallibility of the omnipotent state in the field of morals scattered through Mr. Blanshard's entire chapter on "Church, State, and Democracy." The quotations given above are, however, doubtless sufficient to set forth Mr. Blanshard's totalitarian philosophy.[3] Careful readers should note that the only documentation attached to the passages quoted above (from p. 50) is a quotation from a papal encyclical which does not support either of them. The encyclical spoke of "laws of the state . . . manifestly at variance with the divine law," not laws which "differ from the rulings of the Church." There is nothing here (or anywhere else in Blanshard's book or outside of it) to show that American Catholics are taught to work to *force the lives* of all people

[3] See discussion of this position of Mr. Blanshard from reviews of his book by Dr. Henry Sloan Coffin, Mr. Will Herberg, and Mr. David Rome in Chap. 15.

(or of any people) into *a pattern* laid down in Rome or anywhere else. It should further be noted that Mr. Blanshard makes no attempt to justify his preference for the moral teaching of the infallible state to the moral teaching of the Catholic, Protestant, or Jewish interpretations of the Ten Commandments.

If the public opinion of the majority is always morally right, then might (political might) makes right. It would be interesting to know what, if any, civic boundaries Mr. Blanshard would require before granting to a majority vote infallibility in the field of morals. Would I or Mr. Blanshard in the *family unit* be morally justified in killing relatives whom the family majority found inconvenient economic burdens; or in the *neighborhood* imprisoning or executing the neighbors who drank cocktails, danced, or played bridge for a quarter of a cent a point, if these actions were ruled immoral by the neighborhood majority? Or would he require *nation, state,* or *county* votes of fifty-one per cent over a vote of forty-nine per cent to make the wishes of the majority morally binding? It is to be regretted that some of the clergymen and professors of philosophy who praised Mr. Blanshard's book in unqualified superlatives did not ask these questions before telling their readers that the Blanshard opus was a sound, fair, scholarly, and courageous defense of *American freedom.*

The nature, formation, discovery, measurement, and uses of public opinion mean that any formulated and examinable opinion is *inevitably* the composite or the amalgam of the private opinions of the people who make up the public. Necessarily, a valid public judgment on a moral question can be formed only by a public the individual members of which are capable of forming valid, private, moral judgments. A sound economic public opinion can be formed on any economic subject only by a public the individual members of which are capable of forming sound private, individual, economic opinions on the subject being dealt with. Sound, competent, valid opinions on all topics in morals, economics, or child training are not inherent or instinctive in human nature. They are, therefore, not to be had simply for the asking from each and every member of the human race to whom a moral or economic problem is submitted for a vote. The development of sound moral and economic opinions is the result of training, learning, experience. The fact that after training, learning, and experience in the realms of economics or morals human beings come to different conclusions, and accept different types of economic and moral codes (and express in theory and observe in practice various moral and economic virtues and vices), should not surprise any scholar or depress any believer in personal, political, or religious freedom. It certainly should not lead to a denunciation of those who teach moral codes or economic theories which happen to differ from Mr. Blanshard's preferences.

So long as America remains an even partially free society, moving toward the ideal of a free society, Mr. Blanshard and his fellow advocates of the omnipotent state will have to accept such elementary aspects of freedom. His surprise and anger, if he wishes to be a good citizen of a free country, should be controlled within such personal limits as not to contribute to the difficulties of promoting freedom and the harmonious living together of all sorts of people in our complex society—even though some of the American people happen to disagree with him. The right to be different (within the limits of decency and public order) is, and should remain, one of the most cherished aspects of American freedom.

Mr. Blanshard's devotion to the omnipotent state is not a new emotion resulting from the fact that American Catholics do not like any form of totalitarianism. In his earlier writings we find evidence wholly consistent with Mr. Blanshard's impatience with personal, political, and religious freedom as expressed again and again (as I have shown above) in the book under discussion.

Any reader who wishes to examine Mr. Blanshard's earlier endorsement of the omnipotent state, in a variety of aspects not covered in detail by his book on *American Freedom and Catholic Power* can find illuminating material in his earlier writings.[4] Obviously he might not

[4] "Socialist and Capitalist Planning," *Annals* of American Academy of Political and Social Science, Vol. 162, July, 1932, pp. 6–11;

Blanshard, Paul, "Socialism, A Moral Solution," *The Christian Century,* Vol. 49, Oct. 19, 1932, pp. 1271–1274;

Blanshard, Paul, "Shall We Scrap the Constitution?" *The Forum,* August, 1935, pp. 69–71;

Blanshard, Paul, "Sex Standards in Moscow," *The Nation,* May 12, 1926, pp. 522–523.

write of these items in the same way today; and the documents with which American Catholics had nothing to do and to which Mr. Blanshard referred in his Catholic Plan for America, might also be different if written today even by the original authors.

Here is a four-point program, taken wholly from Mr. Blanshard's book, with accurate documentation, which I suggest is implicitly the Blanshard Plan for America:

1. Moral standards for all citizens to be decided by popular vote; no person to have any right (moral or civil) to refuse obedience to the laws of the majority, regardless of the individual's moral standards or conscience (see above referring to Blanshard, pp. 45–47 and 51).

2. Anyone teaching or advocating opposition to laws considered by some to be immoral in education, religious doctrine, or personal liberty would be considered disloyal (same reference).

3. There would be only the "public school, from kindergarten through college" (see Chapter 7), with no freedom of parents to select the education of their children (p. 304).

4. No further cooperative contacts between government and religion. In the words of Justice Rutledge (quoted by Mr. Blanshard with approval): "Complete and permanent separation of the spheres of religious activity and civil authority" (pp. 90–91). The figurative "wall of separation between church and state" would be kept "high and impregnable" (p. 90), contrary to total American practice, law, and *constitutional* provisions down to date. No religious education or chaplains in army, navy, or government hospitals would be recognized or provided for in federal or state laws. No tax exemption for churches, synagogues, or religious schools. All of these American practices are in violation of the Rutledge doctrine which Mr. Blanshard endorses. Secularism would be the established (government-favored) position in regard to religion throughout the country.

Anyone who desires such a plan for the future of America must necessarily have abandoned most of the American traditions of personal liberty, religious freedom, and freedom of education—if the government set up by a democratic majority should pass laws doing away with these American freedoms. Such a person must be ready, regardless of his private conscience, to yield "submission to law" (see Blanshard, p. 51). He must accept the "statistical morality" of the political majority, or be considered disloyal. "American freedom" will become less and less distinguishable from the slavery that passes for liberty in the totalitarian countries.

If American freedom is to be preserved, those who understand it and believe in it must use their best efforts to defend it against the moral and political dictatorship of a dominant majority. This danger is more real than that of an enemy from outside our borders. And both are more real than the fantastic and uninformed fear which calls for organizing a "resistance movement" against the imaginary, unproved threat of Catholicism to American Freedom.

APPENDIX

A Review by James M. O'Neill of "Communism, Democracy and Catholic Power" by Paul Blanshard

(From the New York Herald Tribune *Book Review,* June 10, 1951)

THIS book has two theses. The first, that Communism is an enemy of democracy and freedom, presents nothing new. All Americans, except the handful of Communists and their fellow-travelers, believe this. The second thesis, the heart of the book, is that the Catholic Church, like Communism, is also an enemy of democracy and freedom. Since Communism is the most active force working today to destroy human freedom, Mr. Blanshard tries to show that Catholicism is like Communism.

Soviet Communism is a world power. It has military might. Army, navy, air force, secret police, concentration camps, firing squads, prisons, and human slavery, are all at its command. So Mr. Blanshard talks about Catholic "power," which he nowhere defines, explains, or illustrates. But since the terror of Communism is its physical power, he attempts to get the gullible and uninformed to believe that the essence of Catholicism is also the threat of its "power" against freedom. The phrase "Catholic power" is simply a name-calling device used by Mr. Blanshard, as his ideological predecessors used "Popery" and "Romanism." "Catholic power" in America means exactly what "Protestant power" or "Jewish power" means—the influence of Catholic, Protestant, or Jewish citizens exercising their common rights as citizens of a free society.

The idea that Catholic public men or citizens "accept policies" and vote as directed by priests on orders from Rome is a childish falsehood for which Mr. Blanshard offers (and can offer) no substantiation of any kind. A casual reader could easily get the idea that the Catholic Church (inaccurately called "the Vatican" throughout Mr. Blanshard's book) has no interest in religion, moral conduct, or the salvation of souls, but only in "world power." Its purpose in accumulating or exercising world power is not made clear. Its mission, as it interprets Christ's teaching, is nowhere presented.

Mr. Blanshard pretends that he is not attacking the Catholic religion or the Catholic people; it is "political Catholicism as a world power which concerns" him. He then proceeds to misrepresent the Catholic religion (and the people who believe in it) in sneering, grossly insulting passages, wholly without any valid proof.

He writes: . . . "the unabashed idolatry . . . the Pope himself is always the central idol . . . and the Catholic people are the slaves who come to worship him . . . all Catholics owe obedience to him 'as to God himself' . . . the Pope can consign human beings to hell for violation of divine law." After a number of paragraphs of this sort of writing, Mr. Blanshard refers to a long footnote (the appearances of scholarship must be kept up). The note continues the discussion, but contains nothing to guide the reader to proof of the nonsense about the idol, the slaves, and the obedience "as to God himself."

Mr. Blanshard continues his attack on religion. The Pope "has power to declare what is right and wrong by divine fiat," "the continuing corruption (by the Church) of human intelligence by systematically cultivated superstition . . . the devices for exploiting relics. . . . The most patent ecclesiastical frauds in the fields of relics and apparitions must be accepted without a murmur. . . . In the Catholic religious orders . . . recruiting, in fact, is largely based on the guilt feelings of youth and adolescence about sex, and the conviction of sin is systematically exploited to induce a commitment to the Religious vocation . . . Monastery life is a mixture of selflessness and egotism, of religious fanaticism and social stupidity . . . Priests are . . . encouraged to play upon the lowest superstitions of their people."

Mr. Blanshard's central theme, however, is that the Catholic Church is the enemy of our American system of government relation to religion and religious freedom, as expressed in the First Amendment. In his attempt to prove this totally unprovable proposition, he misrepresents both the American system and the attitude of Catholics toward it.

He writes: "No true Catholic can agree with the doctrine of church-state separation in its American constitutional form and remain true to Vatican policy [*sic*]." American Catholics, laymen, priests and bishops have been accepting, endorsing and supporting our whole constitutional system including the First Amendment ever since it was written with the help of Catholic statesmen. From the first Catholic bishop, John Carroll, down to the formal statement of all the Catholic bishops in November, 1948, there has not been any important exception among the more than 500 Catholic bishops in the United States. But Mr. Blanshard pretends to believe that this universal testimony is sheer hypocrisy. He offers nothing, and can offer nothing, to prove this.

Mr. Blanshard deals only with the superlatively ambiguous phrase "the separation of church and state," which is not in any American constitution. Church-state separation in its American constitutional form means two things: "No law respecting an establishment of religion," nor any prohibition of the "free exercise" of religion. So says the First Amendment, and all of the state constitutions have similar provisions, many of them in the same language.

Mr. Blanshard assumes that the First Amendment does not mean what it says, but "a complete and permanent separation of the spheres of religious activity and civil authority by comprehensively forbidding every form of public aid or support for religion." This is the language of the Rutledge dissent in the Everson bus case which became the basis of the court's opinion in the McCollum case.

The First Amendment has never been so interpreted either in language or in action, by any President from Washington to Truman, by any Congress in our history, by any relevant Supreme Court decision prior to the McCollum case, nor by the outstanding scholars in constitutional law from Joseph Story to Edward S. Corwin.

The United States government started to use government funds in aid of religious activity in various ways in the First Congress. It has continued such use down to today. Every state in the union has used state funds, personnel and facilities in aid of religion and religious education from the day of its origin and is doing so today. But neither the Federal government nor that of any state has ever set up "an establishment." So we have always had "separation" in the sense of no one religion in a position of exclusive favor as compared with all other religions. All Americans, including the Catholics, believe in this type of separation. By referring to this regular, traditional, literal, historical meaning of the religious clause of the First Amendment as "the Catholic interpretation," Mr. Blanshard seeks to arouse the ignorant against the Constitutional provision and the Catholic Church, both of which are under the cloud of his displeasure.

Perhaps Mr. Blanshard's most inexcusable distortion is his treatment of Al Smith's statement in the Presidential campaign of 1928. There Smith gave an ordinary statement of belief in the American system, such as substantially all American Catholic bishops and laymen have used over and over again. It is in essence identical with the statement of all the Catholic bishops in November, 1948.

Basically Mr. Blanshard's attack is broader than simple anti-Catholicism. It is anti-religion. He advocates the omnipotent state. He denounces as Catholic "imperialism" and "civil rule" over American Catholics, the doctrine that the laws of God are entitled to obedience over the laws of a state legislature when the latter violate the conscience of the citizen. He believes in what Mr. D. W. Brogan called Mr. Blanshard's theory of "statistical morality"—the infallibility of majority decisions in moral questions. Strangely, for an ordained minister, he seems not to realize that all positive religions, specifically and emphatically Protestantism and Judaism, as well as Catholicism, refuse to surrender their moral codes if a political majority rejects them. The "majority of the people have the right to determine our future by choice based on free discussion" is one of many expressions of this position. Americanism to Mr. Blanshard means militant secularism; religious influence is "un-American."

It would take many times the space here available to correct Mr. Blanshard's distortions of Catholic doctrine and practice out of which he gets such terms as "absolute monarchy," "subjects of a foreign power," "thought control," and "censorship." Nor does he approach accuracy in his remarks concerning the dictation, or even the "teaching" of the Church in various fields. He must know that the Church does not teach medicine, economics, government, or international relations. The Church teaches morals. It does not teach a surgeon how to perform an operation, or what he can or cannot do in his practice, but what he should or should not do to live up to the moral code of the Church. The Church has no "power" to prevent him from doing what he pleases, or to punish him for what he does. It has only the force of its persuasion, its instruction, and the privilege of its sacraments. If any man wishes to receive the sacraments of the Catholic Church, or a degree from Harvard University, he has to meet the requirements of the Church or of Harvard. Neither the Church nor the university can dragoon him if he is not interested in what they have to offer. Mr. Blanshard's book exhibits a fundamental misconception of American freedom in religion and in education, and the privileges of the individual American in relation to both.

BIBLIOGRAPHY

The page numbers following each item give the pages *in this book* on which the listed item is referred to.

I Books

Acta et Decreta Concilii Vaticani. Freiburg: Herder, 1892. (Pages 164, 171, 172, 173.)

Acton, Lord, *Correspondence.* (Page 171.)

Acton, Lord, *Essays on Freedom and Power.* Boston: Beacon Press, 1948. (Page 167.)

Acts and Resolves, etc., Massachusetts Bay, Vol. I, 1869. (Page 8.)

Attwater, Donald, *A Catholic Dictionary.* New York: The Macmillan Company, 1943. (Pages 60, 160.)

Bates, M. Searle, *Religious Liberty: An Inquiry.* New York: Harper & Brothers, 1945. (Pages 75, 77, 218.)

Bauscaren and Ellis, *Canon Law.* Milwaukee: Bruce Publishing Company, 1947. (Pages 204, 252.)

Beale, Howard K., *A History of Freedom of Teaching in American Schools.* New York: Charles Scribner's Sons, 1941. (Pages 52, 106.)

Benton, T. H., ed., *Annals of Congress.* New York: D. Appleton-Century Company, 1858. (Pages 22, 23, 45.)

Billington, Ray A., *The Protestant Crusade.* New York: The Macmillan Co., 1938. (Page 107.)

Binchy, D. A., *Church and State in Fascist Italy.* New York: Oxford University Press, 1941. (Page 92.)

Blanshard, Paul, *American Freedom and Catholic Power.* Boston: Beacon Press, 1949. (Since continual reference is made to this volume throughout most of the present book, individual page numbers are not cited here.)

Boyman, *History of Maryland.* (Page 9.)

Burns, J. A., and Kohlbrenner, Bernard J., *A History of Catholic Education in the United States.* New York: Benziger Brothers, 1937. (Page 6.)

Bury, J. B., *History of the Papacy in the Nineteenth Century.* London: The Macmillan Company, 1930. (Page 167.)

Butler, C., *The Vatican Council.* London: 1930. (Pages 164, 173.)

Cadoux, C. J., *Catholicism and Christianity.* London: George Allen and Unwin, 1928. (Page 167.)

Catholic Encyclopedia, Vol. V. (Pages 161, 216, 218.)

Cecconi, E., *Histoire du Concile du Vatican.* Paris: 1887. (Pages 164, 170, 172, 173.)

Commission on American Citizenship, *Better Men For Better Times.* Washington: Catholic University of America Press, 1943. (Pages 135, 146, 147.)

Congressional Globe, Thirty-ninth Congress, Part 2. Washington: Congressional Globe Office, 1866. (Page 47.)

Corwin, Edward S., *The Constitution—What It Means Today.* Princeton: Princeton University Press, 1947. (Page 49.)

Corrigan, Raymond, *The Church and the Nineteenth Century.* Milwaukee: Bruce Publishing Company, 1938. (Pages 70, 72, 86, 168, 216.)

Curran, Francis X., *Major Trends in American Church History.* New York: America Press, 1946. (Pages 70, 71.)

Cushman, Robert E., *Leading Constitutional Decisions.* New York: F. S. Crofts and Company, 1937. (Page 222.)

Dictionary of National Biography. London: Oxford University Press, 1922. (Page 162.)

Ebersole, Luke, *Church Lobbying in the Nation's Capital.* New York: The Macmillan Company, 1951. (Page 184.)

Elliot, Jonathan, ed., *Debates on the Adoption of the Constitution.* Washington: J. Elliot, 1836–1845. (Page 25.)

Encyclopedia Britannica. (Page 168.)

Farrand, Max, *The Framing of the Constitution.* New Haven: Yale University Press, 1913. (Page 17.)

Garrison, William E., *Catholicism and the American Mind.* Chicago: Willet, Clark and Company, 1928. (Page 168.)

Geiger, Mary V., *Daniel Carroll, A Framer of the Constitution.* Washington: Catholic University Press, 1943. (Pages 20, 21, 22.)

Gibbons, James Cardinal, "The Church and the Republic" in *Retrospect of Fifty Years.* Baltimore: John Murphy and Company, 1916. (Page 33.)

Granderath-Kirch, *Histoire du Concile du Vatican.* Brussels: 1907. (Pages 164, 167, 170, 171, 172.)

Griffin, Martin J., *Catholics and the American Revolution.* Ridley Park: Griffin, M. J., 1907–1911. (Page 7.)

Guilday, Peter, *The Life and Times of John Carroll.* New York: The Encyclopedia Press, 1922. (Pages 7, 12, 13, 15, 16.)

Harding, Samuel Bannister, *The Contest Over the Ratification of the Federal Constitution in Massachusetts.* New York: 1896. (Page 25.)

Harrise, *Jean and Sebastian Cabot.* Paris: 1882. (Page 5.)

Hughes, Emmet J., *Report from Spain.* New York: Henry Holt and Company, 1947. (Page 91.)

Hunt, Gaillard, *The Writings of James Madison.* New York: G. P. Putnam's Sons, 1904. (Page 28.)

Ireland, John, *The Church and Modern Society*. St. Paul: Pioneer Press, 1905. (Pages 33, 61.)

Kelly, Alfred H., and Harbison, Winfred A., *The American Constitution*. New York: W. W. Norton and Company, 1948. (Pages 18, 26, 28.)

Leonard, Lewis A., *A Life of Charles Carroll of Carrollton*. New York: Moffat, Yard and Company, 1918. (Page 14.)

Lydon, P. J., *Ready Answers in Canon Law*. New York: Benziger Brothers, 1934. (Page 250.)

Mallock, William H., *Is Life Worth Living?* New York: G. P. Putnam's Sons, 1879. (Pages 162, 203.)

Maynard, Theodore, *The Story of American Catholicism*. New York: The Macmillan Company, 1948. (Pages 12, 14, 70, 71, 169.)

McGucken, W. J., *The Catholic Way in Education*. Milwaukee: Bruce Publishing Company, 1934. (Page 109.)

McMahon, Francis, *A Catholic Looks at the World*. New York: Vanguard Press, 1945. (Page 63.)

McQuade, V. A., *American Catholic Attitudes on the Child Labor Amendment since 1891*. Washington: Catholic University of America Press, 1938. (Page 65.)

"Members of American Hierarchy," *The National Catholic Almanac*. Paterson, N. J.: St. Anthony's Guild, 1950. (Page 191.)

Milner, John, *The End of Religious Controversy*. Baltimore: John Murphy and Company (no date). (Page 7.)

Morison, Samuel Eliot, and Commager, Henry Steele, *The Growth of the American Republic*. New York: Oxford University Press, 1950. (Pages 4, 7, 12.)

Newman, John Henry Cardinal, *Letter to the Duke of Norfolk*. London: Longmans, Green and Company, 1874 (1907). (Pages 84, 87, 163, 203.)

O'Brien, John A., *Catholics and Scholarship*. Huntington, Ind.: Our Sunday Visitor, 1938. (Pages 111, 113, 114.)

Ollivier, E., *L'Eglise et l'Etat au Concile du Vatican*. Paris: 1879. (Pages 164, 174.)

O'Neill, J. M., *Religion and Education Under the Constitution*. New York: Harper & Brothers, 1949. (Pages 26, 27, 28, 36, 42, 44, 45, 46, 48, 49, 52, 106, 239.)

Padover, Saul K., *The Complete Jefferson*. New York: Duell, Sloan and Pearce, 1943. (Pages 28, 46, 52.)

Perry, Ralph Barton, *Puritanism and Democracy*. New York: Vanguard Press, 1944. (Page 30.)

Quirinus, *Letters from Rome*. London: Rivington's, 1870. (Page 171.)

Report of Bureau of Education. Washington: 1903. (Page 6.)

Reynolds, I. A., ed., *The Works of the Right Rev. John England*. Baltimore: John Murphy and Company, 1849. (Pages 32, 159.)

Riley, Arthur J., *Catholicism in New England to 1788*. Washington: Catholic University of America Press, 1936. (Pages 8, 24, 25.)

Rommen, Heinrich A., *The State in Catholic Thought*. St. Louis: Herder Book Company, 1947. (Pages 61, 62, 103, 255.)

Ryan, John A., *The Catholic Church and the Citizen*. New York: The Macmillan Company, 1928. (Pages 85, 87.)

Schaff, David S., *Our Fathers' Faith and Ours*. New York: G. P. Putnam's Sons, 1928. (Page 166.)

Scharf, *History of Maryland, Maryland Archives*. (Page 9.)

Schmidlin, Joseph, *Geschichte der Päpste*, II, 109. Freiburg: 1933–1938. (Page 61.)

Shea, John Gilmary, *The History of the Catholic Church in the United States*. New York: John G. Shea, 1886–1892. (Pages 11, 14, 15, 19, 24, 202.)

Shea, John Gilmary, *The Catholic Church in Colonial Days*. New York: John G. Shea, 1896. (Pages 5, 8.)

Sheppard, Vincent F., *Religion and the Concept of Democracy*. Washington: Catholic University of America Press, 1949. (Pages 59, 137.)

Smythe, Albert Henry, ed., *The Writings of Benjamin Franklin*. New York: 1905–1907. (Page 13.)

Sparks, Jared, ed., *Correspondence of the American Revolution*. IV. Boston: 1853. (Page 25.)

Storer, Mrs. Bellamy, *In Memory of Bellamy Storer*. Privately Printed, 1926. (Page 72.)

Story, Joseph, *Commentaries on the Constitution of the United States*. Boston: Hilliard and Company, 1833. (Page 49.)

Sweet, William Warren, *The Story of Religions in America*. New York: Harper & Brothers, 1930. (Page 10.)

The Tabloid Scientist. Feb. 1, 1935. (Page 114.)

Van Doren, Carl, *Benjamin Franklin*. New York: Viking Press, 1938. (Pages 12, 13.)

Van Tyne, Claude H., "Influence of the Clergy and of Religious and Sectarian Forces on the American Revolution," *American Historical Review*, Vol. XIX. (Page 12.)

Van Tyne, Claude H., *The Loyalists in the American Revolution*. New York: P. Smith, 1929. (Page 12.)

Warren, Charles, *The Making of the Constitution*. Boston: Little, Brown and Company, 1928. (Page 26.)

Who's Who in America. Chicago: A. N. Marquis Company, 1948. (Page 135.)

Will, Allen S., *The Life of Cardinal Gibbons*. New York: E. P. Dutton, 1922. (Pages 71, 169.)

Wynne, John J., *The Great Encyclical Letters of Pope Leo XIII*. New York: Benziger Brothers, 1903. (Pages 63, 70, 72, 205, 262.)

Yates, *Secret Proceedings of the Convention*. Albany: 1821. (Page 19.)

II Periodicals and Newspapers

American Bar Journal, Vol. 34, no. 6. Chicago: American Bar Association, 1948. (Page 49.)

Bennett, J. C., "New Conception of 'Separation,'" *Christianity and Crisis*. New York: 1948. (Page 56.)

Billington, Ray Allen, "American Catholicism and the Church-State Issue," *Christendom,* V, 1940. (Pages 31, 107.)

Blanshard, Paul, "Answer to T. Robert Ingram," *The Atlantic Monthly*. Boston: February, 1950. (Pages 127, 190, 238.)

Blanshard, Paul, "The Catholic Price for Cooperation," *The Christian Century*. Chicago: May 5, 1949. (Page 144.)

Blanshard, Paul, "Answer to Father Dunne," *The Humanist*. New York: August, 1948. (Page 190.)

Blanshard, Paul, "Father Connell and the Scholarship of Paul Blanshard," *Cornell Law Quarterly*. Ithaca: Winter, 1951. (Page 196.)

Blanshard, Paul, "Sex Standards in Moscow," *The Nation*. New York: May 12, 1926. (Page 270.)

Blanshard, Paul, "Shall We Scrap the Constitution?" *The Forum*. New York: August, 1935. (Page 269.)

Blanshard, Paul, "Socialism, A Moral Solution," *The Christian Century*. Chicago: October 19, 1932. (Pages 259, 268.)

Blanshard, Paul, "Socialist and Capitalist Planning," *Annals of American Academy of Political and Social Science*. New York: July, 1932. (Pages 259, 267.)

Boas, George, "Review of 'American Freedom and Catholic Power,'" *Philosophical Review*. Ithaca: January, 1950. (Page 225.)

Brewster, Owen, "Protestants in Spain," *The Sign*. Union City, N. J.: Passionist Fathers, June, 1950. (Page 80.)

Brickman, William W., "The School and the Church-State Question," *School and Society*. May 6, 1950. (Page 109.)

Brogan, D. W., "The Catholic Church in America," *Harper's Magazine*. New York: May, 1950. (Pages 83, 140, 240.)

Chase, John W., "Review of 'American Freedom and Catholic Power,'" *The New York Times Book Review*. New York: May 9, 1949. (Page 235.)

"The Church and Fascism," *London Tablet*. London: September 24, 1938. (Page 253.)

Clinchy, Everett R., "A Letter in Answer to Paul Blanshard," *America*. New York: May 7, 1949. (Page 144.)

Clinchy, Everett R., "A Letter in Answer to Paul Blanshard," *The Christian Century*. Chicago: June 1, 1949. (Page 144.)

Coffin, Henry Sloane, "Review of 'American Freedom and Catholic Power,'" *Christianity and Crisis*. New York: May 2, 1949. (Pages 225, 244, 265.)

Connell, Francis J., "Review of 'American Freedom and Catholic Power,'" *Cornell Law Quarterly*. Ithaca: Spring 1950. (Pages 196, 197, 198.)

Conway, Bertrand C., "John Carroll, First Archbishop of Baltimore," *Catholic World,* CXVI (1922). (Page 23.)

Döllinger, J. J. I., "The Pope and the Council." *Allegemeine Zeitung,* Augsburg: March, 1869. Reissued as a pamphlet, Leipzig; August, 1869.

Drinan, Robert F., "The 'Novel Liberty' Created by the McCollum Decision," *The Georgetown Law Journal*. Washington: Georgetown University, 1951. (Pages 49, 53.)

Dunn, Edward S., "Catholics in the Seventy-ninth Congress," *American Sociological Review*. Chicago: Loyola University, December, 1946. (Page 129.)

Farrell, James A., "Thomas Fitzsimmons, Signer of the Constitution." Philadelphia: American Catholic Historical Society of Philadelphia, *Records,* 1928. (Pages 20, 21.)

Fleck, Stephen, Snedeker, Elizabeth F., and Rock, John, "The Contraceptive Safe Period—A Clinical Study," *New England Journal of Medicine*. Boston: December, 1940. (Pages 152, 153.)

Fleet, Elizabeth, "Madison's Detached Memoranda," *The William and Mary Quarterly,* 3rd, Ser. III, October, 1946. (Page 32.)

Francis, Dale, "Catholics in the Eightieth Congress," *The Commonweal*. New York: January 14, 1949. (Page 131.)

Garrison, William E., "Religious Liberty in Spain," *The Christian Century*. Chicago: October, 1950. (Page 79.)

Garrison, William E., "Review of 'American Freedom and Catholic Power,'" *The Christian Century*. June 8, 1949. (Page 225.)

Hall, Clarence W., "Review of 'American Freedom and Catholic Power,'" *The Christian Herald*. July, 1950. (Page 225.)

Harrigan, Edward A., "A Catholic Looks at Lutherans." Reprinted from *America,* December 3, 1949, in *St. Ansgar's Bulletin*. New York: 40 West 13th St., June, 1950. (Page 4.)

Herberg, Will, "Review of 'American Freedom and Catholic Power,'" *Commentary*. New York: American Jewish Committee, August, 1949. (Pages 235, 265.)

Higgins, George G., "The Yardstick," *The Catholic Transcript*. Hartford: June 29, 1950. (Page 141.)

Ingram, T. Robert, "Review of 'American Freedom and Catholic Power,'" *Atlantic Monthly*. Boston: February, 1950. (Page 237.)

Katz, Leo J., and Reiner, Emil, "Further Studies on the Sterile and Fertile Periods in Women," *American Journal of Obstetrics and Gynecology,* XLIII, 1942. (Page 153.)

Kirkpatrick, Clifford, "Review of 'American Freedom and Catholic Power,'" *Annals of American Academy of Political and Social Science.* Philadelphia: University of Pennsylvania, January, 1950. (Page 225.)

Konvitz, Milton R., "A Plea for Religious Freedom in Israel," *Commentary.* New York: American Jewish Committee, September, 1949. (Page 78.)

Larrabee, Harold A., "Review of 'American Freedom and Catholic Power,'" *The Standard.* February, 1950. (Page 225.)

Lehman, Hal, "Religion by Fiat in Israel," *Commentary.* New York: August, 1949. (Page 78.)

Loeb, James, Jr., "The Catholic Vote," *The Commonweal.* New York: June 16, 1950. (Page 134.)

Maier, Walter A., "Radio Address, International Lutheran Hour," *The Pilot.* Boston: November 6, 1948. (Page 154.)

Maryland Journal. October 16, 1787. (Page 22.)

Murray, John Courtney, "Reply to Dr. Bowie," *The American Mercury.* New York: September, 1949. (Page 139.)

Nelson, Ansgar, "Stifled Liberties," *The Voice.* Baltimore: St. Mary's Seminary, January, 1951. (Page 79.)

New York Times, June 24, 1948. (Pages 119, 120, 121, 123.)

O'Neill, J. M., "Is There a Catholic Constitutional Position?" *Thought.* September, 1949. (Page 50.)

Peterson, Lawrence, "Catholics in Sweden," *The Sign.* Union City, N. J.: Passionist Fathers, June, 1950. (Page 79.)

Pribilla, Max, "Dogmatic Intolerance and Civil Toleration," *The Month.* London: Longmans, Green and Company, October, 1950. (Pages 83, 189.)

"Protestantism and the Public School," *The Christian Century,* April, 1946. (Page 99.)

Editorial, "Protestants Take Catholic Line," *The Christian Century.* Chicago: The Christian Century Foundation, 1948. (Page 57.)

Protestant Ministers, "Statement on Church and State," *Christianity and Crisis.* New York: June, 1948. (Page 56.)

Rome, David, "Review of 'American Freedom and Catholic Power,'" *The Congress Bulletin.* Montreal: Canadian Jewish Congress, July, 1949. (Pages 243, 244, 265.)

Shaver, Erwin L., "Three Years after the Champaign Case," *Religious Education.* Oberlin: Religious Education Association, 1951. (Pages 49, 53.)

Sheridan, Edward F., "A Note on Mr. Blanshard," *Thought.* New York: Fordham University, December, 1950. (Pages 165, 166, 170, 171.)

Shipler, Guy Emory, "Review of 'American Freedom and Catholic Power,'" New York: *Lawyers Guild Review,* Winter, 1950. (Page 194.)

Washington Post, February 2–3, 1951. (Page 185.)

Weigle, Luther A., "Religion in Education." New York: *Christianity and Crisis,* July 24, 1950. (Page 99.)

West, Herbert, "Review of 'American Freedom and Catholic Power,'" *Dartmouth Alumni Magazine.* Hanover, N. H.: October, 1949. (Page 225.)

World Telegram and Sun. New York: January 6, 1950. (Page 156.)

III Pamphlets

Catholic Bishop of the United States, *The Christian in Action.* Washington: National Catholic Welfare Conference, 1948. (Pages 35, 55.)

Dunne, George H., *Religion and American Democracy.* New York: America Press, 1949. (Pages 108, 151, 157, 190.)

Francis, Dale, *American Freedom and Paul Blanshard.* Notre Dame, Ind.: Ave Maria Press, 1950. (Pages 260, 261.)

Garrison, William E., *Religion and Civil Liberty in Roman Catholic Tradition.* Chicago: Willet, Clark and Company, 1946. (Page 62.)

Hartnett, Robert C., *Equal Rights for Children.* New York: America Press, 1948. (Page 99.)

La Piana, George, "A Totalitarian Church in a Democratic State," *The Shane Quarterly.* Indianapolis: April, 1949. (Page 186.)

Murray, John Courtney, "Governmental Repression of Heresy," *Proceedings, American Catholic Theological Society.* Washington: Catholic University of America, 1948. (Page 89.)

Research Bulletin, Vol. XXIV, No. 1, National Education Association. Washington: 1946. (Page 49.)

Scott, Martin J., *No Pope Can be Wrong in Teaching Doctrine.* New York: America Press, 1941. (Page 168.)

IV Law Cases

Bradfield v. Roberts. 175 U. S. 291 (1899). (Page 50.)

Everson bus case. 330 U. S. 1. (Pages 41, 42.)

McCollum released time case. 333 U. S. 203. (Pages 42, 52, 221.)

Meyer v. Nebraska. 262 U. S. 390. (Page 222.)

Pierce v. Society of Sisters. 268 U. S. 510. (Pages 96, 221.)

V Letters, Press Releases, Advertisements

Connell, Francis J., "A Letter." January 12, 1951. (Page 242.)

Costantini, Celso, *A Letter.* Vatican City, March 7, 1950. (Page 183.)

Dewey, John, "Review of 'American Freedom and Catholic Power,'" Advertisement. Boston: Beacon Press, 1949. (Page 225.)

Herberg, Will, "A Letter" (about *American Freedom and Catholic Power*), *Commentary*. New York: American Jewish Committee, March, 1950. (Page 237.)

Holmes, John Haynes, "Review of 'American Freedom and Catholic Power,'" Advertisement. Boston: Beacon Press, 1949. (Page 225.)

Johnson, F. Ernest, *Weekly Information Service*. New York: Federal Council of Churches of Christ in America, Nov. 27, 1948. (Page 121.)

Johnson, Willard, Press Release, July 14, 1948. (Page 120.)

McCarthy, Thomas J., *A Letter*. Information Bureau. Washington: National Catholic Welfare Conference, 1951. (Page 182.)

McNicholas, John T., "The Catholic Church in American Democracy," Press Release. Washington: National Catholic Welfare Conference, 1948. (Pages 34, 57.)

Morrison, Charles Clayton, "Review of 'American Freedom and Catholic Power,'" Advertisement. *New York Herald-Tribune,* October 15, 1950. (Page 225.)

Sugrue, Thomas, A Letter, November 1, 1950. (Page 183.)

Wright, John J., A Letter. March 31, 1951. (Page 192.)

INDEX

Publications cited in this book are not included in this index. They are listed in the bibliography and the numbers of the pages on which each publication is referred to *in this book* are there printed after each item.

Abortion, 150, 151, 241
Absolute obedience to Pope, 163-164
Absolute sovereignty of the people, 63
Academic freedom, 123
Act concerning Religion, 9
Adams, James Luther, 165
Advertising, 211
Agency, 175
  of the State, 68
America, ruling of, 207
American Association of University Professors, 123
American Catholic complacency, 114
American Civil Liberties Union, 123, 141
"American" doctrine, 101
American Gynecological Society, 186
"Americanism," heresy of, 70 ff., 187
Anti-Catholicism, colonial, 8, 237
  in Protestants and Other Americans United, 185
  Maryland, 10
  waning, 24
Anti-democratic Catholics, 61
Anti-discrimination bill, 110
Anti-semitism, 252
Appeal to Reason and Conscience, 122
Artificial insemination, 150
Assumptions, fundamental, 214
Attacks on religion, 232-233
Authentic Catholic doctrine, 196
"Authentic Catholic statements," 127
Authoritative sources, 231-232
Auxiliary services, 100

Backus, Isaac, 24
Baltimore, Lord, 8 ff.
Beacon Press, 226
Betting, 193
Bible reading, 212
Bigotry, 237
Bill of Rights, 19, 26, 27, 28, 29, 75, 128
Bill of Rights, Spanish, 218
Bingo, 193
Birth control, 152 ff.
Bishops, selection of, 194
Bjornson, Vladimar, 4
Black, Justice, errors, 42
Blakely, Father Paul, 209
Blanshard on Catholic Education, 104
Blanshard's attack on religion, 119
  program for America, 267
Bryson bill, 49

Cabots, 5
Calvert, Leonard, 9
Calvin, 7
Canada, 244
Candles, 213
Carroll, Charles, 12, 13, 14, 17, 27, 31
Carroll, Daniel, 11, 17, 20, 21, 22, 27
Carroll, John, 11, 13, 19, 21, 202
Catholic Action, 219
Catholic, "censorship," 115 ff.
  children in public schools, 95, 105
  Church as "totalitarian," 69
  as teacher, 97, 150, 230
  conservatives, 139
  criticism of Catholics, 102
  "documents," 215
  encyclopedia, 210
  laymen and Bill of Rights, 30
  liberals, 137 ff.
  "meaning" of First Amendment, 50 ff.
  "medical code," 142-143
  nurses, 142
  opinions, 260
  "people," 233-234
  policies, 188

Catholic—*Continued*
positions on Federal aid to education, 100-101
power, 241
press, 139
schools, 93, 209
self-criticism, 188
support for Blanshard, 187-188
"vote," 129, 134
Catholicism and forms of government, 63
Catholics and "a foreign power," 68
Catholics and Democracy, 59
Catholics and Jews, 251
Catholics, "help" to Blanshard, 182-183
in Congress, 129 ff.
in Spain, 63
official American, 199
poor showing in scholarship, 111 ff.
"real," 198
Censor Deputatus, 60
Censorship, 115, 239
of movies, 117
Charm, primitive, 246
Chase, Samuel, 12
Child Labor Amendment, 65
Christian denominations, number, 191
Church, and Democracy, 64
and force, 97
and state, 209
and United States government, 262
sacraments of, 98
Civil, allegiance, 206
laws, 255
laws and Catholic sacraments, 203
Colleges, non-Catholic, 209
Columbus, 3
Common religion for America, 192
Communism, 228, 238
Communist Party, 230
Communists, 269
Compulsory public schooling, 221
Concordat, defined, 217
Vatican-Italian, 217
Confessional, 210, 247-251
Congress, Eightieth, 131
Eighty-first, 133
Seventy-ninth, 129
Connell, Francis J., 196 ff., 199
Conscience, priority of, 84-85, 150, 202
Conservative Catholics, 139
Constitution, hypothetical, of U. S. 214
Italian, 218
ratification, 25 ff.
signers of, 17 ff.
Constitutional democracy, 217

Declaration of Independence, 14
Democracy, 244, 259
constitutional, 217
Dickinson, Robert Latou, 185
Dictation, 230
Dictatorial power, 264
Discovery of America, 3
"Divisive" influences, 93
Doctrine, 242
and policy, 188
authentic, 196
official Catholic, 215
principles of, 227
Documentation, and validity, 243
Blanshard's on Vatican Council, 165 ff.
praised, 232
spurious, 201
worthless, 215
Documents, authentic, 215
Catholic, 215
Dogmatic intolerance and civil toleration, 83
Dominicans, 60

Education laws, 110
Encyclical, defined, 160
Endorsements, of the Blanshard book, 224
Eric the Red, 3
Ericson, Leif, 4
"Erroneous ideas," 200
Established religions, 208, 216
Establishing the Church, 218
Establishment, national, 47
"Establishment of religion" traditional meaning, 36-37, 45, 50
Euthanasia Society, 186
Everson case, 36, 41, 43
Ex-Cathedra statements, 215-216
Experts, panel of, 183-187

Fascism, 91
Fair Deal, 66, 138
Faithful Jew, 193

Faithful Protestant, 193
Federal Council of Churches, 121
First Amendment, 226
  language of, 42
  purpose of, 42 ff.
Fitzsimmons, Thomas, 17, 20, 27
Florida, 5
Footnotes, Blanshard's, 192
Force, instruments of, 150, 230
Fourteenth Amendment, 48
Franciscans, 6
Franklin, Benjamin, 11
Free society, 223
Free will, 150
Freedom of press, 231

Gambling, 193
Gardar, See of, 5

Haas, Francis J., 135-136
Hamilton, Alexander, 28
  and Bill of Rights, 46
Harvard University, 257
Heretic, 254
Hierarch and social services, 142, 145 ff.
Hierarchy, and Bill of Rights, 29, 35, 54, 55, 58
  and *The Nation,* 125, 231
  defined, 181
  not "assimilated," 182
  speaking for itself, 191, 218
  work of, 191
Holy Shroud of Turin, 158
Holy water, 213
Hooton, Earnest A., 156
House Committee on Education and Labor, 101

Imperfections in Catholic affairs, 101
Imprimatur, 60, 90, 127, 190, 195-196, 213, 232
Infallibility, 205, 215
  and "character of the Popes," 175
  defined, 159
  scope of, 163
Irishmen, legendary, 3
Israel, 78, 220
Italian Constitution of 1947, 218

Jansen, William, 119
Jefferson, Thomas, 28
  and Bill of Rights, 46
Jew, American, 220
  faithful, 193
Jews, 236
  and Catholics, 251
Johnston, Eric, 117
Judaism, 78
Judges of scholarship, 224
Judicial legislation, 103

Kirchwey, Freda, 120, 125
Knox, 7
Kremlin and Vatican, 185

Lammenais, 62
La Piana, George, 186
Latin America, 91, 241
Legion of Decency, 118
de Leon, Juan Ponce, 5
Levy, average on Catholics, 197-198
Liberal Catholics, 137 ff.
Liberalism, 73
Loyalty, 190, 239
Luther, 7
Lutheran, American, 220

McCollum case, 36, 42, 43, 51, 53, 54, 187, 221

MacLeish, Archibald, 125
Madison, James, 28, 31
  and Bill of Rights, 46
  Memorial and Remonstrance, 32
  statement of purpose of religious clause of First Amendment, 45
Magic, 246
Marriage, mixed, 125
  valid, 255
Maryland assembly, 9
Maryland colony, 9 ff.
Mass tax, 210
Masses, pay for, 210
  prices for, 194
Medals, 213
Medievalism, 246
Mexico, 220
Military precision, 219
Miracles, 157
Monolithic Liberals, 138
Moral infallibility of state, 264
Morality, statistical, 241
Mosaics, 259-260

Murray, Wagner, Dingell bill, 142
Mussolini, 223

Nation, The, 231
in New York schools, 118 ff.
National Conference of Christians and Jews, 143 ff.
"Natural" liberals, 140
New Deal, 66, 138
New Mexico, 6
Neutrality toward God, 99
Newfoundland colony, 9
Nihil obstat, 60, 194
Non-Catholic marriages, 203
Non-Catholic schools, 208
Norsemen, 3
Nurses, 242
Catholic, 142

Obedience, absolute, to Pope, 163-164
to Pope, 204-205
O'Dwyer, Mayor William, 124
Official American Catholics, 199
Omnipotent state, 94, 222, 260
Opinion polls, 154
Opinions, Catholic, 260
Oregon school case, 221-222
O'Toole, Monsignor, 209
Oxnam, Bishop, 120, 156, 181

Panel of experts, 183-187
Papal encyclicals, 216
Parental authority in education, 96
Parochial schools, increasing, 97
Pay for forgiveness of sin, 210
Persecution, 6
Pinckney, Charles, 19, 20
Pioli, Giovanni, 183
Plagiarism, 259
Planned Parenthood Association, 186
Policies from Rome, 190
Policy and doctrine, 188
Political power, 206
Politics in Catholic pulpit, 65 ff.
Pope as God, 204
Pope Gregory XIV, 61
Pope Leo XIII, 63, 73, 205, 261
Pope Pius VI, 13
Pope Pius IX, 61, 165-168, 170-173, 209
Pope Pius XII, 136
Pope's political power, 206
Popes, some, and the Separation of Church and State, 50
Population, 1787, 17
Poteat, Edwin M., 184
Pre-council discussion of infallibility, 169 ff.
Presidents of the United States and First Amendment, 48
Press, Catholic, 139
Pressure, Catholic, 231
Pretense of Catholic approval, 226
Priests' control, 246
Primitive charms, 246
Priority of conscience, 84-85, 202
Private schools, 222
Production code in moving pictures, 117
Program for America, 267
Propaganda, non-Catholic clerical, 227
Protestant-Catholic agreement, 57, 238-239
Protestant-Catholic-Jewish agreement, 261
Protestant, colleges, 102 ff.
establishments, 78 ff.
faithful, 193
ministers on "Separation," 55-56
Protestantism in public schools, 106
Protestants and Other Americans United, 34, 184 ff.
Public opinion, 265
Publishers' refusal to publish, 117-118
Purgatory, 211

Quebec Act, 12

Racial equality, 5
"Real" Catholics, 198
Reform in Sweden, 82
Relics, 213
Religion, common, for America, 192
Religions, established, 208
variety of in U. S., 191
Religious, freedom, 7, 9, 29, 73, 74, 90, 217
freedom, complete, 207
leaders, 228
liberty, 218
test for office, 18
Repression of heresy, 89
Ridicule, 246
Right to be different, 266

Rights, intellectual, moral, legal, 48
Roots of Protestantism, 101
Ruling America, 207
Rutledge, Justice, 41
  doctrine, 49, 226

Sacrament of marriage, 253, 256
Sage School of Philosophy, 230
St. Thomas Aquinas, 213
Salvation outside the Church, 202
Scapulars, 213
School case, Oregon, 221, 222
Schools, compulsory public, 222
  first in U. S., 5
  private, 222
Scott, William Rufus, 185
Secularism, 244
Self-criticism by Catholics, 188
Separation of Church and State, 41, 209, 220
Social, doctrine, 136
  policy, 246
  welfare state, 244
Society, free, 223
South America, 220
"Sovereignty" of the Pope, 67
Soviet government, 228
Spain, 220, 241
  and Sweden, 74, 79 ff.
Spanish, Bill of Rights, 218
  Catholics, 5
  Inquisition, 7
  law of succession, 217
Spaulding, Francis T., 122
Spurious documentation, 201
Standard prices, 246
Statistical morality, 241
Statues, adoring, 211
Sterilization of feeble minded, 148, 150
Subversive doctrines, 95
Sugrue, Thomas, 183-184
Support, of church, 198, 218
  of Catholic schools, 209
Suppression, 240
Syllabus of Errors, 85, 86, 87, 88, 209

Taste, bad, 211
Teaching sisterhoods, 107
Ten Commandments, 140, 151, 257
Tenth Amendment, 23
Tests for accuracy, 233
Thought control, 98, 229-230
Totalitarian state, 257
Totalitarianism, 69, 223, 229, 243, 261

Ultimate sovereignty, 262
Un-Americanism, 260

Valid marriage, 255
Vatican, and Kremlin, 185
  Council, 215
  "espionage," 185
  State, 69
Veneration, 211
Veuillot, 61
Vilification, 240
Votes in the Vatican Council, 171-172

Wall of Separation, 26, 52
Washington, George, 11, 15, 16, 19
Wise, Rabbi Stephen A., 181